Hinduism and the Diaspora

Hinduism and the Diaspora

A South African Narrative

P. Pratap Kumar

RAWAT PUBLICATIONS

Jaipur • New Delhi • Bangalore • Hyderabad • Guwahati

ISBN 978-81-316-0527-1

Published by
Prem Rawat for **Rawat Publications**
Satyam Apts, Sector 3, Jawahar Nagar, Jaipur 302 004 (India)
Phone: 0141 265 1748 / 7006 Fax: 0141 265 1748
E-mail: info@rawatbooks.com
Website: www.rawatbooks.com

New Delhi Office
4858/24, Ansari Road, Daryaganj, New Delhi 110 002
Phone: 011 2326 3290

Also at *Bangalore, Hyderabad* and *Guwahati*

Typeset by Rawat Computers, Jaipur
Printed at Chaman Enterprises, New Delhi

To my loving wife

Vasantha

for her constant support

Contents

	Introduction	1
1	Indians: A New Community Settles in South Africa	7
2	A New Religious Tradition on the South African Soil	22
3	Consolidation of the Tradition: Temples and Priesthood	34
4	Centrality of Ritual: Temple and Domestic Practices	49
5	Religious Celebrations	66
6	Goddess Worship	86
7	Community Organisations, Schools, Rituals and Language	103
8	Some Reflections on the Major Neo-Hindu Organisations	123
9	The Arya Samajists	137
10	The Saiva Siddhantists	150
11	The Ramakrishnaites	159
12	The Divine Life Society	174
13	The Hare Krishnas	184
14	The Satya Sai Baba Followers	197
15	Afterword	208
	Appendix: Perceptions and Attitudes of South African Hindus	217
	Bibliography	234
	Index	242

Introduction

South Africa is a land of cultural diversity. It is one of the most cross-culturally rich and powerful countries. One could take a walk through the main streets of Downtown Durban and feel the profound reshaping of western and eastern cultures in the crucible of an African ethos. One is simultaneously passing through a multidimensional worldview. It is in the context of this multidimensional worldview that one has to understand the uniquely reshaped Hindu culture outside its original home, India. With all their temples, institutions and organisations, the Hindus have created a niche for themselves in South Africa. They have lived in this country for more than one hundred and thirty years and have been amazingly successful in perpetuating their worldview in an alien land. It is against this backdrop that the present study is conducted.

This book is about the South African Hindus. I have tried to present their worldview to the extent they have enabled me to see it, hear and read about it. But, in the process, the two, that is, 'they' and 'I', have fused to the extent that what follows here is an 'intersubjective' (to borrow the term from Habermas[1]) reflection.

Some Methodological Considerations

Documenting and interpreting the worldview of a people is rather a tricky enterprise. No single book or person can give us a complete picture of what we are looking for. It comes to us in bits and pieces, often in incoherent and disconnected forms. Perhaps, all those pieces are there in that society. But looking for them is not easy because in the first place, it is not easy to evaluate what is central and what is peripheral. One needs some background understanding of who the subjects of our study are, what their religious traditions are, what their myths, beliefs, hopes and socio-economic conditions are. Even if we know a great deal about the general background of their religious tradition, it is still not easy to grasp the specific idiosyncrasies of a particular social group.

The researcher needs to live, participate, and enter their worldview and tirelessly pursue their ways of thinking and perceiving things. For nearly a decade, this is what I have done. The time frame is perhaps not adequate to understand something that has gone on for several generations. But like all time-bound projects, I have come to a point when I have to put my observations, thoughts, reflections, and interpretations in writing.

I have lived and moved among the South African Hindus for the last few years. Although, as an Indian, I hold a similar worldview, I found the South African Hindus unique in their way of thinking. Things that I have noticed, observed and found out were often those that either I did not come across in India in the region where I lived, or even if I did, perhaps I did not pay much attention to them until they presented themselves to me quite conspicuously among the Hindus here.

When I first started on my project, I had little idea where to begin. I could not simply take it for granted that what the South African Hindus do and believe is much the same as what one reads in any text on classical Hinduism. There were hardly any written documents that I could consult. Even those inadequately and carelessly preserved documents relating to their immigration to South Africa and what happened to them here, etc., did not contain any significant details regarding their religious traditions. So the best option for me was to go and look around for the most conspicuous things that I could see, the stories, the myths, beliefs, etc., that I could hear. The most conspicuous phenomena were the amazing number of temples in the places where the Hindu community lived. That could be a staring point. I decided to begin with an attempt to identify with them and began to talk to people, eat with them, worship with them and participate in everything that they did. What fascinated me was the continuous cycle of temple rituals and domestic rituals. Most of them are what might be considered part of the non-Brahminical traditions. In the course of my field research, I have also come across innumerable temple societies, and religious organisations that might be considered neo-Hindu vis-à-vis their approach to Hinduism. Thus, my study of the South African Hindus takes into account mainly the ritualistic traditions and some major neo-Hindu organisations.

In many ways, this study departs from the traditional ways of writing about the religion of a people. That is to say, it resists from drawing upon mainly the written texts of the people. Although the South African Hindus do have many written texts which they consider as their scriptures, I have taken the option of studying the oral tradition to a large extent because I have realised that the text does not always tell us what is actually happening. The myths and rituals, perhaps belong to the age-old tradition and are documented in the texts, but the South African Hindus seemed to have taken them from the oral tradition, not in the sense of Vedic tradition but simply bringing together what their forefathers saw and remembered in their homeland before they came to South Africa. A majority of them came from non-Brahmin communities and they relied heavily on what they had witnessed in the region of their origin. These included both Brahminical rituals as well as folk and village rituals that are outside the orthopraxis of the Brahmins. Thus, it is the context that has informed me and not so much the text. Nevertheless, I have tried to bring some comparative perspective to what I saw both in the light of the textual traditions and the contextual traditions that exist in India at the present time.

In approaching the subject matter, I have combined a variety of methodological approaches in view of the complexity of the material. In general, I have drawn on the phenomenological and historical methods, especially in describing and interpreting the ritual traditions and the philosophical background of the Hindus, that is, both the traditional and the neo-Hindu groups. In view of my extensive field research, I have also made use of methods followed in social and cultural anthropology, especially, the method of participant-observer. (In the course of my interviews, I have used the questionnaire method, especially to get some statistical data on the perceptions and attitudes of the Hindus. The statistical data is used only to help me to understand the various trends that I have noticed in the course of my interviews.)

Besides, I have made use of ethnographic data, found in the government documents, books, theses, etc. I have researched all the literature that I could have access, such as pamphlets, announcements, brochures, souvenirs which are found in the temples, and religious organisations/institutions. The major portion of the data comes from the people themselves, that is, their stories, their experiences and their memories of their forefathers.

In giving shape to the mass of material that I have accumulated, I have been guided by two basic queries: what is it that they do, and what is it that they think. Perhaps, the result is a multidimensional picture. However, I have chosen to concentrate and convey to my readers matters related to two of those significant dimensions, namely, the ritualistic and the philosophical. The dominant form that I have discussed here is the ritual. Of course, it is naive to call it a two dimensional picture because it is not as simple as it appears to be. Within the two dimensions many different layers are embedded. They include related symbols, myths, stories, what they say and what they don't, what they show and what they don't and so on. It is between the hidden and the obvious that I have searched for the material and tried to put it together to provide a coherent understanding of the South African Hindus.

In classifying the data, I have also been guided by traditional distinctions such as Brahminic and non-Brahminic, centre and periphery, popular and orthodox, traditional and modern. Nevertheless, as will be shown in the section on rituals, these polarised distinctions are in essence problematic in the case of the South African Hindus. I have made use of those distinctions to draw the attention of the reader to the absence of those distinctions rather than their presence. For instance, what might be considered an exclusive Brahminical activity is no longer considered so in the case of the South African Hindus. This becomes obvious in the case of the priesthood and the performance of the rituals by the devotees.

An Overview

The first two chapters trace the beginnings of the South African Hindus, and the emergence of Hinduism in South Africa. Chapter 3 deals specifically with the Hindu temples and priesthood in South Africa. It throws light not only on the various aspects of the temples, such as worship patterns, architectural backgrounds, etc., but also on the problems related to priesthood. Chapter 4 discusses various rituals performed in the temples and in the homes. Apart from dealing with the commonly observed rituals, it throws light on the rituals that are peculiar to various linguistic groups. It also identifies rituals that are usually common within the Brahminical tradition and others that are common among the non-Brahminical traditions. Furthermore, it also points out the ritual orientations within the neo-Hindu groups. Chapter 5 deals with rituals that are specifically related to the various Hindu festivals. The festival related rituals usually have the same features, such as bathing and dressing up the deity, carrying the festival images in a procession, etc. This chapter also throws some light on the myths that are commonly associated with those festivals, especially those that are remembered among the South African Hindus. Chapter 6 deals with the rituals and festivals related to the worship of the goddess. Goddess worship is a major phenomenon among the South African Hindus. The chapter highlights the intrinsic relationship that can be seen between the material pursuits of the Hindus and the worship of the goddess. Goddess worship is also seen in relation to healing, both physical and psychological. The chapter also deals with some of the local myths related to goddess worship in South Africa. Furthermore, it is pointed out how the goddess phenomenon presents South African Hinduism in its multiple forms. Chapter 7 discusses the intrinsic relationship between ritual and language and points out how each enables other to survive. The chapter also focuses on the different linguistic orientations that are found in South Africa.

Chapter 8 presents an overview of the role and distinguishing features of the various neo-Hindu organisations in South Africa. The presence of the neo-Hindu organisations has led to the emergence of "denominationalism" among the South African Hindus. However, the neo-Hindu organisations can be seen to play an important role in Hindu society (e.g., fostering the Hindu culture among the younger generations). Although most of them have the potential to enter into dialogue with other religions, only the Ramakrishna Centre is found to be involved in an inter-faith dialogue programme. Chapter 9 deals with the Arya Samajists. They were the first ones to bring a new dimension to South African Hinduism which, until then was mainly ritual oriented. As such, they were also the ones who created the distinction between the Sanatans and the Arya Samajists. However, their contribution to the propagation and preservation of Indian culture and the Hindi language is remarkable. Chapter 10 deals with the Saiva Siddhanta Sangam of South Africa. The chapter provides both the background of the Saiva Siddhanta philosophy and local developments. Chapter 11 focuses on the work of the founder of the Ramakrishna Centre of South Africa. The chapter provides an insight about the man behind the organisation, his spiritual struggles and mystical tendencies among other things. The reason for focusing on the founder rather than the organisation is because his life and work illustrate the philosophical foundations of the Ramakrishna Centre better. Chapter 12 discusses the role of the Divine Life Society in South Africa. It highlights the Sanatani tendencies of the Divine Life Society. Their role is seen, apart from their social welfare activities, in the areas of publishing and distributing Hindu religious material. The worship of the goddess is seen as one of their characteristic features. Chapter 13 discusses the role of the Hare Krishna movement in fostering Hindu culture in South Africa. It highlights both their Sanatani (traditional) tendencies as well as some of their distinguishing features. Chapter 14 deals with the followers of Satya Sai Baba in South Africa. The Sai followers are seen to be on the rise in South Africa and the ability and willingness of the devotees in sharing their experiences of Sai Baba seem to help the rapid growth of the Sai Foundation. In that sense, the miracles of Sai Baba seem to play a vital role in spreading his message. Although there is an umbrella body under which the various branches of the Sai Foundation operate, they seem to be pretty much independent in their activities.

The last chapter focuses on some theoretical issues rather than summarising things in the form of conclusions. In this study, although some general tendencies are noted, there are no conclusions as such. However, as a result of the focus given to two types of religious orientation, namely, the ritualistic and the intellectual activity, a theoretical issue is prompted in the form of queries. How are ritual activity and cognitive activity integrated both within the experiences of the Hindus in South Africa and also in the interpretive process rendered by the scholar? It is this theoretical discussion that is taken up in the last chapter. For the sake of a general understanding, I have also included a sample survey of perceptions and attitudes of the South African Hindus on various issues as an 'Appendix' at the end of the book. This survey is not meant as a precise indicator, but merely provides a general picture of the Hindu perspective on various social issues.

Note

1. Jürgen Habermas. *The Theory of Communicative Practice,* Vol. 1: *Reason and Rationalization of Society.* Tr. By Thomas McCarthy. (Boston: Beacon Press, 1984).

1 Indians

A New Community Settles in South Africa

The Indian community in South Africa is now over 150 years old. They celebrated this landmark event in their history and culture in 2010. At this point of time it is perhaps useful to place their history in the context of global developments. South Asians are the second largest immigrant community in many parts of the world, including North America and Europe, trailing behind the Chinese. While many of them are now migrating to western countries, the earlier emigration of mid-nineteenth century was within the context of the movement of human labour throughout the European colonies. As such, the history of South Asian diaspora is closely intertwined with the colonial history of Europe. The purpose of this chapter is to bring to the attention of the reader the basic background against which the Indian community developed and the ways in which their religious traditions were established in South Africa. I have not, however, dealt with all the historical details of that background, but have only highlighted the emergence of South Asians as a new community in South Africa. For exactly one hundred and one years the Indian community in South Africa remained without being granted citizenship since their arrival in 1860. Since 1910 they were neither British subjects as South Africa became a republic that year, nor were they South African citizens until 1961 when they were formally recognised as citizens of South Africa.

Placing them in the Global Context

The European colonies initially developed a system of labour called "slavery". By 1833, the system of slavery was abolished in the colonies. At the same time by the mid-nineteenth century, the British Empire grew enormously thereby requiring labour force to work on the plantations in the colonies. The growing need for labour force in the colonies was coupled with the growing poor economic conditions in India, especially during the mid-nineteenth century. T.N. Thomas points out that "[T]he situation in India was ripe for exploitation by British and French planters in the former slave-owning colonies ...". Thomas also notes that the slump in cotton industry in India created large-scale unemployment. This was further compounded by the drought during the nineteenth century (Thomas, 1). Many Indian labourers could find jobs neither on the farm nor in the industrial sector. And many of them were ready to sell their labour to anyone anywhere. So it seemed like a perfect match between the growing need for labour in the colonies and the poor economic conditions in nineteenth century India. Although, by and large, many scholars advanced this line of reasoning for the Indian emigration to other countries, M.D. North-Combes offers another line of argument that forces us to see the Indian emigration of the nineteenth and early twentieth centuries in the context of British imperialism which necessitated the movement of labour from one place to another to sustain the colonial economy (North-Combes, 13). There were certainly other reasons such as growth in urban population in India as more and more people in the rural areas left for cities in search of employment and new economic opportunities. Others left rural life to escape the rigid social system centred on caste hierarchy. It was certainly a period of significant new ventures and explorations.

In view of the abolition of slavery, the colonies had to use a different system of labour which became common in South American colonies. This new system of labour came to be known as the "indenture system." Thomas defines this new system in the following way, "Under this system, labour was recruited for the planters by their agents to work for a certain period of time (usually five years), during which the employer was legally obliged to provide fixed wages, medical attention and other amenities for the labourers" (Thomas, 1).[1]

This new system of labour looked very attractive to many Indians because it provided an opportunity to seek employment opportunities beyond India. It was first introduced in Mauritius in 1834. Even before it was introduced in South Africa, many of its inherent flaws became apparent. As a result, during those few preceding decades before being introduced in South Africa, the rules of the system were revised many times attempting to strike a balance between fairness to the labourer on one side and the employer on the other. Nevertheless, the system of indenture continued to pose many problems in the South African context.

Indentured Indians Arrive in Natal

After many discussions in Natal, India as well as England and after passing many laws, particularly the laws 13, 14 and 15 of 1859 which laid down rules of the indenture system to be applied in Natal, the first group of Indian workers left Madras for Natal on October 11, 1860 and arrived on November 16, 1860.[2] The first group came from the Madras province. During 1860 and 1866, about 6,445 indentured labourers were brought to Natal from Madras and Calcutta ports in India (Motwani and Barot-Motwani, 13; Bhana, 18ff).

The emigration process was stopped during 1866 and 1874 due to the ill-treatment of labourers hired under the new system in Natal (Thomas, 25). When it was resumed in 1874, the immigration department in Natal placed advertisements in India to attract labourers. Among other things, they guaranteed that "Your religion will in no way be interfered with, and both Hindoos and Mahomedans (*sic*) are alike protected" (Henning, 49). But there was no law specifically for the purpose of the protection of their religion and culture except the provision of a Protector of Immigrants who would generally look into the needs and complaints of the indentured workers (Y.S. Meer, 229). The advertisement also states that there were already more than five thousand Indians in Natal thus pointing to the fact that a community of Indians had already begun to develop in South Africa.

In order to protect the interests of the indentured labourers, the powers of the 'Protector of Indian Immigrants' were strengthened under Law 19 of 1874 (Henning, 54). Law 20 of 1874 further provided for the protection of the future immigrants. Despite all these laws, there were many irregularities and promises made to the indentured labourers were not fulfilled (Henning, 55). As indentured labourers became free, some of them were re-indentured and some freed themselves and either returned to India or engaged in other self-employment activities there itself. Among those who became free of the indenture system, some moved into rural areas to pursue market gardening, selling fruits and vegetables, while others pursued whatever vocations were available to Indians at that time in the service sector in order to survive in the alien land.

Indian Traders Arrive

During 1874 and 1911, nearly 146,000 new immigrants came to Natal in 364 ships (Henning, 56). Joy Brain (251) notes that during a period of 51 years between 1860 and 1911: 152,184 Indians including women and children arrived in Natal. About 24 per cent of them returned to India by 1911. It was during this period that many "free passenger" Indians also arrived in Natal. They were mostly traders holding British passports who entered Natal at their own expense. Most of them came from Gujarat and a significant number of them were Muslims. The Muslim traders who came from Gujarat spoke Gujarati, but those who came from other parts of North India spoke Urdu (Motwani and Barot-Motwani, 17). Thus, by this time, i.e., during 1874 and 1911, we had three distinct categories of Indians within South Africa—those who were still part of the indenture system; others who had become free of the indenture system and had taken up special services and those who had come as free passengers or what Maureen Swan (273) calls 'the merchant class'. With the arrival of the merchant class, the relations between Indians and native Africans began to change as the Indian merchants began trading and supplying groceries and other items to Indians and native Africans. In the eyes of the latter the Indians began to appear not merely as their fellow workers but also as their employers as many Indian merchants began to employ them.

Indians Move Beyond Natal

Once the freed indentured labourers and the merchant class began to enter the small trading enterprises, their economic interests clashed directly with those of the European merchants. By 1990, a strong anti-Indian feeling had emerged among the European settlers (Henning, 82f; Brain, 257).[3] The general increase of the Indian population coupled with the arrival of a new merchant class sent waves of alarm among the European colonists. By this time the Indian community had already spread to other colonies, such as Transvaal, Cape and Free State (Henning, 81).

Many Indians, especially the merchant class, protested against the harsh treatment and discrimination meted out to them by the European colonists. At the same time from 1890 onwards, there was a clash of interest between the planters in Natal and the colonists. The planters wanted the indenture system to continue, but the colonists saw the Indian community as a threat to their economic interests. In 1893, Natal was given the status of

Responsible Government (Motwani and Barot-Motwani, 15; Brain, 261). This relative freedom from the British enabled the colonists in Natal to intensify the anti-Indian feeling among the Europeans resulting in Act 17 of 1875 which required, *inter alia,* that indentured labourers be repatriated upon completion of their contract. But if they stayed on, they must pay a £3 penalty annually and £1 poll tax per person annually (Motwani and Barot-Motwani, 16).[4]

By this time Gandhi had already arrived in South Africa (1893) and had got involved in merchant politics.[5] The year 1895 saw the formation of the Natal Indian Congress which spearheaded the Indian struggle against the oppressive laws in Natal. A number of protests were launched by the Indians. Swan's book highlights the fact that much of the struggle centred on merchant interests and the concerns of the indentured labourers were taken as a cover to lobby for the merchant class. By 1908, the English merchants in Natal were demanding the repatriation of Indians by introducing the 'Asiatic Trading Bill.' But, in 1909, the British Government intervened to allow Indians to appeal to the Supreme Court (Motwani and Barot-Motwani, 19).

The discovery of diamonds in 1867 attracted many Indian traders to move to the Cape Colony. The laws pertaining to the Indian traders were less oppressive in the Cape Colony. So, by 1910 there were about 10,000 Indians in the Cape Colony. The Orange Free State attained independence from the British in 1854. During the 1880s, some "Arab" merchants[6] tried to set up business there but they were soon prevented from doing so by the stringent restrictions (Motwani and Barot-Motwani, 20). In the Transvaal, the 1899 Anglo-Boer war created a great deal of confusion about the status of a number of Indians. During the war thousands of British subjects including Indians, left Transvaal. After the war many Indians returned as refugees. But when the refugees began to return, government officials were unable to determine as to who had the permit to enter the colony and who did not. That was the time when finger printing was required for Indians. Gandhi and his associates protested against it (Motwani and Barot-Motwani, 21). It is beyond the scope of this study to go into all the details of that struggle, but suffice it to point out that by the time the Transvaal received its status of Representative Government in 1907, there were already a significant number of Indian traders living there. The period between 1907 and 1910 witnessed a barrage of protests from Indians in Transvaal and the role that Gandhi played during that period was quite significant.

The period between 1900 and 1910 is quite crucial for our understanding of the Hindu presence in South Africa. In 1903, *Indian Opinion* the first Indian newspaper was started by Gandhi in both Gujarati and English. In 1904, the Arya Samaj was formed, in 1905 Prof. Bhai Paramanand of the Arya Samaj visited South Africa and the same year the Pretoria Tamil League was formed. In 1907, the Surat Hindu Association was formed, in 1909, the Young Men's Hindu Association was formed, and in 1910, the Pretoria Hindu Seva Samaj and the New Castle Tamil Association were formed (Motwani and Barot-Motwani, 25). These developments certainly confirm that the Indians were in South Africa to stay.

End of Indian Immigration

The year 1911 heralded a new phase of experience for Indians when all the colonies joined to form the Union of South Africa in 1910. It put an end to Indian immigration to South Africa. From now on the question was not so much about the immigration of the Indians but their repatriation. While the South African Government viewed it as repatriation, the Indians took it as expatriation. In the light of this situation, many new organisations and lobbies supporting the Indian cause came into existence. In 1911, the Colonial Born Indian Association and the South African Indian Committee were formed. In 1910, Prof. G. Gokhale of the Indian National Congress introduced a resolution in the Imperial Legislative Council, which sought the prohibition of future immigration of indentured Indians to Natal. In 1912, Prof. Gokhale paid a visit to South Africa at the invitation of Gandhi. In 1913, Indian immigration finally ended (Pachai, 31). On October 29, 1913, Gandhi led what was called the 'Great March' to oppose the £3 tax (Motwani and Barot-Motwani, 26). After a great deal of political involvement, Gandhi finally left for India on July 18, 1914 to lead the freedom struggle there.

New Developments

One of the most significant developments of the period after Gandhi's departure from South Africa was the visit of Mrs Sarojini Naidu in 1924. She voiced her opposition to the Class Areas Act of 1924 (Pachai, 37). Then, in 1926, V.S. Srinivasa Sastri arrived in South Africa as part of a delegation from India. He appealed to the South African Government to improve the living standards of the Indian people. When he returned to South Africa in 1927 as the Agent-General of the Government of India, he played an important role in the development of Indian education. In 1930, Sastri College was started to provide education to Indians (Motwani and Barot-Motwani, 27). During his visit Sastri went around the country and gave public lectures in many South African universities on topics related to Indian philosophy. Thus, Sastri's visit provided an occasion for the European community to become aware of Indian religions and philosophy. In fact, Jan H. Hofmeyr, the then minister of the Interior, spoke highly about the contribution of Sastri (Naidoo and Bramdaw, viii–ix).

Although many Indian children began to take advantage of the educational opportunities, there was not much encouragement for women in the Indian community due to many traditional prejudices. However, the role of Lady Maharaj Singh, wife of the Agent-General Kanwar Maharaj Singh, who came after Sastri, was instrumental in motivating more women to take advantage of the educational opportunities. Subsequently, many other educational institutions, such as Springfield Training College in Durban, College of Education in Durban, and M.L. Sultan Technikon in Durban were established (Motwani, 27).

Beginning of a New Struggle

With the availability of new educational opportunities, Indians in South Africa progressed gradually. But, a major setback to their progress came in 1950 when the Nationalist Party introduced the Group Areas Act. Under this Act, the non-European communities were moved to separate locations according to their ethnicity. By 1950, the Indian population was about 500,000 and at least 150,000 were relocated. Henning says, "Of all the non-White groups in South Africa, by 1950 the Indians were the most advanced group and, therefore, were hurt the most by the act" (Motwani and Barot-Motwani, 30). In 1952, a passive resistance movement was launched to oppose the Group Areas Act (Pachai, 54).

The Indian Question Settled

In spite of all the restrictions, the Indians in South Africa continued to stake their claim to the citizenship of the country. Since 1947 the Indian Government had taken up the question of repatriation of Indians in South Africa with the United Nations. While the South African Government insisted that the question was a domestic matter, both India and Pakistan applied strong pressure on South Africa to accept the Indians in South Africa as citizens (Bhana and Pachai, 240). Finally in 1961, one hundred and one years after their first arrival in 1860, the South African Government declared that all

Indians in South Africa were citizens and that was the end of the saga of repatriation of the Indians (Motwani and Barot-Motwani, 32).

In 1961, the Department of Indian Affairs was set up (Pachai, 57). The next two decades were the years of Indian consolidation in South Africa. In 1964, an Indian Advisory Council was formed, and in 1966, a National Indian Council was appointed. It was renamed the South African Indian Council later. In continuation to these developments, the Tricameral Parliament[7] which gave the Indians some political representation was set up in 1984 (Motwani and Barot-Motwani, 33). There have been many interpretations of how much the Tricameral Parliament was a real help to the Indians. Popular support from the Indian community to the new Tricameral Parliament was minimal. Nevertheless, under the Tricameral Parliament the House of Delegates "represented" the Indian interests in the national Government of South Africa.

Beginning of a New Era

The end of the eighties marked a major development in the political history of South Africa. With the western government placing sanctions and many major multinational companies pulling out, international pressure increased on the South African Government. These measures certainly had an effect on the sustainability of the dominantly white political system in South Africa. This brought about a significant rethink in the political hierarchy. In 1990, President F.W. De Klerk lifted the ban on all political parties that were fighting against apartheid. In the same year, Nelson Mandela was released after more than 27 years in prison (*Year Book of South Africa,* 15). Things changed dramatically for all ethnic groups in South Africa when in June 1991 the Group Areas Act was removed from the statute books (*Year Book of South Africa,* 15). For the first time a multi-party forum discussed the process towards democratisation of the country for nearly three years. As a result of those deliberations the Transitional Executive Council was appointed in 1993 to oversee the governmental matters until a "legitimate" government was elected. Besides, an Independent Electoral Commission was established in April 1994 to supervise the electoral process of multi-party elections.

All these new developments altered the Indian situation in South Africa radically. Their future was intrinsically tied with the future of all ethnic groups and for the first time they were able to participate in the democratic process of the country in electing a government of national unity. According to the 1996 census report the total population of Indians in South Africa was 1,045,596 (total South African population was 40,583,573) and as per the 2001 report, the population of Indians in South Africa was 1,115,467 (total South African population was 44,819,778). Of the total population of South Africa in 1996 the Hindus were 1.4 per cent (516,227 Hindus against 236,315 Muslims). Within the Indian community, this translates to 49.8 per cent Hindus against 22.8 per cent Muslims. In 2001, they were 1.2 per cent of the total population (527,353 Hindus against 274,932 Muslims). Within the Indian community it translated to 47.3 per cent Hindus against 24.6 per cent Muslims. A comparison of the figures of 1996 and 2001 shows a drop of roughly 2 per cent within the Indian population whereas nationally there was a drop of 0.2 per cent. Correspondingly, there was an increase of about 2 per cent among Muslims within the Indian community and an increase of about 6 per cent in the Christian population within the Indian community. This is often interpreted in relation to the conversion strategies of the Muslim and Christian groups. However, a careful sociological analysis of conversion and its impact on population changes is needed before any conclusions are drawn. Such an analysis is beyond the scope of the present study. Here it is sufficient to show how Hindu population figures stand in relation to their significant counterparts (these statistics are as per the *South African Government Statistics of 1996 and 2001*).

1996 Census

SA Population	*Indians*	*Indian Hindus*	*Indian Muslims*	*Indian Christians*
40,583,573	1,045,596	516,227 (49.9%)	236,315 (22.8%)	181,468 (18.6%)

2001 Census

SA Population	*Indians*	*Indian Hindus*	*Indian Muslims*	*Indian Christians*
44,819,778	1,115,467	527,353 (47.3%)	274,932 (24.6%)	269,128 (24.4%)

Source: (As per the South African Government Statistics of 1996 and 2001).

Note: Percentages of Hindus, Muslims and Christians above are in relation to the total Indian population and not the total SA population. This is to indicate how within the Indian community the three major religious groups are distributed.

Cultural Background of the Indian Immigrants

There were two major ports in India from where indentured Indians were shipped—Madras which sent mainly Tamil- and Telugu-speaking people and Calcutta which sent mainly Hindi-speaking people. The passenger Indians or traders came largely from Gujarat and Bombay (present Mumbai).[8]

The lists of persons who travelled to South Africa from the Madras port between 1860 and 1877 do not give us any details regarding the castes of Indians. Up to 1877 all Hindus coming from Madras were listed under the generic term 'Gentoo'.[9] From 1878 onwards, however, lists of the ships coming from Madras contained details of the castes of the people travelling in them. Therefore, it is not easy to find out exactly which caste groups came from South India during the early period of the immigration.

On the other hand, the lists of the ships coming from Calcutta give some details of caste. However, most of the last names of the South Indian groups do indicate their caste background. Both in the case of North Indian and South Indian groups, there seems to have been some mobility in terms of caste background. Often the documents of individuals reflect caste names that do not match with their family names. For instance, in one of the documents a person is listed as belonging to the Vanniya caste which is a non-Brahminical caste equivalent to the Vaishya in the four-fold classification of the Indian castes. But the same person's last name "Iyer" is a specific Brahminical caste name in South India. In another instance, a person with the last name Thakur, is listed as Maharaj (Brahmin). Such anomalies, however, need to be carefully investigated and studied by social scientists to see whether some individuals had claimed higher caste status by changing their last names and for what reasons.[10] Such investigation would help us understand how social mobility might have been a feature among the South African Indians.

In general, the Madras group constituted of around 12 per cent Muslims, 5 per cent Christians, 5 per cent Rajputs (warrior caste) some Pillais (traders) and the rest were labourers of low social rank. The Calcutta group constituted of about 5.5 per cent Rajputs, others were either from the Lohar caste (blacksmith) or Koris (weavers) or some other underprivileged caste. The first group comprised not so much of agricultural labourers as service providers, such as, mechanics, servants, gardeners, traders, carpenters, barbers, accountants, and grooms (Ferguson-Davie, 13). Thus, the Indian community which eventually settled in South Africa might be divided along cultural lines into North and South Indians.

When the Indian labourers arrived in South Africa, they were allocated to different employers, some in the sugarcane industry, others in the railways and so on. The employers then took them away to their respective locations of work. Although there seems to be no documentation as to what linguistic group went to which area, some indirect evidence could be proffered to show that a significant number of families coming from the same language group could have gone to the same area. For instance, one could take a look at some areas, such as Verulam and Tongaat where mostly Tamil- and Telugu-speaking people seemed to have settled. A survey of the background of the early temples in those areas gives some indication as to which language group might have been present there in the early days. So by taking a careful inventory of the older settlements, one could, perhaps, find out the settlements of various linguistic groups. However, more careful field study is required to find out the exact situation in terms of linguistic background in each Indian settlement in the early period.[11]

Although linguistically speaking there are several groups (e.g., Hindi- and Gujarati-speaking people in the North Indian group; Tamil- and Telugu-speaking people in the South Indian group), in general all North Indians shared a similar cultural milieu, while all South Indians shared a similar cultural milieu. This trend might be identified in the observance of festivals.[12] One could notice distinct South Indian and North Indian styles in temple architecture. Mikula et al. (1982) note those distinct architectural backgrounds.

In terms of the religious background, the Indian community may be divided largely into Hindus and Muslims and a small group of Christians and Parsees. The Christian group was the result of the nineteenth century mass conversion in India. However, subsequent conversions did occur in South Africa. The 1996 and 2001 statistical figures indicate reduction of Hindus, some of which could be attributed to conversion to other religions. In recent years, townships like Chatsworth and Pheonix witnessed significant growth of Pentecostal Christianity among Indians.

The present Hindu community in South Africa may be considered largely as belonging to four language groups.[13] These are, as identified earlier: (i) Tamils, (ii) Telugus, (iii) those speaking Hindi, and (iv) Gujaratis.[14] There seems to be a greater awareness of their respective linguistic identity today than there was during their initial period. Therefore, the linguistic group identities seem to be becoming reified. However, such observations need to be qualified as often these reified identities are reflected in debates around larger interests of radio broadcasts and cultural programmes on the television and other such matters when one or the other cultural group would complain against another. On another level of youth participation, there seems to be less emphasis on narrow linguistic identity among Hindu youth. Nowbath and others point out that during the earlier time the North Indian groups were not aware of the fact that the Telugus and the Tamils were groups distinct from each other in terms of language and culture. They point out:

> In the early days of indenture, the Tamils and the Telugus were regarded by the Hindis and the rest of the Indian community as one people, Madrasis. Those who were neither Tamil nor Telugu were not aware of the fact that the Madrasis consisted of their separate identities, who had their different customs, practices and rites and who in their domestic lives lived apart. In public they seemed to be one people. Over the last 30 years, however, the Telugus have more and more established and forwarded their own separate identity. (Nowbath, Chotai and Lalla, 18)

Nevertheless, it must be noted that over the years there was a great deal of assimilation between the Tamils and the Telugus, perhaps more from the side of the Telugus.[15] In other words, a great many Telugus appropriated Tamil culture and tended to identify themselves with Tamil society. This trend may be clearly noticed among persons belonging to the Reddy community and those from Naidoo community who seem to have come largely from the Tamil-speaking regions in India. But those who came from the coastal regions of Andhra seem to have a greater awareness of their identity as Telugu-speaking and it is groups like that who were more actively involved in the Andhra Maha Sabhas, cultural organisations that catered to the cultural needs of Telugu speakers.

Much of the information on the geographical backgrounds was gathered from a random survey that I was able to conduct during my oral interviews with people. This information was further corroborated by the immigration documents that I was able to obtain (Bhana, 1984 and 1985; also *cf.* Bhana, 1991 and Meer, 1980). I noted the following areas as the origins of the Hindu Indians. The Tamil group came from places like Chittoor, Tanjore, north and south Arcott districts, Tiruvannamalai, Madurai and the greater suburbs of the then Madras port. The Telugus came from Tirupati, Chittoor (both bordering Andhra and Tamil Nadu), Guntur, and present Rayalaseema (Cuddapa—pronounced as Kadapa) area, the Godavari delta area of Andhra Pradesh and along the east coast of Andhra Pradesh up to the Orissa border. The Hindi group seems to have come largely from Uttar Pradesh—61 per cent (Allahabad, Varanasi/Benares, Gorakhpur, Lucknow, Barielly, Kanpur, Agra), Bihar—31 per cent (Patna, Gaya, Arrah, Monghyr). There were about 6 per cent from Bengal and 2 per cent from central India (Madhya Pradesh). The Gujarati people came largely from two main areas in Gujarat, namely, Surat and Kathiawad in Gujarat on the western coast of India.[16] A newly established documentation centre in Verulam (Verulam Documentation Centre) which was started as a project of the 1860 Indentured Labourers Foundation, is attempting to assist Indians in South Africa to trace their lineage through their computerised system (see "Story of proud Indian heritage" in *Sunday Tribune*, November 7, 2010).

Notes

1. There were also other systems of labour used in different colonies. In Malaysia and Sri Lanka the system of labour was known as Kangani (from the Tamil word 'kanakni' meaning overseer) system. It was abolished in 1938. The other system of labour was known as Maistry system used in Burma. Under the Kangani system, an Indian himself recruited the labourers and supplied them to the employers. The Maistry system functioned on the basis of a gradation of middlemen beginning from the employer to the labourer at the bottom. See Prakash C. Jain. "Five Patterns of Indian Emigration." in *Global Migration of Indians*. Edited by Jagat K. Motwani and Jyoti Barot-Motwani. 1989: 7.
2. During the year 2010 a series of commemoration events took place throughout South Africa and culminated in November in the Province of KwaZulu Natal hosting a major event on 4 December, 2010 at the People's Park adjoining the Moses Mabhida Stadium in Durban where a commemorative plaque was unveiled in honour and memory of the early

Indian settlers and for their contribution to the economic and cultural life of the Province.

3. Also see Henning's article on "The Indian South African 1860–1989' in Motwani 1989: 15.
4. According to Gandhi's *Autobiography,* initially the Natal Government tried to tax the Indians £25 annually. Subsequently, it was reduced to £3. Gandhi says, "The Congress could not regard it as any great achievement to have succeeded in getting the tax reduced from £25 to £3. The regret was still there that it had not completely safeguarded the interests of the indentured Indians" (Gandhi, 118; Also see pp. 116–117). For the exact details of the Act 17 of 1895 see Y.S. Meer, 690.
5. Gandhi was brought to Natal to represent an Indian business person in a legal dispute with another Indian merchant. It is beyond the scope of this chapter to go into details of Gandhi's life in South Africa, suffice to say that his initial encounter with European racism on the train on his way to Pretoria began a story that eventually culminated in his launching a movement that he called Satyagraha that subsequently played a pivotal role in achieving independence for India.
6. In the colonial records, Indian Muslims were often called 'Arabs' by mistake.
7. The Tricameral Parliament refers to the structure which facilitated representation for Indians, Coloureds and the Whites, with the last of the three as the dominant political force.
8. Y.S. Meer makes a reference to the Indians coming to South Africa during the 17th and 18th centuries from Bengal and Madras. They were brought as slaves to the Cape colony. However, no reliable source is cited (see Y.S. Meer, 4).
9. The term "Gentoo" is used in many of the early ship lists (ships that came from Madras, and not Calcutta) to refer to the Hindus. The term is found under the column of caste. The colonial officials seem to have identified the term "Gentoo" as a caste category. Cf. Y.S. Meer 1980. The term seems to be corruption of the word "Gentile" as Hindus were generally referred to by the European Christian missionaries of that time. In 1776, a book on the Hindu code of law appeared in English. The book is entitled *A Code of Gentoo Laws or Ordinations of the Pandits*. It is a translation of a book *(Vivadarnavasetu)* compiled by the Indian pundits at the request of the British East India Company. See, Klaus K. Klostermaier. *A Survey of Hinduism* (New York: State University of New York Press, 1989), 22. This text was translated by Nathaniel Brassey in 1776 into English (see Sugirtharajah, 23). The term seems to have been used in the 17th century alongside Banian, which it replaced. The Old English Dictionary gives the etymology as from the Portuguese

"Gentio". Thus, it seems that the early colonial officials in India (at least in South India) seemed to know the term "Gentoo", and used it as a caste category rather than a religious category.

10. R.K. Jain, an anthropologist from the Jawaharlal Nehru University, India, suggested during my discussions with him that such acquisition of last names from Brahminical castes did occur in Malaysia and other places where Indians had settled. He thinks that such changes in the last names indicate that a person has taken on a priestly role in the community.
11. For more caste details see S. Bhana 1991. Also see C.G. Henning, 1993: 72–74; 84–109.
12. It is not so easy to divide the Hindu community into North and South Indians on the basis of cultural variations, although such distinctions might explain some religious phenomena among them. In actual religious practice, however, the Telugus in certain instances seem to follow the Hindi-speaking people more closely (e.g., in terms of their general tendency toward Vishnu worship) and in certain instances seem to follow the Tamil traditions more closely (e.g., Kavadi, and fasting during Parattassi month). But, culturally they are closer to the Tamils. This may be seen, for instance, in the way they celebrate festivals (e.g., *Divali*), and in their general tendency toward Vaishnava rather than Saiva faith.
13. For the purpose of this study I am not dealing with the Muslim groups but only the groups that may be identified as Hindu.
14. Although there were other linguistic groups (e.g., Malayalis, Marathis) during the initial years of immigration, soon they lost their identity due to their negligible overall numbers.
15. V. Prabhakaran has identified in her research the extent to which the Telugus have borrowed Tamil words in their common usage in South Africa (see Prabhakaran, 26–31). However, it must also be remembered that in the nineteenth century many of the Telugus came to South Africa either from the Tamil-speaking areas or from the coastal regions of Andhra. Thus, the Tamil influence on the Telugus, either linguistically or culturally, seem to pre-date their settlement in South Africa.
16. It must be borne in mind that at the time the Indian immigrants left the country, the formation of modern states along linguistic lines did not exist.

2 A New Religious Tradition on the South African Soil

The immigration of indentured labourers and the passenger Indians to South Africa from the mid-nineteenth century to the early twentieth century resulted in the establishment of new religious groups, such as Hindus and Muslims, among others. There was also a small number of Christians among them. Since 1994 the Hindu community has come to occupy a significant place among the minority religious groups. With the new Constitutional provisions giving recognition to many other religious practitioners, including the small groups such as practitioners of Paganism and Scientology, *inter alia*. In order to place them in the context of their broader religious background, I present here the historical development of early temple building activities and their role in shaping the future of Hindu practice in South Africa.

Traditionally, temple building among Hindus was patronised by the local kings or the feudal lords, who were generally from the ruling class or economically powerful communities who controlled land and agriculture in the context of India. The architectural details were supplied by the Brahmins. Once it was built, the temple and the land around it came under the jurisdiction of the local Brahmins who performed rituals there daily. The common folk from the lower order of society did not have much involvement in these activities except performing their caste obligations in the context of ritual. For instance, the musicians played musical instruments in the temple. Similarly, the potters, the washermen, the *pariahs*, all performed their duties in accordance with the prescriptions laid down by the Brahminical practice.

The non-Brahminical castes also performed certain rituals that were unique to their local customs along with their respective duties in the context of Brahminical rituals. They maintained their local shrines independent of Brahminical jurisdiction. Brahmins did not have much role to play in those rituals. But as time went on they gradually became involved in those ritual activities, and eventually Brahminized some of the elements of those rituals. By the time the British arrived in India, there was already a great deal of Brahminical elements that had become part of the rituals of the caste groups that lived outside the Brahminical worldview. However, much of the ritual retained its local customs and practices. Over a period of time Brahminical rituals also seem to have been influenced by the non-Brahminical aspects of rituals.

As indicated in the previous chapter, the majority of Hindus in South Africa belonged to the non-Brahminical castes.[1] They, however, shared the worldview of the Brahmins. Their knowledge of the Brahminical aspects of Hinduism is only indirect, *via* the oral tradition. Nevertheless, the Hinduism that they have been able to create and perpetuate in South Africa is a remarkable blend of both non-Brahminical and Brahminical elements. It would be interesting to study how Brahminical and non-Brahminical elements have become integrated in the Hinduism practised in South Africa. In what follows, I shall trace the emergence of Hinduism in South Africa which stands as a living memory of the nineteenth century Hindu worldview of India.

Although some documents, such as Lord Russell's despatch in 1840 which indicate the intention of the Natal Government to provide "the means of performing their own heathen rites" (Bell and Morrell, 413), evidence is lacking on whether subsequently, the Indian labourers, when they finally arrived in South Africa, were provided with such means. The popular rhetoric of course reinforces the view that there was no such assistance given to the Indians when they arrived in the mid-nineteenth century. In 1874, when the Natal Government advertised for indentured labourers from India, they did include an assurance in the advertisement that their religion would not be interfered with.[2] But, apart from that there was neither a law that was provided specifically for the protection of their religious freedom nor one that safeguarded the practise of their religion. In fact, documents reflect the general tendency of the whites to become vexed with the religious festivals of the Indians because they were supposed to have been noisy and created law and order problems (Brain, 213).

There is, however, an oral tradition that survives among the Indian communities in South Africa, according to which the first thing that the immigrant Indians did, as soon as circumstances permitted them, was to set up religious and cultural institutions in order to perpetuate their religious practices. They seem to have made great efforts to preserve their old 'life-world' within South Africa. Although officially the government did not seem to have provided either for the educational or cultural activities of Indians, individual employers were sometimes sympathetic to the religious and cultural needs of the Indian immigrants and provided land and partial financial support for their activities. For example, the Ganesha temple at Mt. Edgecombe was built with partial assistance from the Campbell family (Fransen, 385).

Beginnings of Hindu Temple Activities

In an article entitled "Some Reminiscences of South Indian Settlers," S.R. Naidoo recalls that the Hindu community followed a dictum: "Live not in any place which is without a temple" (Nowbath, Chotai and Lalla, 77). This dictum, perhaps, explains the presence of many Hindu temples in Natal alone.

Although, the Natal Government instructed their agents not to send Brahmins, between 1860 and 1911 as Brain points out, a small number of Brahmins did eventually come to South Africa and most of them seem to have been from North India. Brain further points out that in 1890 a priest from Ladysmith applied for land to build a temple for the railway workers. In 1901, one Chottey Singh, a Brahmin priest, was released from indenture in order to allow him to function as a priest at the Depot Road temple. Brain further notes that on Sundays workers used to meet to discuss their problems and it is possible, she suggests, that those evenings were used for worship as well (Brain, 211).

Temples began to appear within a few years of the arrival of the Indians. As indentured Indians became free, they moved to the outskirts of the towns and established their settlements or what came to be known as townships. At the same time they also seemed to have made provision for relatively small shrines built with wattle and daub. Brain makes reference to the establishment of a small Indian village near Ottawa (outside Durban) by 1869 (Brain, 212).

Some of the earliest temples built in the area around Durban date back to 1864.

The following temples were built between 1864 and 1910 in the greater Durban area—Umzinto temple (1864), Umbilo temple (1869), Isipingo Rail temple (1870), Mount Edgecombe temple (1875), Tongaat temple (1880), Cato Manor temple (1882), Umgeni Road temple (1885), Newlands temple (1896) and Sea View temple (1910) (Brain, 212). In the midlands region temples were built between 1880 and 1885 because of the railway workers of Indian origin there (Brain, 213).

Brain notes that by l880s both the Tamil and the Telugu communities began to set up small schools to teach and the two languages gave their children a religious education. In fact in the early 1870s efforts were made to build temples and teach vernacular languages to the children in an effort to make them retain their culture. In one of the documents collected by the Coolie Commission in 1872, there is a reference to a temple built at Riet Valley. The report dated June 26, 1872 was made by one C. Behrens, Esq. He says, "The Coolies at Riet Valley call the manager their father; and have built a Hindoo temple, where they celebrate their own feast days" (Y.S. Meer, 141). Another report filed on June 23, 1872 by one Rangasammy, also shows that there were requests for permission to build temples and have holidays for celebrating their festivals (Y.S. Meer, 139). Only after 1893 the Hindi schools began to appear i.e., when the Natal Government provided Indians with primary education. Religious education became part of the school curriculum (Brain, 213). These early temples and schools seem to have become centres of religious and cultural activities. Reading of the scriptures, story telling and staging religious plays became the activities of these centres where people could meet, not only for social activities but also religious ones. These centres seem to have provided the much needed sense of belonging to Hindus as members of the same community. After the nineteenth century, the Hindu temples were built mainly by the professional builders from India.

Some Professional Builders

Names of the early Indian patrons are not readily available. The reason for this, it seems to me, is that there was no single Indian patron as such, but the entire Hindu community shouldered the responsibility of building temples. As pointed out earlier, some of the white employers (e.g., the Campbell family, the Tongaat group, *inter alia.*) assisted their employees financially and in other ways. Most of the names that one finds today on many plaques in temples are those of recent donors. Therefore, with that caveat, I shall present some details of the people involved in the actual construction of the temples, namely the builders. Some historical accounts are available on some of these people, both in the oral tradition as well as in the written documents.

One of the most well-known builders in South Africa was Kistappa Reddy (1863–1941). He came to South Africa from the Madras Presidency in 1898 as a bricklayer for Mt. Edgecombe. As mentioned earlier, Kistappa Reddy was commissioned in 1899 to build a Ganesha temple for the Indian farm workers. Fransen offers a beautiful description of the temple which reflects the skill of Kistappa Reddy as follows:

> It is an intimate little shrine consisting of a single square *cella* with tower (decorated with 'rings of fire'—Symbols of Creation) and an open pergola in front, in place of the usual hail, set inside a tight compound wall of which the axial entrance assumes the form of a low barrel-vaulted and exquisitely decorated *gopirum* (sic). (Fransen, 385)[3]

This small temple is presently a national monument. After completing his indentureship, between 1906–8, K. Reddy built the Narainsamy temple (named after the donor) at Newlands. It is a Vishnu temple. Its dome is beautifully decorated with the 'rings of fire' and Garuda birds (vehicle of Vishnu). Grossert (28) provides a list of temples built by K. Reddy:

(i) Ganesha temple (Mt. Edgecombe, 1899)
(ii) Subramaniar temple (Umbilo, 1903–4, this temple is now in ruins)
(iii) Narainsamy temple (Newlands, 1906–8)[4]
(iv) Sri Subramaniar and Mariamman temple (Pietermaritzburg, 1909–11, Reddy built only the towers)
(v) Empangeni temple (1914–16)
(vi) Perumal temple (Mt. Edgecombe, 1922–23)
(vii) Perumal temple (Esperanza, 1925–26)
(viii) Wyebank temple (1933–35)
(ix) Perumal temple (Umhloti, 1936–38)[5]

Paul Mikula et al., in their book *Traditional Hindu Temples in South Africa* (15) attribute some of the workmanship at the Cato Manor temple (known as the Second River temple) to K. Reddy.

Another significant name is that of Kothanar Ramsamy Pillay (1863–1938). He was also from the Madras Presidency. He came before K. Reddy in 1885 via Mauritius as an independent passenger. According to Fransen (385), Pillay might have built a temple in Port Elizabeth. The Siva Subramaniar temple in Mt. Edgecombe was his first. He seems to have been influenced by K. Reddy's architectural styles. Fransen points out that the barrel and vaulted dome (*sikhara*) indicates a strong influence of K. Reddy (Fransen, 385). According to the list provided by Mikula et al. (15), K.R. Pillay built the following temples:

Subrahmaniar temple (Port Elizabeth, 1893), Ganesha temple (Park Station Road, 1900), Second Umbilo temple (jointly with Reddy, 1905), Siva temple (Umgeni Road, 1910), Dundee temple (1910), Subramaniar temple (Pietermaritzburg, 1915), Subrahmaniar temple (Mt. Edgecombe, 1912), a private temple at Columbine Road (1924) and Railway Barracks temple (1924)—all three in Durban.

Alaga Pillay was another builder from the town of Madurai in the Madras Presidency. He was first known for his work at Umgeni (Vishnu temple) in 1911. His best remembered work, however, is the Vishnu temple at Umzinto (1932). The other temples built by him include Ganesha temple (Ladysmith, 1916), Vishnu temple (Park Station Road, 1930), Siva temple (Umzinto, 1931) and Magazine Barracks temple (1937) (Mikula et al., 15).

Barasathi Naiker (1872–1962) was originally a resident priest at Sirdar Road temple (Durban), but worked as a sculptor as well. He sculpted the figures on the Sirdar Road temple and became known for his craftsmanship. The temples associated with his skill are: Siva temple (Sirdar Road, 1924), Angalamman temple (Dromore Road, 1930), Hindu temple (Cato Manor, 1932), Siva temple (known as Manning Place temple, Brickfield Road, 1938), South Indian Kali temple (now in ruins at Coughlan Crescent, 1942), Murugan temple (Clairwood, 1945) and Vishnu temple (Kwadabeka, 1946; Mikula et al., 1982: 16).

S.P. Chetty was another prominent building contractor who worked with Barasathi Naiker. He was born in South Africa. However, very little is known about his personal background. He was associated with the construction of the following temples: Angalamman temple (Dromore Road, 1930), Hindu temple (Cato Manor, 1932) and Saiva temple (known as Manning Place temple, Brickfield Road, 1938) (Mikula et al., 16).

Finally, Ramjee, a Gujarati passenger is associated with the following temples (Mikula et al., 16): Sri Gopalal temple (Verulam, 1913—this temple was reportedly inaugurated by M.K. Gandhi), Lakshmi temple (Sirdar Road, 1920—this temple is now in ruins, but the idols were recovered and installed at the Merebank temple), (Mikula et al., 76) and Shree Sanathan Dharma Mandir (Randles Road, 1923) et al. On the basis of the similarities in style and structure Mikula et al. think that Ramjee also built the Mariamman temple at Isipingo (1912). Although Fransen (387) thinks that Gandhi inaugurated the Isipingo Mariamman temple, there is no recorded evidence to corroborate this, except the fact that the builder happens to be the same Ramjee who built the Gopalal temple at Verulam.

Arrival of Religious Leaders

Beside the temple culture which contributed to the establishment of Hindu practices, by the turn of the century there were many Hindu religious leaders from India visiting South Africa. Many of them went around the country, visiting mainly Natal and Transvaal where they delivered lectures on Hindu ideals, practices, customs and so on. Some of them favoured a sectarian form of Hinduism, while others supported reformed Hinduism. Most of the religious leaders who visited South Africa at the turn of the century were part of the Arya Samaj movement in India. I shall discuss the contributions of neo-Hindu movements to South African Hinduism in subsequent chapters. Here I shall identify some of the early religious leaders who provided an impetus to the Hindu faith and practice in South Africa.

By the turn of the century, the indentured Indians and the passenger Indians felt that religious teachings were not being imparted properly. Whatever the early Indian settlers remembered and practised with regard to religion was not adequate for the new generation. They were looking for more and naturally turned to their motherland, India for the same. As a result many religious leaders were invited from India and they visited South Africa. The Veda Dharma Sabha records in its history the arrival of Prof. Bhai

Paramanand in 1905. He travelled all over Natal and Transvaal for nearly five months, and lectured on the Vedic Dharma and strengthened the newly established Arya Samaj. Although he was an Arya Samajist himself, he established the Hindu Young Men's Association (in Pietermaritzburg) to achieve "unification of all the different linguistic and denominational groups of Hindus ..." (Nowbath, Chotai and Lalla, 83). In 1908, Swami Shankaranand arrived in South Africa, and began preaching about the significance of Hindu festivals, ceremonies, myths, etc. This resulted in the establishment of the Veda Dharma Sabha in Pietermaritzburg in 1909. In 1912, he established the Hindu Maha Sabha.[6] As Hindus began to organise themselves initially under the Arya Samaj and Hindu Maha Sabha, they began to demand religious holidays. It was mainly because of Swami Shankaranand's campaign that by 1910 *Divali* was declared a public holiday for the Hindus. Brain makes reference to the celebration of *Divali* by the railway and municipal workers in Durban in 1910 (Brain, 214).

His work was later continued by a South Africa born religious leader Pandit Bhavani Dayal (Nowbath, Chotai and Lalla, 84). He did not limit himself to teaching the principles of Arya Samaj, but went on to help Hindi language and culture to spread by establishing Hindi Pracharani Sabhas. He also participated in political activities and was imprisoned with Gandhi for his involvement in the *Satyagraha* Movement. In 1938, he was elected the president of the Natal Indian Congress (Nowbath, Chotai and Lalla, 84). Another religious leader who visited Natal in 1913 was Swami Mangalanand Puri. Although his visit was a short one, his contribution to the Hindu culture in South Africa is considered remarkable. In 1921, another learned scholar arrived in Natal at the invitation of the Arya Yuvak Sabha. He was Pandit Ishwardutt Vidyalankar. He demonstrated to the South African Hindus "the correct way of performing the *havan* and the *samskaras*" (Nowbath, Chotai and Lalla, 84)[7] according to the principles of the Arya Samaj.

Thus the Hindu community strengthened its faith and practice with the spiritual help coming from visiting leaders. It would be worth noting some of the ways in which this revitalisation of the Hindu faith has been achieved. It has been noted that the following means were adopted to revitalise the Hindu faith: (i) lectures and sermons delivered by the visitors, (ii) observance of festivals, (iii) performance of rituals, and (iv) the study of the vernacular (Nowbath, Chotai and Lalla, 22).

Gandhi in South Africa

Gandhi's presence for nearly 21 years in South Africa exerted tremendous impact on the Hindu-Indians there. He arrived in South Africa in 1893 as a lawyer to represent a Muslim businessman in a legal dispute which ended in an out-of-court settlement. It would be worthwhile to note his encounters with the Christian missionaries and his European colleagues who thought he might make a good Christian in order to understand his role in upholding the cause of Hindus in South Africa.

Gandhi thought of himself as a devout Hindu, although he was willing to experiment with other religious traditions. His first encounter with Christians in South Africa was with one Mr Baker, the attorney of Dada Abdhulla who had hired Gandhi to represent him. In his first meeting with Mr Baker, Gandhi told him:

> I am a Hindu by birth. And yet I do not know much of Hinduism, and I know less of other religions. In fact, I do not know where I am, and what is and what should be my belief. I intend to make a careful study of my own religion and, as far as I can, of other religions as well. (Gandhi, 100)

This rather polite disclosure gave hope to Mr Baker that Gandhi would be a good target for conversion. So, he at once invited Gandhi to attend one of his prayer meetings. Gandhi attended these prayer meetings and had conversations over cups of tea at the house of two old ladies Ms Harris and Ms Gabb who lived together. Mr Coates, a Quaker also joined them during these conversations. Gandhi used to show a great deal of enthusiasm in the books that they suggested for him to read. After reading each one of those books, Gandhi invariably felt that they had no effect on him.

In all those encounters in South Africa, Gandhi does not come off as a "superstitious"[8] Hindu. When Mr Coates offered to break his Vaishnava necklace, he refused to let him do so not on the grounds of religious belief but on the grounds of his love and trust for his mother. His response was:

> I do not know its mysterious significance. I do not think I should come to harm if I did not wear it. But I cannot, without sufficient reason, give up a necklace that she put around my neck out of love and in the conviction that it would be conducive to my welfare. (Gandhi, 103)

It is, perhaps, because of this simple faith and trust that he was not convinced by an argument that made sin its central focus. He rejected the argument that one's sins could be washed away only through the worship of Jesus Christ. Gandhi refused to value the truth of a religion on the basis of sin. His quest was not the redemption from the consequences of sin, but sin itself. And he was willing to remain restless in his sins until he found redemption from sin itself (Gandhi, 104). Commenting on Gandhi's reaction to efforts to convert him into a Christian, B.R. Nanda says, "The first impact of Quaker proselytizing in a strange country was doubtless strong on him, but he was in no greater hurry to become a Christian in Pretoria than he had been to become a Theosophist in London" (Nanda, 5). The more he was exposed to the Christian and Muslim efforts to convert him, the more the latent Hindu worldview in him came to surface and his Hindu identity began to take shape in South Africa. It is on this Hindu identity that Gandhi stood firmly to the end of his life. Nanda points out, "Years later, Gandhi confided to a group of Christian missionaries: 'Hinduism as I know it entirely satisfies my soul, fills my whole being and I find a solace in the *Bhagavad Gita* which I miss even in the Sermon on the Mount'" (Nanda, 5).

To many South African Hindus, Gandhi set a model in countering the attractions of Christian missionaries. Many Hindus in South Africa praised him not only for his political role, but also for being a loyal Hindu. The Hindu Maha Sabha honoured his memory by building the Gandhi Memorial Hall in Durban and many Hindu temples, especially in places where Gujarati families live in large numbers, have installed statues of Gandhi in the vicinity of the temple complex (e.g., Vishnu temple in Ladysmith). Many South African Hindus claim that they were the first to honour him with the title 'Mahatma' (the Great Soul). In the course of my interviews in South Africa, I also came across people who profess Gandhism more as a religion than as a socio-political ideology.

Their respect for Gandhi borders on veneration accorded to a deity. This is not to say that there are no critics of Gandhi in South Africa. When I first arrived in South Africa, I ran into a journalist who pointed out to me in the course of our conversation that Gandhi represented mostly the interests of the Gujarati business people and not the concerns of the indentured labourers. Some of the members of the Veda Dharma Sabha tend to consider Mahatma Gandhi's South African political involvement as favouring mostly the Gujarati merchants (both Hindu and Muslim) and not the indentured labourers of the time.[9] The leader of the Arya Pratinidhi Sabha, whom I interviewed in Durban, however pointed out that Gandhi's struggle against 'poll tax'[10] clearly shows that he fought for the indentured labourers. Gandhi himself records in his *Autobiography* that he became a friend of the indentured labourers after he dealt successfully with the case of an indentured labourer who was beaten very badly by his master. Gandhi took up his case and saw to it that the labourer was transferred to another employer (Gandhi, 128). Many prominent members of the Arya Samaj in South Africa are staunch followers of Gandhi and were also actively involved in the Gandhi centenary celebrations which took place there in June 1993. Whatever other perceptions of Gandhi exist in South Africa, the fact remains that Gandhi became a symbol of Hindu pride within the country. Both his critics and fans see him as a model Hindu whose self discovery began in South Africa. Perhaps, it is this very discovery of his Hindu identity that might be seen as his contribution to the emerging South African Hinduism.

Notes

1. J.B. Brain points out that the colonial government instructed their agents in India not to send Brahmins (see J.B. Brain, 211).
2. I have noted the details of the advert in Chapter 1 of this book.
3. *Gopirum* should read as *gopuram*—it refers to an arch-shaped dome on the upper section of the temple building (clarification mine).
4. There might have been an earlier construction of the temple at Newlands dating back to 1896.
5. The dates mentioned are approximate and based on the information from Grossert (1942).
6. It is interesting to note that the Hindu Maha Sabha was originally established under the auspices of the Arya Samaj leadership. However, it gradually came to represent the Sanatana Hindu practices in South Africa.
7. *Samskaras* refer to the 16 Hindu ceremonies, such as birth, marriage, death, and so on.

8. That was how in general Europeans at the time of Gandhi understood Hinduism to be. It most certainly represents the 19th century Christian missionary attitude.
9. The leader of the Veda Dharma Sabha (VDS) whom I interviewed in Pietermaritzburg had not read Maureen Swan's book on Gandhi (Swan, 1985) nor did he know of it until I brought it to his notice. Maureen Swan presents Gandhi precisely from that point of view which is expressed by the leader of the VDS at Pietermaritzburg.
10. In 1894, the indentured labourers were brought under heavy taxation. According to Gandhi's Autobiography, the Natal Government initially tried to tax the Indians twenty five pounds annually. Subsequently, it was reduced to three pounds. To quote Gandhi, 'The Congress could not regard it as any great achievement to have succeeded in getting the tax reduced from £25 to £3. The regret was still there that it had not completely safeguarded the interests of the indentured Indians' (Gandhi, 118; also see 116–17).

3 Consolidation of the Tradition

Temples and Priesthood

The significance of temples is undoubtedly great for the South African Hindus. Even a casual tourist might be able to perceive how pervasive the Hindu temple culture is within South Africa. In the previous chapter, we have seen the extent of temple building activity during the early days of Indian settlement. It laid the foundation for the Hindu religion in an alien land. The significant role that Hindu temples played in preserving and spreading Hinduism is further testified by the fact that even today the building of temples seems to continue uninterrupted. Each generation of Hindus, as they move to new locations in South Africa, ensure that their children are rooted in the temple culture; something that they consider very important. New temples that are constantly emerging in many new locations in South Africa testify to that fact. For instance, in an Indian suburb (Palmridge) in Johannesburg, there are two temples within the radius of a kilometre. The newly established Indian community is making efforts to organize a Hindu society in order to build a new Hindu temple in Umhlanga earlier a whites only location. As wealthy Indians continue to move to historically White suburbs, the presence of Hindu temples in these new locations is bound to make a deeper cultural impact on South African society.

Almost all their life seems to be guided by the temple activities. From birth to death, an average Hindu passes through a series of temple ritual activities. Temple rituals attract Hindus of all background, regardless of their education and economic status. In my research experience, I found many economically well to do Hindus involved in temple committees. Whether they are involved in the temple activities for their spiritual progress or social status is another matter altogether. But the fact remains that many rich Hindus tend to patronise Hindu temple activities. From the time of the first generation to the present, temple activity has been continued by Hindus in South Africa. Nevertheless, many changes have taken place both in the nature of the temple ritual practices, customs as well as in the priesthood. In the present chapter, I shall discuss some of these changes in South Africa.

Structure of the Hindu Temples

Within the traditional mode of Hinduism in South Africa, temple worship is the most dominant feature. As pointed out earlier, most of these temples were built during late nineteenth and early twentieth centuries, mostly by the South Indian indentured labourers.

The Hindu temples of South Africa reflect a wide variety of traditions. From the architectural point of view, there are two types of temples, namely, the South Indian style and the North Indian style. Among the older ones, most Natal temples reflect the dominant South Indian style. In general, the South Indian and North Indian styles are distinguished by the shrine (*cella*), the tower (*sikhara*) and the flag post (*kodi*). According to Mikula, major design criteria for a South Indian style building are the following: 'orientation (generally east-west), the square plan form of the shrine (*cella*), the axial alignment of an external altar and the stylised flagpole (*kodi*)' (Mikula et al., 10). The North Indian style (known as the Nagara style) temples are marked by much more plain and simple designs. Some of the basic elements include:

> [t]he freestanding, single *cella* and the emphasis on verticality in the design. The same east-west orientation applied, but much emphasis was placed on the idea of circumambulation for which purpose some hardened walkway or in later versions, a veranda was provided. No lineal external alters and *kodi* poles were provided at all. In later versions under the influence of the Islamic, Victorian, and Edwardian architectural styles a curious hybrid form of temple developed which nevertheless retained its Hindu quality. (Mikula et al., 10)

Although the characteristic features mentioned above are more applicable to the temples in India, one does find stylistic architectural distinctions (as in North and South India) in South

Africa as well. Nevertheless, most of the temples in South Africa have a curious mixture of both. The older South Indian temples have been built in the typical South Indian style. But in temples built more recently one finds a mixture of both elements. Commenting on the later temples Mikula et al., point out:

> North Indian temple builders, with their basic understanding of the Nagara style, were constructing South Indian temples and vice versa. Elements such as the circumambulatory passage around the *cella,* the emphasis on the vertical line and blind arches were introduced into Dravidian temples. Southern deities dressed in *Gujarati* dress adorned the buildings and Islamic domes appeared over shrines. North Indian temples, already heavily influenced by western architecture, received external altars and *kodi* poles often making it difficult to distinguish one from the other. (Mikula et al., 11)

Such syncretistic approach to sacred space and rituals, though not unique to South African Hinduism, is nevertheless significant in South Africa.

From a religious point of view broadly speaking, there are three types of temples in South Africa: the Siva temples, the Vishnu temples and Amman (Mother goddess) temples or Sakti temples. Often all these types are set in one single temple complex. However, there seems to be a structural pattern in the way the various types are combined. Usually in each temple complex, there is one dominant deity and others who are peripheral. The dominant deity occupies the sanctum sanctorum, whereas the peripheral ones are located in individual shrines. For instance, if the dominant deity is Siva, the other deities related to him would be placed in the shrines that are in closer proximity, and the idols of other distantly related deities (e.g., Vishnu, Lakshmi) would be placed in shrines a little farther. In some smaller temples there are no separate shrines for the peripheral deities. Those idols are placed around the dominant deity. The most universal deity in all temples is Ganesha or Vinayaka (also known as Vighnesvara) and Lakshmi.[1]

One point of interest is the way the deities and their consorts are placed in the temples, whether Saiva or Vaishnava. In Saiva temples, if the presiding deity is Siva, his image occupies the sanctum sanctorum. Normally his consort is placed in the shrine left of the sanctum sanctorum. Sometimes no separate shrine is provided to the consort, she would be depicted with Siva in another place or as part of the images that are carried during a festival procession (*utsavamurtis*).[2] In the Vaishnava temples, sometimes Vishnu stands alone in the sanctum sanctorum (e.g., the Maha Vishnu temple or Emperumal temple, Canelands). His consorts, Lakshmi and Bhudevi are placed in the shrine left of the sanctum sanctorum (e.g., Sri Maha Vishnu temple, Newlands). In some temples, Vishnu and his consorts (Lakshmi and Bhudevi) are depicted together. In other Vaishnava temples, Vishnu and his consort Lakshmi are depicted as Lord Krishna and Radha (e.g. Gokula temple, Tongaat and also at the Radha Radhanath temple of Understanding in Chatsworth). In some temples, Lord Krishna stands alone in his universal form (the Jagannatha temple at Tongaat in Durban).[3] Vishnu in his incarnation as Rama is always depicted with his consort Sita and brother Lakshmana. The images of Rama, Sita and Lakshmana are found in a smaller shrine outside the main temple of Jagannatha in Durban. An image of Hanuman is also found in this temple. Usually Hanuman seems to have a special place in temples built by the North Indian community.[4]

One of the striking features of the South African Hindu temples is the mixing of the Brahminical and the non-Brahminical deities. In the temples in India, the non-Brahminical goddesses (e.g., Draupadi Amman and Mariamman) are not part of the Brahminical temples. In the South African context, the non-Brahminical Amman (goddess) temples are built next to the Brahminical temples within the same complex. However, a careful observation of the general pattern of the temple complexes reveals an interesting structure. Where the Brahminical temples and the non-Brahminical temples are combined in one complex, the Brahminical temples take the central position, whereas the Amman temples are located in the periphery of the complex, usually on the right hand side (e.g., Umgeni temple complex in Durban, and Sivasubramaniar and Mariamman temple complex on Longmarket Road in Pietermaritzburg).

One of my informants suggested that one reason why the various types of Hindu tradition are combined in one single complex is that the indentured labourers attempted to achieve consensus and unity within the Indian community by catering to all the various backgrounds of people, especially in the religious sphere. Another informant suggested that the iconography and rituals in many Brahminical temples do not match. In other words, it is suggested that although the iconography seems Brahminical, the worship pattern, the ceremonies, the festivals, etc., do not always reflect the Brahminical tradition, but rather a mixture of Brahminical and non-Brahminical traditions. For instance, on any festival occasion, rituals are performed not only to the main deity concerned but also to the peripheral deities. Even though the festival belongs to the Brahminical tradition, the non-Brahminical goddesses are also worshipped, and vice versa. At the Karttikaidipam festival at Umgeni temple, I noticed that the priest who is a Brahmin trained in Sri Lanka, performed rituals not only in honour of the main deities (Siva and Parvati), but also performed rituals at the non-Brahmin goddess temple on the periphery of the complex. Similarly, during Amman festivals, rituals are performed in honour of Siva, Ganesha, and other deities as well.

Patterns of Worship

Patterns of worship in the South African Hindu temples are largely a mixture of Brahminical and non-Brahminical rituals. They reflect the social reality within the Hindu fold. The earlier patterns of worship in South Africa were clearly dominated by the non-Brahminical aspects. It is only in the last two decades or so that the temple worship patterns are becoming Brahminised. As pointed out earlier, one way it is done is by bringing Brahmin priests from Sri Lanka. Since 1993 there are diplomatic ties between India and South Africa. As a result there are attempts to bring priests from India. To understand the pattern of worship in the Hindu temples, we need to recognise the fact that the individual sectarian patterns are not clearly visible. In other words, all temples, whether Saiva or Vaishnava, have a similar pattern of worship.

Most of the Saiva temples in South Africa were built by the South Indian immigrants, as noted in chapter 2. This is evident in their architectural design (the *gopura* type), the observance of rituals, the language used in the ritual context, the priesthood, and the general linguistic background of the worshippers at the temples.[5]

Saiva temples include, those dedicated to the worship of the following deities: Siva, Ganesha and Subramania (Murugan). The other deities associated with them are Parvati (Siva's consort), Valli and Devayani (consorts of Subramania). Ganesha stands alone as he is considered a celibate. Almost all Saiva temples that I visited have shrines for the images of Vishnu, Lakshmi and Sakti or Amman.[6]

The worship pattern in the Saiva temples at present follows the South Indian Saiva Agama worship closely. This is mainly because of the presence of the Sri Lankan priests who are trained in those traditions. The older worship pattern seemed to be simpler, and involved mainly Tamil prayers and *bhajans,* the priest being an elder of the community who depended mainly on the oral tradition.

The presiding deity is the main one to be worshipped. Just as the placing of the deities is in terms of the presiding one taking precedence and the others in the periphery, the pattern of worship also follows the same hierarchy. If it is Siva who is presiding, he occupies the chief place in the worship. The ritual, however, begins with the worship of Ganesha whether the presiding deity is Ganesha or Siva or Murugan. All the other deities are worshipped after prayers are offered to the main deity.

In the Vaishnava temples, worship is offered mainly to the presiding deity, namely, Vishnu, and then to his consort, Lakshmi. Deities, such as Siva, Murugan, and others are also offered worship. Invariably Ganesha is the first to be worshipped. All the Vaishnava priests are local people, none from India. Vaishnava ritual texts (Agamas) are not followed during the prayers as the local priests are not trained Brahmins. In fact, in many of the Vaishnava temples, on major occasions, such as the Kumbhabhishekam, the Sri Lankan priests trained in the Saiva Agama worship, have been found to conduct rituals in their own way. Thus, the Vaishnava temples are slowly becoming influenced by the worship pattern followed by the Sri Lankan Saiva priests.

One of the unique practices in South African temples is the worship of the Navagrahas (nine deities associated with the nine planets). Without circumambulating the nine deities (Navagrahas) the worship is not complete. The ritual usually begins with the worship of Ganesha and ends with prayers offered to the nine planetary deities. The worship of the nine deities is also known as "bad luck prayers" in South Africa. While Ganesha is believed to remove all obstacles, the nine planetary deities are believed to remove all bad luck. However, I have also noticed that some devotees do not worship the nine planetary deities every time they worship at a temple, but only when they have taken special vows.

Another interesting feature of worship in the South African temples is the presence of a "banyan tree" which is considered sacred. In South Africa, it is often known as the "marriage tree".

Newly married couple go round the tree and pray for children. Barren women also circumambulate the tree in the hope of having children. One notices white cotton thread wound around the tree as a mark of circumambulation. It also symbolises a bond between the woman and the tree such as the one that exists between husband and wife. Tying the thread round the tree is seen as reminiscent of a husband tying the sacred thread (*mangalasutram*) round the neck of the wife in a Hindu marriage, especially in South India.

The smaller shrines/temples are not open daily as there are no permanent priests there. Only when devotees visit or there is a festival they are opened for worship. In bigger temples, such as Cato Manor or the Umgeni Road temple, the priest performs rituals daily in the morning, afternoon and evening. Special prayers are offered when the devotees visit the temple. Typically, in all the bigger Hindu temples worship begins with the ritual bathing of the images, anointing, clothing and decorating them before the people visit the temple. This happens in the morning. Then, as the devotees visit the temple, special prayers are offered on their behalf.

Changes in Ritual Observation

In the course of their continued existence, they seem to have modified many rituals perhaps in an attempt both to simplify them as well as to make them relevant and in some way comprehensible to the people. For instance, in some of the temples, the priest explains the significance of various symbols and the meaning of various prayers in English. Also in some marriage ceremonies, the priests wear garments that resemble the cassocks of the Christian priests. In some temples, one finds sign boards that say "lighting camphor inside the temple not permitted", "clean the coconut before bringing into the temple", etc. I have noticed some of these restrictions in the Hindu temples in the USA also. This consideration for the modern building codes and health codes in the vicinity is a tendency that seems peculiar to the Hindu temples outside India.

Changes in Customs and Practices

As Hindus settled in South Africa and elsewhere continued with their religious activities, it soon became apparent that some of their religious practices and customs needed modifications to suit the place of their adoption. One of the changes that has taken place is in the area of the religious calendar. The South African Hindus hold most of their religious ceremonies and festivals either on a Sunday or a Saturday for the sake of the convenience of the people. Although special consideration is given to the auspiciousness of the time, it is not always possible for the Hindu community to observe it meticulously. In the case of India, according to the orthodox Hindu custom, when fixing the day or time for a ritual, or a social festival like marriage, Brahmin pundits are consulted to check the auspicious time (*muhurtam*). This auspicious time is extremely important in India. I attended Hindu weddings in India sometimes in the middle of the night because that point of time was considered auspicious. In the South African context, there is a general religious calendar that mentions uniform auspicious times and inauspicious times. They do not, however, specify the exact time. For instance, the calendar in South Africa (incidentally most of them are supplied from India) provides a general guideline and not specific time—on Sunday between 3:00 p.m. and 4:00 p.m. it is auspicious time, and between 4:30 p.m. and 6:00 p.m. it is inauspicious. It is generally assumed to be the same on all Sundays unlike in India where orthodox Hindus look at each day and find out which is the auspicious time and which is not. Given the specific situation of the Indian community in South Africa, it is quite understandable why it is difficult to practise religious ceremonies observing all the minute details. The observance of most auspicious occasions on Sundays is generally explained as a result of the early practice when indentured Indians were given permission to take leave for such events only on Sundays. Generally, the South Asian diasporic Hindus seem to hold most of the social ceremonies and celebrate festivals on Sundays in western societies as it is convenient.

At the beginning, Indian labourers working on the farms did not get holidays on account of festivals. The only day off was Sunday. So they shifted their religious activities to that day. At present, Saturday and Sunday are days on which most religious ceremonies are performed. In recent time the Indian community have been able to lobby for some holidays for festivals through the intervention of the House of Delegates (the parliamentary body for the Indian community).

In South Africa, among Hindus in general, and the South Indian Hindus in particular, fasting during the *Parattassi* month (September 17–October 17) is common. Most of the South Indian Hindus however fast on Mondays and Fridays, whereas North

Indian Hindus fast on Tuesdays and Saturdays. Almost all the Hindus in South Africa refrain from eating meat and fish on these days. In India, non-vegetarian Hindus normally do not eat meat and fish on Tuesdays and Saturdays. There are the days when most Hindus in India visit temples. In certain parts of North India, Friday is the day on which most Hindus, especially women visit the temples. It is perhaps useful to note that unlike Muslims, fasting in the case of Hindus involves abstaining from avoiding non-vegetarian food if one has them otherwise. If one is a vegetarian it means avoiding certain vegetarian foods that are considered not conducive to spiritual well-being. For instance, followers of the Hare Krishna movement generally abstain from eating certain lentils during certain seasons, and avoid garlic and onion at all times as they are not found to be conducive to the spiritual well-being.

Priesthood in Hindu Temples

For an understanding of worship patterns in South African Hindu temples, it is important to understand the priesthood of the temples also. When one refers to the title "Brahmin" in the South African context it must be kept in mind that one is not necessarily referring to the caste that goes by the same name, but rather to the function of the priest. Thus, a Brahmin in South Africa is someone who performs the role of a priest either in the temple, or in the context of religious ceremonies, such as marriage, funeral, etc. This distinction is important because it distinguishes the Hindu priesthood in South Africa from its counterpart in India. In India, Hindu priesthood is vested exclusively in the hands of the Brahmins, except the goddess worship by those with a non-Brahminical background which often allows women into priesthood mostly from the non-Brahminical groups. Tantric worship also allows women as well as those who are not Brahmins to become priests.

As for traditional Hindu rituals, only Brahmin priests perform them in India. Priesthood in India is hereditary, and children are often trained from the beginning in a particular school of ritual tradition. For instance, most of the priests in the Saiva temples in South India belong to a school of priesthood called 'Gurukal or Sthanikal' (the current Hindu priests who are brought from Sri Lanka belong to the former group. For this reason in South Africa they are often called 'Gurukal'). Another important distinction is that in India, the priest who worships in a temple does not preside over marriage ceremonies. A priest who performs marriage ceremonies does not take part in funeral ceremonies. There are important caste distinctions within the Brahmin group to identify these levels of priesthood.

In the South African context, however, these fine distinctions have become irrelevant, perhaps, for the simple reason that the trained Brahmin priests did not constitute the group of early settlers. Even if there were some who belonged to the Brahmin caste, they did not have the necessary priestly training. Therefore, the Hindu priesthood in South Africa is drawn from highly differentiated group from among the Hindu community. In the process, it even crossed the traditional Hindu caste barriers. In fact the majority of the priests seem to be drawn from the non-Brahmin caste groups (e.g., Naidoo, Naiker, Pather, etc.). But this situation could change in the wake of the increasing number of Brahmin priests from Sri Lanka and India.

Training of Hindu Priests

In the beginning, Indian settlers in South Africa depended on their own memories of tradition. The ritual acts, prayers, chants (*mantras*), myths, symbols, beliefs and various religious practices were carried over to this country as part of their experience. Whatever ceremonies they observed in India, they remembered and transmitted with relative accuracy. It is only much later, almost at the turn of the century that some religious books were brought by visiting religious leaders. Also, whenever the Indian immigrants went to India to visit their relatives, they brought with them some of the religious texts in regional languages, some English translations (by this time, i.e., the nineteenth century, a significant number of Hindu religious texts had been translated into English and other European languages by western indologists. For instance, Gandhi speaks of his reading of the *Bhagavad Gita* and some of the *Upanishads* and their influence on him). Some Hindus visited India to learn some of the basics of their religious practices. At present, there are attempts to bring more priests from India and Sri Lanka. Because of the lack of diplomatic ties between India and South Africa until 1991, those attempts were not very successful. Nonetheless, in some temples Sri Lankan priests are employed on a contractual basis (as at Cato, Manor temple, Durban, and Siva

Subramania temple in Pietermaritzburg). After the 1994 elections and with the emergence of the democratic government, there is a gradual improvement in the situation, in that some priests from India are beginning to come to South Africa, as in the case of the Sri Maha Visnu temple in Havenside, Durban.

For an understanding of the situation in South Africa with regard to the Hindu priesthood, it may be worthwhile to look at the case of a young priest. He was from Benoni, an Indian suburb of Johannesburg. His grandfather and great grandfather were involved in temple activities. As a result, he developed an interest in temple rituals, cultural activities and Tamil from his boyhood. He gradually grew to realise that he should become a priest. His parents also encouraged him. He found that the training opportunities and facilities in South Africa were not adequate to become a good Hindu priest. So he approached the local temple organisations and eventually found a sponsor in Mobeni Heights (Durban). A rich Indian businessman, V.M. Reddy agreed to sponsor his studies in India. So the young man set out to India and arrived in a small temple town called Chidambaram (in Tamil Nadu) where he spent the next three years studying Tamil literature, the Saiva Siddhanta philosophy and Indian music. He was eventually initiated into the priesthood[7] in Chidambaram and trained in all the technical aspects of conducting rituals in the Saiva Agama tradition.[8] He also learned the Sanskrit *mantras* which are recited in the context of Hindu rituals.

Most of the Hindu temples still continue to have non-Brahmin priests, and many of them are not adequately qualified to conduct rituals in the temples. They learnt by observing the older generations. There is no organisational network that would facilitate the training of traditional Hindu priests in South Africa.[9] Consequently, the South African Hindus either have to depend on foreign priests or be content with the local priests who are engaged in this profession as a part time job.

Some Mixed Feelings about Priests from Abroad

Currently there are two schools of thought in South Africa, among the Hindus regarding priests coming from India or Sri Lanka. There are those who feel that the only way to re-establish Hindu rituals properly and perform them meaningfully is to bring priests from either India or Sri Lanka. They are worried about the lack of proper knowledge of ritual procedures, the accompanying *mantras*, etc., among the priests in South Africa. Let us examine this line of thinking in some detail.

In general, the South African Indians have always looked towards India not only for cultural and religious purposes but also for general educational reasons. The apartheid laws in South Africa have prevented Indians from pursuing higher education and, thus, moving upward on the social ladder. For the last two or three decades a significant number of Indians, have sent their children to India to pursue studies in medicine and other cultural and religious disciplines. For instance, most of the Indian staff in the departments of Indian languages, religion, music, dance, etc., at the University of Durban-Westville have been trained in the Indian universities. This was not only due to the lack of opportunities for Indian students within the country, but also due to the widely held notion that in terms of the languages, culture, religion, etc., India has better facilities and opportunities. Students of medicine went to India certainly because of the lack of opportunities and encouragement within the country. The students of culture, religion, etc., went to India in pursuit of a better knowledge which is not available within South Africa. While this trend continues to persist to this day, surprisingly no attempts seem to have been made to send people to be trained as Hindu priests. As mentioned earlier, so far there is only one young man sent to India to be trained as a priest. The Indian Hindu community in South Africa certainly displays a profound interest in religious and cultural matters. But in the face of discouraging apartheid laws in the past, they had undoubtedly placed economic goals ahead of everything. And this should explain why, on the one hand, large numbers of Indians went abroad to pursue higher studies in the field of medicine and other professions and almost none to be trained as priests. The trend toward bringing priests from India and Sri Lanka is relatively recent.

Some Hindus certainly feel that bringing priests from India or Sri Lanka is not always a viable option. It is such Hindus who constitute the second school of thought. Let me now examine their fears and anxieties at some length. The Hindus that came to South Africa belonged to nineteenth century of India, and brought with them traditions that existed mainly outside the Brahminical practice. As a result, they developed a distinct, non-Brahminical practice in South Africa. Whatever Brahminical elements they had brought were drawn mainly from what they witnessed during the nineteenth century. They made not only a mixture of the Brahminical and non-Brahminical traditions, but also an eclectic mixture of traditions from various linguistic groups. As such, the Hindi-speaking, the Telugu-speaking and Tamil-speaking indentured labourers, living side by side, exchanged their local customs and practices and developed a unique blend of Hindu religious practice. This was facilitated by the fact that the early indentured labourers were bent on preserving what little they had brought with them by assimilating each other's customs and practices mutually, instead of being exclusivistic. The indentured labourers, coming from various linguistic backgrounds and living in an alien land among alien people, had one thing in common, that is their being Hindu. They realised that the only way they could preserve their Hindu culture was to assimilate each other's Hindu practices consciously. So they celebrated each other's local festivals and participated in each other's local ceremonies. Thus for instance, today Kavadi is not an exclusively Tamil Hindu ritual but is practised by many Hindi speakers and others. Another example is the celebration of the Maha Shivaratri festival. In the greater Durban area at least more than 20 temples that cut across North Indian-South Indian cultural distinctions and denominational differences have this year (2011) celebrated the festival (see *Tribune Herald*, February 27, 2011, p. 2).

This unique blend of non-Brahminical and Brahminical aspects on the one hand, and the various local customs and practices of different linguistic groups on the other, is beginning to be at stake. Some Hindus see the introduction of Brahmin priests from outside as detrimental to the existing practices of South African Hindus. Besides, some feel that the introduction of a "Brahmin" as priest is to reintroduce an element of caste structure into the South African Hindu society. Some social scientists like Hilda Kuper argue that caste within the Hindu community in South Africa is virtually non-existent.[10] Although the introduction of the Brahmin as a priest in South Africa so far has not made any significant difference in the Hindu society in terms of caste change, some Hindu members seem to be concerned about the long term effects of such a practice. Perhaps, their fears are not totally unfounded. In the long run, the existing unique practices of the South African Hindus are bound to be modified by the "properly" trained

Brahmin priests. Nevertheless, the South African Hindus will continue to develop a type of Hinduism that is perhaps unique to them. Although the reintroduction of caste into the South African Hindu society may not be an easy possibility, the consciousness of linguistic affiliations seem to be increasing.[11]

Notes

1. Ganesha is associated with the removal of hurdles in life (his name, Vighnesvara, indicates the same—*vighna* means hurdle, *Isvara* means lord, thus Vighnesvara means the lord who helps to cross hurdles). The Hindus believe that worshipping Ganesha is essential before worshipping any deity. He is believed to place obstacles if he is not worshipped before the other deities. Hindus therefore believe that proper worship of Ganesha will result in the removal of all difficulties.
2. Utsavamurtis (festival images) are the images set apart for the festival procession. They are mobile unlike the fixed image in the sanctum sanctorum.
3. The image in the Durban temple of Jagannatha is perhaps the tallest and bears very little artistic intricacies. In fact it looks very plain and simple. The temple is more than hundred years old. It is said to be modelled after the temple in Puri, Orissa in India. The custodianship and the priesthood of this temple are held by a Maharaj family who live in a house next to the temple. According to their own claim, they originally came from Uttar Pradesh in India but belong to Bihar.
4. Hanuman is the son of Pawan—the Wind God. However, in the Dravidian tradition, Hanuman and Ganesha are considered sons of Siva. See W.T. Elmore. *Dravidian Gods in Modern Hinduism.* (New Delhi: Asian Educational Services, 1984, first published in 1913), p. 6. Murugan is the other Son of Siva.
5. Although almost all Hindu temples today draw Hindus of all linguistic backgrounds, my reference here is to the dominant presence. For instance, at the Cato Manor temple and Umgeni Road temple, I have noticed that not only the temple officials and priests, but the devotees are also predominantly Tamil-speaking South Indians. In both these temples, the priests are Tamil-speaking Sri Lankans, most members of the committees are South Indians (either Telugu or Tamil), and the language used in rituals is Tamil, though Sanskrit *mantras* are also recited.
6. In the Ganesha temple at Mt Edgecombe, Vishnu is seated on the southern side of the *gopuram*, in the Sri Subramania Alayam of Verulam Lord Venkatesvara (manifestation of Vishnu) has a shrine on the eastern side within the main temple hall, in the Siva-Subramania and

Mariamman temple (Pietermaritzburg), there is a separate shrine for Vishnu on the eastern side.

7. Without initiation one is not entitled to enter the temple and perform rituals. At the time of initiation, the initiate is invested with a thread which should always be worn as a mark of his initiation.
8. In all the Saiva temples in India, rituals are performed according to the Saiva Agama tradition. There are three ritual traditions in India, namely, the Saiva, Vaishnava, and Sakta ritual traditions. Although the Agamas have claimed Vedic lineage, they are considered a distinct class in the ritual traditions in Hinduism. They seem to have assimilated a great deal of Tantric ritual procedures as part of the temple and domestic rituals.
9. The Arya Samaj is an exception to this. See the chapter on the Arya Samaj.
10. See Hilda Kuper. *Indian People in Natal* (Pietermaritzburg: Natal University Press, 1960). It must be noted, however, that Kuper's observations do not seem to reflect all sections of the Hindu community in South Africa. Among the Gujaratis, there seems to be a definite caste consciousness. For instance, the Cape Town Gujaratis have two Vishnu temples, one for the *mochis* (shoemakers) and another for the Patels (business class). Among the Hindi-speaking Hindus also there is some caste consciousness, especially among those who have their last names as Singh and Maharaj. Although the Maharaj community belongs to the Brahmins, it forms the lower strata within the Brahmins and perform the functions of cooking at the Hindu ceremonies, such as, weddings etc. But in South Africa, it has taken up, in some cases, the priesthood in Hindu temples, and as such considers itself higher than the rest of the Hindus. While these caste groupings are visible within each linguistic community in various degrees, the South African Hindus in general tend to claim that caste is not an important factor any more in their social relations. As shown in the last section on "Perceptions and Attitudes of Hindus in South Africa", the majority of Hindus (80% male and 79% female) across the board claimed that caste is no longer a factor among the Hindus.
11. In South Africa, marriages are usually encouraged within the same linguistic group. There is, however, some flexibility between the Tamil and the Telugu groups.

4 Centrality of Ritual

Temple and Domestic Practices

In a survey study on 'Religion in a South African Indian Community' conducted by J.H. Hofmeyr and G.C. Oosthuizen (Durban: University of Durban-Westville, No. 12, October 1981) it is noted that (i) "the traditional forms of ritual Hinduism are being eroded" (Hofmeyr and Oosthuizen, 4); (ii) because of western education the younger Hindus "will use the traditional temple less and less as the ritual religious style with which the temple is associated" (Hofmeyr and Oosthuizen, 14); (iii) "the better educated older Hindu uses the temple significantly less regularly than the less educated ones" (Hofmeyr and Oosthuizen, 14); (iv) the survival of Hindu temple rituals depends on the broadening scope of the neo-Hindu movements. But such movements "will not be that of the traditional ritual Hindu style, it will be modelled on the "meeting houses" of groups like that of the Arya Samaj" (Hofmeyr and Oosthuizen, 14); (v) "Hindus worship together as a family far less regularly than Muslims or Christians" (with the exception of the neo-Hindu groups, such as Divine Life Society, Ramakrishna Centre, etc.) (Hofmeyr and Oosthuizen, 20); (vi) with regard to the domestic rituals "men were significantly less inclined to participate than women" (Hofmeyr and Oosthuizen, 27).

While all the above conclusions are supported by statistical data, the authors of the study seem to miss an important aspect of the Hindu tradition, i.e., historically Hinduism has always survived because of its ritual orientation and not so much for its doctrinal orientation. Although the Hindu ritual has certain corporate aspect to it, by and large it is individual oriented in contradistinction to the Christian and Islamic worship.

Although doctrinal and philosophical aspects are important for any religious tradition, it must be firmly grounded in the ritual in which it is expressed in a concrete form rather than in abstract terms. This is not to suggest that one is more important than the other, but rather to affirm that ritual is what provides a concrete expression to a religious tradition. The abstract is concretised in ritual. In the case of the Hindu tradition, ritual is much more pronounced than other dimensions. The conclusions that are arrived at by the above mentioned study are based on sociological and statistical data taken at a given point of time. Besides, some of the questions that the authors asked of the informants of various religious groups are misleading. For instance, one of the questions that the authors asked was regarding the regularity of attendance in respective places of worship among Hindus, Muslims and Christians. The data reveals higher incidence of attendance among the Muslims and the Christians than among the Hindus (Hofmeyr and Oosthuizen, 29).

On the basis of the above observation the study points out that there is a breakdown in "the traditional ritual temple function" (Hofmeyr and Oosthuizen, 28). Although the study does take into account the fact that the "temple of Hinduism functions differently", (Hofmeyr and Oosthuizen, 13) the authors have tended to conflate the issue of Hindu temple worship with that of the Muslims and the Christians. This way of posing uniform questions to different religious groups would be to mix apples and oranges. Thus, the study fails to take into account a historical continuum which would give us a better sense of how to understand the Hindu tradition. In understanding a religious tradition, a sense of its historical development, therefore, is more useful to grasp as to how a religious tradition expresses itself. This historical approach provides us with a coherent understanding of the tradition.

To illustrate the point I might use the case of the South Indian Vaishnava tradition. During the early centuries of the Common Era, it arose out of the devotional tradition of the Alvar singers. During the medieval times it became a sophisticated philosophical tradition in the hands of the early teachers, such as Yamuna, Ramanuja, et al. But simultaneously, it also became grounded in a ritual tradition called the *Pancaratra Agama* tradition. Today, if one were to go, for instance, to Melkote or Srirangam, or visit any typical Vaishnava community in India one would find a highly ritualistic Vaishnavism. If one were studying only the Alvar singers, a natural conclusion would be that the South Indian Vaishnavism is a more devotional religion.[1] But then one fails to see the subsequent changes. We notice a pattern in the case of the South Indian Vaishnavism. Ritualism therefore is an essential aspect of Hinduism that needs to be taken into account in understanding South African Hinduism as well.

Turning to the above mentioned study once again, I am hesitant to accept, the general conclusion that "the traditional forms of ritual Hinduism are being eroded" among the South African Hindus in the light of the sustained historical trend in Hinduism. In her recent study on the Hindi-speaking South Africans, U.D. Shukla attempts to show that the Hindu rituals among the Hindi-speaking South Africans are very much alive. She argues:

> The finding that there was religious degeneration amongst Hindus as postulated by Naidoo who cites Pandit Naradev Vedalankar and Prof. Hilda Kuper in support of his contention that the religious observances of those early Hindus were "so grotesque as to be totally devoid of any real religious meaning" (Naidoo, 67) is firmly rejected by the writer, whose findings indicate that meaningful Hinduism was kept alive through ritual and ceremonies. (Shukla, 174–75)

In another recent study titled "Hindu Firewalking Ritual in Natal", Alleyn Diesel points at the increasing popularity of the ritual among Hindus in the Natal area. Refuting Kuper's statement that "There is a definite trend towards abandoning non-Sanskritic village rites," Diesel argues, "However, it would appear from the increasing numbers of people who attend the firewalking and other similar festivals that they are growing in popularity rather than diminishing" (Diesel, 30). If history is our guide for the future, I feel that the Hindu ritual will survive and perhaps take deeper roots in the South African context.

The Hindu ritual survives not on the basis of numbers, how many persons are present in the temple and how often the Hindus visit the temple. It survives because of their need to perform rituals in order to achieve something, whether it is something mundane (e.g., good health, prosperity, etc.) or the ultimate goal of release from worldly attachments (*moksha*). In many traditional societies, no matter how religious or non-religious people might appear, they seem to participate in rites often involuntarily and unconsciously. Many South African Hindus today are as westernised as any other people living in the twenty-first century. And yet their lifestyle is replete with rites. For instance, Hindus in general believe that wealth and prosperity is associated with the goddess Lakshmi. Whether they are very religious or not, whether they belong to a Sanatanist Hindu background or a reformed Hindu organisation, there is a certain behaviour noticed in the way, for instance, money is received by the South African Hindus—with the right arm stretched while the left palm is in contact with the right elbow—a posture followed in receiving sacred items in the temples or at ritual ceremonies. This religious behaviour is transferred into secular dealings quite unconsciously [or perhaps quite consciously because earning money and aspiring for prosperity is part of the sacred duty of a Hindu. That is why the Hindu religious goals include both prosperity (*artha*) and carnal enjoyment (*kama*)].[2]

Again, I have observed in South Africa that whenever Hindus come across a temple, their instant reaction is to turn toward it for a second and bring their two palms together in the gesture of saluting the deity. Such actions are predetermined in a society. They link their mundane life with their religiosity. Often people are not fully aware of their ostensible religious behaviour. As we shall notice in the last chapter, many South African Hindus claim to have done away with a number of ritualistic actions either because of their association with a reformist movement, or because they are highly educated. And yet one would notice hundreds and thousands of Hindus gathering at the temples, especially on festival days, and performing rituals in order to fulfil the vows they had taken sometime in the past. Many of them also display their religious behaviour in front of the pictures of various deities in their homes. The pervasiveness of ritual activity directed to the various deities is recorded by a student researcher who interviewed a self-styled reformer named P.A. Pillay in 1985. The student notes:

> Between 1962–1963 Mr Pillay visited most of the existing temples in South Africa in an effort to have Saivism[3] adopted in one of these temples. This failed for one very important reason. Most of these temples were not prepared to part with their many idols, viz., Hanuman, Krishna, Murugan, etc. (Bhana, 9)

He further notes that the *Kavadi* worship is so pervasive that people do not want to give it up. The centrality of ritual for Hindus may be seen in that even after their conversion to another religion they tended to be attracted to some form of ritual and tried to find such ritual activity in the new religion that they have adopted. In the cases where some Hindus converted to Roman Catholicism, it is observed that "[T]hough none of the converts could be described as being excessively obsessed with the external rituals of the Church ... they are susceptible to the attraction of ritual to a marked degree" (Currin, 175). Furthermore, the dramatic character of the Hindu ritual is noted by Oosthuizen, "Hindu rites have a highly dramatic character" (Oosthuizen, 184). It is this dramatic appeal of the ritual on the Hindu mind that draws the Hindu towards observance of rituals from time to time in order to re-establish his ties with the deity and the tradition of his community.

In the present chapter, I shall show the types of the temple and domestic rituals that have survived thus far among the South African Hindus. I shall consider the Hindu rituals under the following group for this purpose: (i) traditional Sanskritic rituals (often termed as Brahminical rituals); (ii) non-Sanskritic rituals (normally termed by anthropologists as "folk" ritual traditions); and (iii) neo-Hindu rituals (this incorporates the neo-Hindu movements). Under the category of "traditional Sanskritic ritual," I shall include rituals performed in connection with deities, such as Vishnu, Siva, Murugan, Ganesha, who are part of the Sanskritic (Brahminical) Hindu pantheon. In the category of "non-Sanskritic rituals," I shall refer to the ceremonies offered to deities, such as Mariamman, Hanuman, Draupadi, all of whom are associated with what is known among scholars as village/folk Hinduism. A fuller discussion on the goddess rituals will be dealt with in another chapter (see Chapter 6). In the category of "neo-Hindu rituals", I shall discuss the worship patterns in the modern reformist religious movements, such as the Arya Samaj, Hare Krishna Movement, worship of Satya Sai Baba, etc.

By dividing Hindu rituals in South Africa in three broad categories, I am making distinctions between first, Sanskritic traditions and non-Sanskritic traditions; second, older Hindu forms and modern Hindu forms of rituals. These distinctions, however, are not to isolate the various forms of Hindu rituals, but rather to use the categories for the purpose of clarifying the complex phenomena of Hindu rituals. Furthermore, the distinctions, that I indicated do not make room for group loyalties and fine sectarian differences. On the contrary, I found on the basis of my observations that members of one form of worship are often found in the other. In other words, those who are involved in the "traditional Sanskritic Hindu rituals" are involved in the other two forms as well. Similarly, those who are involved in either "neo-Hindu rituals" or "non-Sanskritic rituals" are also found in the other groups. In general, those who call themselves Sanatanists (traditional) in South Africa perform both the Brahminical and the non-Brahminical rituals. In India, however, the distinction between Brahminical and non-Brahminical rituals is much clearer, especially in the Brahminical temples.

In the case of the distinction between "traditional Sanskritic rituals" and "non-Sanskritic rituals", I found that the broader location of the rituals is often the same (e.g., the Mariamman rituals are performed in the precincts of the same temple as the Sanskritic or Brahminical rituals). The difference, of course, is that the particular shrine of the deity to whom the ritual is offered becomes the focus of worship at that point of time. The locus of the neo-Hindu rituals, however, is distinct and separate. Nevertheless, it must be noted that at least two reformed Hindu organisations in the Natal region began their initial activities and worship in a traditional Hindu temple (e.g., the Divine Life Society and the Ramakrishna Centre, both started their worship activities in the Vishnu temple on Umgeni Road, Durban). In other words, the neo-Hindu organisations and temples are not poles apart but rather there seems to be some cooperation between the two types.

Traditional Sanskritic Rituals

The use of the term "Traditional Sanskritic Rituals" must be defined clearly in the context of South African Hindu temples. Earlier I noted that the priesthood in South African temples is of a mixed nature, incorporating both Brahminical and non-Brahminical, but predominantly non-Brahminical elements. Therefore, when I speak of the "Traditional Sanskritic Rituals" I mean that historically these temple rituals belonged to the Sanskritic (Brahminical) tradition. But in South Africa, what one finds is that temple rituals are performed by priests who neither have a knowledge of Sanskrit nor any Brahminical background. Therefore, many priests perform the ritual acts without much regard to the accompanying chants (*mantras*). Often they are substituted with spontaneous and extemporaneous words that the priest utters as he performs certain acts, such as washing the image.

In the predominantly Tamil-oriented temples (e.g., most Saiva temples), Tamil chants and lyrics have replaced the Sanskrit chants (*mantras*). In most Tamil temples, one finds Tamil books that guide the priest in the process of performing rituals. In most Gujarati- and Hindi-speaking temples, Sanskrit *mantras* are used. Most members of these communities have memorised the *mantras*. In the Tamil and Telugu groups too most members have memorised the lyrics and chants. Thus, the participation of the devotees in the process of ritual is impressive by virtue of the fact that they have memorised the chants and lyrics appropriate for the occasion. The lack of understanding of the meaning of various ritual acts and symbols do not seem to have prevented their continuation in South Africa. The meaning and the intent of a ritual will, perhaps, be recovered as the members of the Hindu community increase their knowledge of their scriptures, ritualistic symbols and so on. But what seems to be important is the performance of the ritual.

The 'Traditional Sanskritic Rituals' in the temples are divided into three kinds in line with the general practice in India: (i) Daily Temple Rituals, (ii) Occasional Temple Rituals and (iii) Festival Rituals. In this chapter, I shall deal with 'Daily Temple Rituals' and 'Occasional Rituals'. I shall deal with festival rituals separately in another chapter.

Daily Temple Rituals

The daily temple rituals consist of all the ritual activities that take place within the temple complex from the time the temple is opened to the time it is closed. Except for the temples where there are no regular priests, Hindu temples are usually open in the morning. The priest or his assistant cleans the temple precincts and then enters it. First, the images are bathed ritually and decorated in colourful garments, ornaments, and flowers. Then the oil lamp is lit in front of the presiding deity and a lamp offering (*arati*) is made to the deity. The temple then is considered open to the public for worship. During the day, the priest performs a variety of rituals depending on the needs and requests of the devotees. Other than those rituals, where there is a properly trained Brahmin priest, such as a Sri Lankan one, rituals are performed in the morning, at mid-day and in the evening. Although the traditional Hindu practice prescribes that rituals in the temple be performed five times a day (morning, mid-day, afternoon, evening and finally when the temple closes at night), in South Africa the practice varies. In some temples where there are no priests, rituals are not performed on a daily basis. Where there is a Sri Lankan Brahmin priest, rituals are performed at least three times a day, apart from the rituals performed as and when the devotees visit.[4] I am not aware of any temple in South Africa where the rituals are performed five times a day.

Domestic Rituals

The South African Hindus, like their counterparts in India, have various domestic rituals performed on various occasions. This again varies from one linguistic group to another. Most Hindi-speaking Hindus perform daily rituals, such as *sandhya* (offering *puja* to one's own deity, often to Surya, the sun god), lighting a lamp in the house in front of the image of a deity or in front of the *Jhanda* (flag).[5] In more traditional Hindi-speaking homes, the daily rituals are followed meticulously. In such homes, worship of Siva is conducted on Mondays, Hanuman worship on Tuesday, Wednesday is an open day for any deity, on Thursday Sarasvati and others and on Friday Lakshmi is worshipped. *Sandhya* prayers are found among the Tamils also. Most Tamils also light a lamp called *kamakshi (kamacchi—Tamil), velukku* (light of the goddess, Kamakshi or popularly known among Tamils as "God lamp").[6] This lighting of the lamp is done both in the morning and evening. Usually a range of deities, namely, Ganesha, Siva, Murugan, Lakshmi and Sarasvati are invoked at these daily rituals. The Telugu community more or less follows the same pattern as the Tamils. The Gujarati community also follows the lighting of the lamp in the morning, etc., rituals.

While Lakshmi worship is common to all linguistic groups among Hindus, one finds that different communities have different favourite deities. For instance, among most Hindi-speaking people, Hanuman is a special deity, and for Tamils Murugan is special. Telugu and Gujarati communities, in general, are Vishnu worshippers, and hence they worship mainly Rama and Krishna, the two most popular incarnations of Vishnu.

Nevertheless, most Hindus try to affirm that all deities are equally important and furthermore, all of them represent one God. To an outsider, it may appear like a contradiction between what they practise and what they believe in. But in the Hindu psyche, there seems to be no such contradiction. And it is rooted both in their ritual and philosophical traditions of the past.

Occasional Temple Rituals

Occasional temple rituals mainly involve those rituals that are performed for fulfilling specific requests of the devotees. In South Africa, as in India, Hindus take vows for various reasons. For instance, the health of an individual member of a family, economic prospects, business venture, surviving an accident, etc., ordinary life-situations can give rise to occasions when the members of a family might take a vow that they would perform special rituals and offer prayers at the temple. Car prayer is one good example of occasional rituals. That is, when a Hindu family buys a car, they would first take the car to the temple and have the priest perform a ritual of protection. Typically, the ritual involves the priest performing *arati* while the members of the family with the new car perform circumambulation around the car, and then the driver of the car symbolically drives three times over the lemons placed under the car tyres. Most *Kavadi* and 'firewalking' rituals in South Africa have to do with the vows that people take. I shall deal with 'firewalking' ritual separately in the chapter on goddess worship. The *Kavadi* ritual is dealt with in the chapter on festivals.

Occasional Domestic Rituals

Occasional rituals also include those that are performed at home during the various stages in one's life: birth ceremonies, house-warming ceremonies (a ritual ceremony performed when a family moves into a new home), marriage ceremonies, funeral ceremonies, etc. In South Africa, not all Hindu domestic ceremonies require the presence of a priest. In most cases, birth ceremonies, name-giving ceremonies and house-warming ceremonies are done within the family often without the presence of a priest. The most common ceremonies in which the presence of the priest is required are the marriage ceremony and the funeral ceremony. These are often performed in the home of the concerned family. According to the traditional Brahminical practice in India, the Hindu priesthood is hierarchically classified so that the priests who perform daily rituals in the temples do not perform marriage and funeral ceremonies.[7] And the one who performs marriage ceremonies does not perform funeral ceremonies. Such rites that are part of domestic rituals are assigned to a different class of priests within the Brahmin caste. On the other hand, in the South African context, since most priests are of non-Brahmin background, such distinctions have no relevance. Often the priest who performs the marriage rituals also performs funeral ceremonies.

The reason for this kind of situation is not simply the lack of a sufficient number of priests, although it is often cited as one reason. But one has to understand the very nature of the social background of the Indian community in South Africa. In certain non-Brahmin communities in India, some public ceremonies, such as marriage, funeral, etc., are performed by non-Brahmin priests. Often they are the elders of the community. The Indian community that came to South Africa reflects a similar background. As such, some of the elders in the Indian community assumed the role of the priest and performed some of the public ceremonies. And to this day the same practice continues to a large extent in South Africa. This trend might eventually change as the orthodox class of priests from India and Sri Lanka take over the Hindu priesthood in South Africa. There is at the moment some discussion among the Hindu leaders on whether to bring Brahmin priests from outside or not.[8]

Among the South African Hindus, birth ceremony (or hair removing ceremony) is an important ritual. It is practised both among the South Indians as well as North Indians. Among Tamilians, it is known as *Katteri*[9] prayer, and is performed in the seventh month.[10] During this ritual, a black rooster and a white hen are sacrificed. After the offering of the fowls, the child's hair is shaved off. It was reported to me that this ritual is usually undertaken when a woman does not conceive for a long time. Thus, the purpose of the ritual is to remove any evil surrounding either the child or the mother. However, it must be pointed out that this ritual is a commonly accepted one among all the Hindus in South Africa, whereas the idea that 'this ritual is performed only when a woman does not conceive for a long time' seems to exist mainly among the Tamil-speaking Hindus. According to Kuppusami, the hair removing ritual is commonly practised among both Tamil- and Hindi-speaking Hindus, though both groups have their distinct ways of observing it. It is pointed out that among the Hindi-speaking Hindus, "the shaving of the head must be done in the presence of the paternal sister (sic)." (Kuppusami, 23).

Regarding the funeral ceremony, there seems to be some difference in the observance of the number of days of mourning before the ceremony after the death of a person. Among the Tamilians, funeral ceremonies are performed usually on the eighth day and the sixteenth day and then at the end of a year. Among the Hindi-speaking Hindus, it is usually performed on the thirteenth day.[11] Some of the Hindi-speaking Hindus also perform the funeral ceremony after one month, six months and then at the end of a year.

Apart from the commonly performed ceremonies mentioned above, some individual families may undertake various other rituals. For instance, among the Hindi-speaking Hindus a special ritual to Brahma (one of the Hindu Trinity, the others being Siva and Vishnu) is performed once a year. Although sometimes it is performed during the time of the *Navaratri* festival, it can be performed at any time of the year. It can be performed either on one's own or officiated by a priest. It is a rather brief ritual and lasts for not more than five minutes. Only the men are entitled to have offerings like sweets etc., which are offered to the deity on this occasion. The ritual is performed by the head of the house. If the father is no more, the eldest son would have to perform it. A two-metre piece of calico cloth is placed before the image (*murti*) of Brahma (the images of the other members of the Trinity are also present). Apart from it, a towel, a handkerchief, special wooden sandals, three kinds of fruit, sweets and some white cotton thread are placed in front of the deity. A lamp is lit and *arati* is performed. If a priest is present, he reads the section of the scripture called 'Brahma p'.[12] Wooden sandals are given to him.

Another more popular domestic ceremony among both Hindi-speaking Hindus and the Gujaratis is the Satyanarayana Vrata *katha*[13] (among the Hindi-speaking Hindus it is simply known as *katha*). This ceremony is held publicly either in a temple complex or in a public hall when the community feels the need for it, or when a visiting specialist in Hindu rituals arrives. It is more commonly held at home, sometimes once a year, once in four years depending on the individual family and its need. Often members of the family take vows to hold the *katha* ceremony. The central activity of this ceremony is the recitation of the sacred narrative about Lord Satyanarayana. I shall describe the procedure of the ceremony in brief.

Like any other Hindu ceremony, the *katha* also requires certain things. They include: five types of fruits, sweets, five types of ambrosia (panchamrita), suji (a sweet preparation made of fine broken wheat/cream of wheat), honey, rose water, perfume water, sour milk, betel leaves, betel nut, *sindhur* (vermilion), white rice, *kumkum* (red powder), *haldi* (turmeric powder), sandal powder, water, flowers, incense, oil and *ghee* (clarified butter). Having obtained all these, a special raised platform (altar) is constructed square in shape. Four oil lamps are placed in four corners. The raised platform is decorated with coloured flour and rice; four bamboo poles are erected in the four corners in such a way that the four bamboos are joined together at the centre of the platform and they are tied together in a conical shape; a white piece of cloth is placed over the bamboo structure; a few garlands are also placed over it; then a Lakshmi lamp, a vessel (*kalasa*) with a coconut inverted on it is placed on the platform; the vessel contains water and some mango leaves; a mixture of turmeric powder and flour and *kusa* grass (a type of grass used in the Hindu rituals); a betel nut is also placed on the platform; the betel nut and the *kusa* grass are said to represent Ganesha. The priest then takes the image of Ganesha and the vessel (*kalasa*) and smears them with *sindhur* (vermilion), sandal paste, *kumkum* and turmeric powder. He then winds a cotton thread around the image of Ganesha and the vessel. Then offerings of fruits, sweets, etc., are made to Ganesha, Lakshmi and Vishnu. Then, Vishnu is especially invoked into the sacred vessel. As the offerings are made to the deities, the lamps are lit and the images of the deities are anointed while the sacred *mantras* are chanted.

The actual recital of the *katha* begins after all these rituals are over and some preliminary prayers have been offered. Five chapters[14] from the story of the Lord Satyanarayana are read. Each chapter concludes with the sound of a conch shell and an offering of flowers and white rice to the sacred vessel (*kalasa*). A *havan* (*homa*) ceremony concludes the narration of the story. At the end, *arati* is offered to the deity and the devotees are blessed. The whole ceremony concludes with the reading of the *Santi Path* (the hymn of peace). There is no bar on either sex in this ceremony, and any number of people can participate in the main ritual. The sweets and other offerings are distributed among the devotees present. The sacred vessel is kept in the house for three days. The bamboos, etc., are immersed in a river.

Closely connected with the *katha* ceremony is the ritual called *jhanda*. A walk around the Indian townships in any town in South

Africa shows green, yellow and red flags in front of some Hindu homes. Although one would find such flags mostly in the Hindi-speaking homes, I did come across some Tamil homes also that displayed them. The word *jhanda* literally means a flag. But from the religious point of view, such flags, as one finds in the front yard of the Hindu homes in South Africa, are usually associated with the deity named Hanuman. Hanuman is a deity with the face of a monkey on a human body. His presence in the Hindu pantheon provides an insight into the multivalent dimension of the Hindu tradition. He seems to combine both the folk and the classical (Brahminical) aspects of Hinduism. Usually, in India, Hanuman's image is found in the outskirts of a village, for he is considered the guardian of the village. This is true of both North and South India. In the well-known epic *Ramayana*, Hanuman is closely associated with Rama, especially in his search for his wife, Sita. Allusions to his character are also made in the epic *Mahabharata*. One of the Pandava brothers (Bhima) is considered the brother of Hanuman in the sense that both of them were born under the influence of the wind god (Vayu). Thus, the flag of Hanuman also figures in the *Mahabharata*.

Usually, the *katha* and *jhanda* ceremonies are held together. They are held in individual homes in the presence of invited guests. They are, therefore, considered private or domestic rituals. They are not temple rituals nor are they festival rituals. There is no particular time in the year for these rituals to be observed. Their observance depends on the vows taken by the members of a family. They can be observed on any day of the week (Nowbath, Chotai and Lalla, 20).

Non-Sanskritic Temple Rituals: Goddess Rituals

Many of the non-Sanskritic rituals are associated with the worship of the goddess in the form of Draupadi Amman, Mariamman, Gangai Amman, and others. Some male deities, such as Mathuraiviran (associated with the folk goddesses) and Hanuman are also part of the non-Sanskritic rituals, although Hanuman does have links with the Sanskritic tradition. In the case of the female deities mentioned above, the most well-known rituals in South Africa are 'firewalking' and the 'six-foot dance'. Both are associated with the Draupadi. In India, these rituals are performed in the non-Brahminical temples during any festival related to the goddess. But in South Africa, rituals like 'firewalking' and 'six-foot dance' are associated exclusively with the Draupadi festival. During my interviews with some of the priests in South Africa, they did, however, indicate that these rituals can be performed at any goddess festival.

In almost all the Amman (goddess) temples, rituals are normally performed according to the non-Brahminical traditions. Only in temples where there are Sri Lankan Brahmin priests, rituals are performed with a combination of Brahminical rituals. Some priests from outside South Africa, though trained in the Brahminical rituals, are willing to perform in accordance with the local customs and traditions of South African Indians.

The non-Brahminical rituals are performed both in the temple complex and the homes of devotees. In some Hindu homes, (mainly Tamil-speaking homes) I have noticed in the courtyard a stone shaped in the *linga* form and a trident behind it. Some turmeric, and *kumkum* (red coloured powder) is applied on the stone and on the trident. There are also private shrines that I have come across in Durban, mainly in the Chatsworth area. Often women are in charge of the priestly functions in these shrines. Devotees with special requests go to these shrines and have some special prayers said for them. These prayers are often referred to as "bad-luck prayers". Whenever something of a negative nature happens in the family, many Hindus in South Africa approach a person who performs these special prayers to ward off evil. There seems to be a growing demand for these semi-priests[15] who say these prayers.

Ritual in the Neo-Hindu Movements: *Satsangh, Havan, Bhajan* and *Arati*

The neo-Hindu groups are largely oriented toward philosophical traditions of the Hindus, and as such ritual in the traditional Hindu form does not find a significant place in their pattern of worship. Nevertheless, some basic forms of Hindu ritual have survived even in these movements. The basic form of the neo-Hindu ritual is centred on what is known as *satsanghs* (literally it means the community of the true ones). Once every week, members of all neo-Hindu organisations gather in their respective organisations (or shrines or temples or meeting places) for worship, singing, and offering *arati* to the divine. Although the neo-Hindu movements generally pay more attention to philosophical discourses, they affirm their faith in a form of divinity that may or may not be understood in anthropomorphic form. It is for this reason alone one should consider the significance of some ritual aspects within their religious practice. Those organisations that subscribe to some form of anthropomorphism of the divine would tend to have ritual substantially present, as in the case of the Hare Krishna movement. Conversely, those who subscribe to abstract forms of the divine tend to minimalise ritual. For most of them, the *havan* is perhaps the most basic and essential one. But in the case of the Arya Samaj which is more inclined to the Vedic tradition, the *havan* is quite central, although they do not subscribe to the worship of many deities as other Sanatani Hindus do, nor do they attach importance to the anthropomorphism of the divine. The *Saiva Siddhanta Sangam* also performs *havan* on certain occasions, although their worship pattern follows the congregational singing of *bhajans* more. The Hare Krishna temples in South Africa observe typical Vaishnava rituals that one would find in any Vishnu temple. The Divine Life Society and the Ramakrishna Mission also have *havans* performed on certain festival occasions.

Satsangh in that sense is another form of congregational worship common to all the neo-Hindu organisations. These *satsanghs* follow the *bhajan* type of worship pattern. In the Ramakrishna Mission, the *satsangh* ends with a special *arati* performed by the presiding Swamiji if it is a general congregation. In the Ashram (at the Asherville Ashram which is dedicated to the women monks) run by the nuns, a woman *sannyasin* performs the *arati*. The Satya Sai Baba centres also follow devotional singing. But in all these *satsanghs*, the lighting of the lamp and offering *arati* to the sacred symbol or image is common practice. In the case of Ramakrishna Centre, the presiding Swamiji of the Ashram performs the *arati* ritual in which the ritual acts, such as hand gestures (*mudras*) and symbols, are quite the same as in any traditional Hindu temple. The uniqueness of the *bhajans* sung in the neo-Hindu movements is that most of these hymns and songs are in praise of their respective gurus, and founders. For instance, the Satya Sai Baba devotees sing *bhajans* in praise of Satya Sai Baba, the Ramakrishna Centre sings *bhajans* in praise of Ramakrishna, and the Saiva Siddhanta Sangam sings in praise of the early Saiva saints. Nevertheless, most of the neo-Hindu groups also sing hymns in praise of Rama, Krishna and other deities.

Notes

1. F. Hardy in his study of the Alvars (*Viraha Bhakti*) arrives at the conclusion that South Indian Vaishnavism is merely Krishna Bhakti. See F. Hardy. *Viraha Bhakti: The Early Krishna Devotion in South India* (Delhi: Oxford University Press, 1983).
2. The four goals of a Hindu are: Too simplistic (*dharma*), prosperity (*artha*), carnal enjoyment (*kama*), and liberation (*moksha*).
3. Saivism here refers to the Saiva Siddhanta philosophy which encourages worship of formless Siva. Less emphasis is placed on ritual activity. Meditation and devotion are the more acceptable forms of worship.
4. In most South African temples, devotees visit temples mostly on a Saturday or Sunday, with some exceptions. Thus devotees rarely visit the temple on a daily basis. Only when there is a need or a special occasion, such as ill-health, starting a new job, buying a new car, etc., the people visit the temple for prayers and blessings. This does not mean that ritual has become less significant in the lives of the Hindus. Historically, in the Hindu tradition, there is no prescription that one should visit the temple either on a daily basis or weekly basis. It is customary that Hindus visit temples mainly on special occasions or when they have special needs.
5. Among the Hindi-speaking Hindus, lighting a lamp in front of the *jhanda* in the yard is done usually on Tuesdays. In most Hindi-speaking homes, one would find a flag (*jhanda*) which represents Hanuman, who is associated with the worship of Rama. It also functions as an identity marker for Hindi-speaking Hindus in South Africa. Of course, non-Indians generally take it as a signification for a Hindu home. This practice of displaying Hanuman *jhanda* by Hindi-speaking Hindus is common in other parts of the world where Hindu diaspora lives, e.g., Trinidad, Mauritius, Fiji and so on.
6. Kamakshi is an epithet of the consort of Siva. In Kanchipuram (South India), Siva's consort is known as Kamakshi (the one with eyes of desire perhaps in view of the belief that she grants the desires of the devotees).
7. A temple priest might occasionally perform marriage ceremony provided it is done in the temple.
8. See Chapter 3.
9. *Kattari* in Tamil means a pair of scissors. The Telugu cognate for it is *kattiri*. The shaving of the head of the new-born child is popularly known as *kattari* prayers. There is also another possibility of interpreting the word "kattari", i.e., by deriving it from the word "kat" meaning the outskirts of the village or the burial ground. It is perhaps due to the fact that some of these rituals in rural India were performed in the outskirts of the village. Hence the name *kattari* prayers.

10. Some have reported that it is done in the ninth month, and some in the tenth month after the child's birth.
11. According to the South Indian Brahminical tradition, the 1st, 2nd, 10th, 11th and the 12th day ceremonies are most important and tend to be longer. It is on the 13th day that the death ceremony is concluded. Cf. Sastri 1988: 39.
12. The details of information about this ritual were supplied to me by my research assistant.
13. Satyanarayana is another epithet of God Vishnu. Literally it means the true Narayana'; *vrata* means a holy practice or solemn vow; *katha* means story. Thus, it means the story of the holy ritual relating to the true Narayana.
14. The five chapters are—the story of the divine sage Narada, the story of a poor Brahmin, the story of a woodcutter, the story of a merchant and the story of king Tungadhvaja.
15. I have classified them as semi-priests because they do not function in temples as regular priests, and they do not have any institutional backing. They are, perhaps, like the private consultants who draw the public because of their special healing and other powers. Their role is analogous to the faith healers in the Christian tradition.

5 Religious Celebrations

The Hindu festivals and seasons are celebrated/observed in South Africa according to the calendars used in India. Although South Africa is in the southern hemisphere and as such the arrival of seasons is in complete opposition to that in India, South African Hindus have not made any changes in their religious calendars. This, perhaps, reflects the orthopraxy of the Hindus in South Africa. The Indian Hindu calendar is prepared in accordance with the movement of the sun in the northern hemisphere. For instance, the Thai Pongal and Maha Sivaratri are festivals that mark the beginning of the sun's entry into the northern hemisphere. In the case of South Africa, it is the beginning of winter. According to the Hindu belief, the sun's entry into the northern hemisphere marks the beginning of the auspicious season. The *Mahabharata* makes a reference to it. When Bhishma was dying, in the final battle between the Kauravas and the Pandavas, he requested Arjuna to make a bed of arrows so that he could lie on it and wait until the sun entered the northern hemisphere at which time he wished to die.[1] Thus, in India, the Hindus consider the season when the sun enters the northern hemisphere auspicious, which means in the case of South Africa, it would mark the beginning of winter. Nevertheless, Hindu festivals are celebrated according to the dates on which they are celebrated in India. This tendency to be orthopractic perhaps helps us to understand South African Hinduism. What seems to be important is that the performing of the rituals and ceremonies according to the ancient tradition is more important than why and when they should be performed. Such theological ramifications are not the most important factors when compared to the actual practice of the tradition. But such adherence to tradition in celebrating key festivals and ceremonies is not unique to Hinduism and is perhaps pervasive in other religions too.

In South Africa, several Hindu festivals are celebrated. The Hindu calendar provides for several festivals during the year. In fact, every month there is some festival or public ceremony. The Tamil calendar, for instance, lists about sixty seven ceremonies in a year. These include smaller and more elaborate ceremonies. All Hindu calendars begin with the New Year festival which occurs in the month of *Caitra* (*Sithirai* in Tamil, April–May). The exact date of the New Year varies for different linguistic communities. For instance, the Tamil New Year occurs in the second week of the month of April, and the Telugu New Year occurs in the first week of the same month. The New Year festivities of South Indians coincide roughly with the festival of *Ramanavami* which is very popular among the North Indians. The Telugus also celebrate *Ramanavami*. Although almost all Hindus celebrate more or less all the festivals regardless of their language background, some are more typical to a particular language group. I shall highlight those festivals that are of greater significance to particular linguistic groups.

As mentioned above, the Tamil festivals begin with their New Year celebrations. It is followed by a season called *Kattiri*. It is considered an inauspicious season and no marriages, business, or other such important matters are transacted during this season. It begins at the beginning of May and is over by the end of May. Another inauspicious season is the month of *Adi* (July–August) during which no important matters are transacted. More typical of the Tamil festivals are: *Mariamman* prayers (in August), *Vinayagar Saturthi* (*Vinayaka Caturthi*, in September) which is followed by *Parattassi* (in September), *Navaratri* (in October), *Karttikaidipam* (in November), *Thai Pongal* and *Thai Pusam, Kavadi* (in January), and *Maha Sivaratri* (in March). Between January and April is the busiest season for South Indian festivals.

Apart from their Telugu New Year, all the other Tamil festivals are also celebrated by the Telugu-speaking people. Besides, they also celebrate some typical North Indian festivals, such as, *Divali, Maha Sivaratri, Ramanavami* and *Sankranti* (the North Indian version of the *Tamil Thai Pongal*). The North Indians (including the Gujarati- and Hindi-speaking people) celebrate *Divali* (in November), *Ramanavami* (in April), *Krishna Jayanti* (in September) and *Hanuman Jayanti* (in January).

Although some of the festivals are more popular among certain linguistic groups, in the South African context there is an attempt to celebrate and participate in the festivals that are not characteristic to them. This idea of celebrating all the Hindu festivals is more common to the organisations that have a pan-Indian perspective in their attempt to unite all Hindus in South Africa. For instance, the Hindu Youth Cultural Association of Pietermaritzburg, a predominantly Hindi-speaking group of youth, has recently celebrated the *Maha Sivaratri*. The Ramakrishna Centre of South Africa also celebrates the *Maha Sivaratri* festival. Thus, celebrating festivals is seen as an important occasion to bring unity and oneness among different groups of Hindus in South Africa.

The most important aspect of the festival ritual is the *havan*. It is a fire ritual which is presided over by a Brahmin priest and assisted by many temple officials. The *havan* is, perhaps, more original of the Brahminical rituals which the North Indian group follows more faithfully. I was told by my informants that in the early days the South Indian groups did not observe the fire ritual (*havan*), but gradually assimilated it into their rituals. Now that the Sri Lankan Brahmin priests are available, it is commonly a part of all the festivals including the South Indian ones.

Basic Structure of a Hindu Festival

In order to understand the Hindu festival, it is useful to get some background of its basic structure in South Africa. In describing the festival, we shall identify the following features:

Marking the Beginning

The Hindu festivals are usually celebrated for a certain number of days. Some are celebrated only for a day and some for nine days and others for a whole month. As such, all festivals have a beginning and an end. In the case of those festivals that last for a longer period, e.g., ten days, the beginning of a festival is usually marked by the "flag hoisting". On the first day, the ritual begins in the temple either in the morning or at an appointed time that is convenient for all the community to gather and at the end of the ritual the flag is hoisted on the flag post (*kodi maram* in Tamil, *dhvaja stambha* in Sanskrit) to mark the beginning of the festival.

In the Hindu ritual tradition, the deity is worshipped in three forms: in the form of a pole (*stambha* or *kodi maram* in Tamil), in the form of an image (*bimba*), and in the form of a sacred pot or vessel (*kumbha* literally means an enclosure around a place of sacrifice, and it is symbolically represented by a *kalasam* meaning a pot or a pitcher). On the first day of the festival at the end of the ritual inside the sanctum sanctorum, the priest approaches the pole in front of the temple and performs a ritual and invokes all the other deities and the presiding deity to become present in the pole and bless the celebration. The pole or the flag post (as it is popularly known) is adorned with a long white cloth with an image of the deity that is worshipped. The long cloth, *darbha* grass and a yellow string are wound around the pole.[2]

In the South African context, the main festival ritual is not always celebrated on the day it falls in view of the fact that most people cannot attend the ceremony on a working day. Thus, usually the following Saturday or Sunday is chosen for the celebration. However, a small ritual is celebrated on the actual day on which the festival falls. It is usually attended by the main committee members of the temple.

The main ritual requires the following materials to be used in the ritual process: a large quantity of water for the ritual bath of the images, milk, honey, curd, turmeric powder, *kumkum*, sandalwood paste or powder, *darbha* grass, *ghee*, wooden spoons, camphor, firewood, pieces of new cloth, thread, powdered dry roots (*vatti* roots), etc.

On the day of the main ritual, the temple priest opens the doors of the temple in the morning at sunrise and prepares the idols for the ritual by cleaning up the inner sanctum, and lighting the lamp in front of the deity. In the evening, or afternoon depending on the appointed time, the priest begins the ritual in the following order: first one to be worshipped is Ganesha (Vinayaka), and then a *havan* ritual is performed with the sacred pot on which a coconut is placed (*kalasa puja*), the sacred bathing of the presiding deity (*abhishekam*—literally means anointment), the offering of lamp (*diparathana* also known as *arati*), the procession of the deity who is present in the festival image (*utsava murti*)[3], and the worship of the flag post (*stambha puja*) are performed respectively.

The most elaborate parts of the ritual in the temple are related to the sacred pot and the ritual bathing of the deity. The sacred pot ritual (*kalasa puja*) is popularly known in South Africa as the *havan kund*. The priest consecrates the elders of the temple[4] by tying a piece of thread round the right wrist and a piece of *darbha* grass to the ring finger on the right hand. All the necessary materials, namely, the firewood, *ghee,* wooden spoons, camphor, etc., are gathered at the venue where the *havan* is performed in the courtyard of the temple. At the auspicious time, the priest, chanting the *mantras,* lights the sacred fire in the *havan kund*. The sacred pot with a coconut placed on it is kept near the *havan kund*. The elders are seated around the *havan* and they assist the priest in pouring the *ghee,* and other ingredients (powdered dry roots, etc., that are mixed with *ghee*).

After the *havan* is performed, the priest enters the temple with the elders and begins the anointing (*abhishekam*) of the images of the deities in the inner sanctum. The presiding deity is ritually bathed in water, milk, curd, honey and sandalwood paste and again with water. The devotees stand in the hall and witness the ritual and try to assist in whatever way they can to partake in the merit of the ritual.

After the ritual bath is over, the priest draws the curtain of the inner sanctum. Only the officiating priest and his consecrated assistants remain inside and drape the image of the presiding deity with new clothes, decorating it further with ornaments and garlands of flowers. Then the curtains are drawn and the priest offers *arati* to the presiding deity and then blesses the people. Throughout the ritual one of the assistants rings the bell.

When the ritual bath of the presiding deity is completed, the priest approaches the *utsava murtis* (festival images) and offers coconuts and camphor (*arati*), and blesses all the devotees individually. All the devotees approach the *arati* and receive blessings by stretching their palms toward the lighted camphor and touching their eyes with their palms again. All the devotees then partake of the meal prepared for them, and those who have brought special offerings in the form of milk, fruits, etc., receive them back after they have been offered to the deity.

Unhoisting the Flag

On the last day of the festival, a similar ritual is performed, although the attendance at the ritual is often limited to the elders and a few keenly religious people. This final ritual marks the end of the festival and the flag is ritually dehoisted.

Meaning of the Ritual

Perhaps, one of the most difficult aspects about the Hindu ritual is the reconstruction of the meaning of the ritual. Many of my informants, though fairly educated, could not tell me the meaning of what goes on in the temple. This observation did not surprise me as I was used to this phenomenon in India as well. The most that people could tell me about the Hindu ritual is the kind of material benefits that one receives by performing certain rituals (e.g., birth of children, prosperity). The most consistent response is that Hindus must perform these rituals in order to maintain their religious and cultural ties and to make sure that the coming generations would continue the tradition of their forefathers.

It is the continuity of the tradition that seems to be very important for the South African Hindus. As such, a separate elaboration of the meaning of a ritual seems antithetical to the very structure and nature of the Hindu ritual practice.[5] From the Vedic tradition to the present, the emphasis seems to be on the performance of the ritual and its continuity. It is precisely because of the emphasis on the performance, that the Hindu ritual is carried out with utmost precision and care for every single detail.

Although most Hindus do not seem to know the meaning of the rituals that they observe, it does not mean that no meaning can be attributed to them. The rituals in many festivals are the same, or at least similar. But they take on different meanings in different festivals and on different occasions. In this sense, the meaning of the ritual depends on what is celebrated and what is remembered in the context of the ritual. This special meaning is preserved in the myth that relates the significance of the festival. Each festival has a myth (often many myths[6]) that provides the meaning of the ritual. Thus, the ritual acts are uniform, but the significance of those acts is different on each different occasion.

The most important aspect of the festival ritual is the anointment (*abhishekam*) of the presiding deity. The presiding deity is given a sacred bath and installed again so that the devotees may have a glimpse (*darsana*). Thus, the deity makes his/her manifestation periodically to sustain and bless the devotees. As a mark of this special manifestation, the deity is taken in a procession round the temple complex and the neighbourhood. At the time of the festival procession, the deity is believed to dwell in the *utsava murti*. At the end of the festival procession, the deity returns to the inner sanctum. This periodical appearance and disappearance (or coming out and going into the inner sanctum) of the deity is marked by the hoisting and unhoisting of the flag. During my conversation, the Sri

Lankan priest at the Siva Subramaniar temple, Pietermaritzburg compared it with the ascending and descending of notes in an Indian *raga* (melody). The scale of the *raga* ascends gradually and then descends. This perennial ascending and descending, appearance and disappearance, is what Eliade calls the myth of the eternal return. Year after year at festival time the ritual is repeated and the myth is recalled and the divine communion with the devotees renewed.[7]

Some Important Festivals

Thai Pongal (Sankranti)

Thai Pongal occurs in the month of January (in the month of Thai in the Tamil calendar). It is also known as *Sankranti* among the North Indian and Telugu-speaking communities. Traditionally, it is a harvest festival and as such associated with the agrarian society. People bring their harvest home and offer it to God for having blessed them with a rich crop. As a mark of abundance, milk is boiled on an open fire until it overflows from the pot. The word "Pongal" in Tamil means to overflow. In South Africa, it is relatively more popular among the Tamil-speaking community.

Thai Pusam (Kavadi)[8]

Thai Pusam occurs a few days after the *Thai Pongal* and is more widely celebrated among the Tamil group in South Africa. People seem to attach more importance to it than to *Thai Pongal* because of the *Kavadi* ceremony associated with it. Most Hindus, mainly the Tamilians and some from other linguistic groups participate in the *Kavadi* ceremony with a great deal of zeal. Some of them take vows and carry the *Kavadi*.

The main deity worshipped during the *Thai Pusam* (*Kavadi*) is Murugan, who is the most popular deity among the Tamilians in South Africa. The festival is celebrated for ten days. The most important part of the ceremony is the carrying of the *Kavadi* by the devotees who have taken vows for various personal reasons with a desire to earn merit for having celebrated it. It is a common practice among South African Hindus to take vows, and if the vows are fulfilled they participate in the *Kavadi* festival and carry the *Kavadi* on their shoulders to thank the deity. The reasons for taking a vow are various. It can be healing of a sick member of the family or success in business. Any such reason can make a devotee take a vow.

The devotees who wish to carry the *Kavadi* notify the temple committee members and reserve a *Kavadi* in advance for a nominal fee. During the ten day festival, those who have taken vows observe a fast. On the day of the *Kavadi*[9] ceremony (which is observed on various days for the sake of the convenience of the public), the devotees who have made their reservations, arrive at the temple with their offerings of milk, fruits, coconuts, etc. The members of the temple committee have the *Kavadis* ready for the devotees. Each devotee is provided with a *Kavadi* and a sacred thread (*kankanam*) which they tie to their wrist. Then the devotees circumambulate the temple, and join the main ritual. The devotees stand near the *havan* in rows, each one with a *Kavadi* in front of him/her. The priest and his consecrated assistants sit around the *havan*. Three pitchers are filled with water and a coconut is placed on top of each. The three pitchers are then placed near the *havan*. They represent Murugan and his two consorts, Valli and Devayani, respectively. Then the ritual is performed by pouring *ghee* and other ingredients into the fire, accompanied by *mantras* and *bhajans*. After the *havan* is completed, those devotees who carry the *Kavadi* approach the *havan kund*, throw the powdered dry roots mixed with *ghee* into the fire and return to their places. The assistants then take the burning coal and place it on an iron plate and throw incense (*sambrani*) on it. Then, they approach each *Kavadi*-carrying devotee who is waiting with two tumblers placed on either side of the *Kavadi*. The assistants take the two tumblers and invert them on the rising smoke of incense in order to consecrate them.

In the meantime, the main *Kavadis* of the temple[10] are ritually bathed and decorated by the assistants. At the same time, the *Kavadis* of the devotees are also washed ritually and decorated by smearing them with sandalwood paste and putting a *kumkum* dot on them. Then, the tumblers that were consecrated earlier are filled with milk and tied to the horizontal pole of the *Kavadi*. The mouths of the devotees are tied up with a piece of cloth. A piece of camphor is lit in front of each *Kavadi*, including the main *Kavadis*. As these various rituals are being performed, the other devotees participate in singing *bhajans* in praise of Murugan. As the devotees continue to sing the *bhajans*, the priest and the temple officials along with those carrying *Kavadis* and the other devotees circumambulate the temple. The procession moves in such a way that all the other shrines in the temple are also covered. After the circumambulation, the devotees and the priest enter the temple. While all the *Kavadis* of the devotees are left outside, the main *Kavadis* of the temple are carried into the hall of the temple and placed at the entrance to the sanctum sanctorum. Some of the devotees carrying *Kavadi* seem to go into a trance at various stages of the ritual.

The priest and the assistants enter the inner sanctum and begin the ritual bathing of the image of Murugan.[11] The ritual bathing is over after the water from the three pitchers *(kalasa)* placed near the *havan* is poured over the images of Murugan and his consorts. Then *arati* is offered to the deity and the devotees shout the praises of Murugan in ecstasy. Curtains are drawn and the idols of the deities are decorated with new clothes, garlands and ornaments. When the curtains are removed, another *arati* is offered and people receive blessings from the priest. *Arati* is offered to the other deities (namely, Vishnu et al.) in other shrines. Finally, *arati* is offered to the festival images (*utsava murtis*) of Murugan and his two consorts, then the images are brought into the temple in a procession and installed at the entrance to the inner sanctum. At the end of the ritual, all the devotees participate in a communal meal.

Maha Sivaratri

Maha Sivaratri is a major festival for those who are of Saivite orientation. In South Africa, most Tamil-speaking people and some Telugu- and Hindi-speaking people are Saivites. Besides, *Saiva Siddhanta Sangam,* a reformed Hindu movement, also considers *Maha Sivaratri* as central to their faith. In the contemporary Hindu society in South Africa, various religious and cultural organisations (e.g., The Hindu Youth Cultural Association of Pietermaritzburg, Ramakrishna Centre of South Africa) also celebrate the festival mainly to foster unity among Hindus and cultivate an interest in the Hindu religion.

The ritual associated with *Maha Sivaratri* has more or less the same components as the other festivals, namely, *Vinayaka puja, kalasa puja, abhishekam, diparathana* also known as *arati,* then the procession of the deity in the festival image (*utsava murti*). There is no flag hoisting ritual separately since *Maha Sivaratri* is celebrated only on one day.

The significance of the festival is related through several ancient myths that seem familiar to the South African Hindus. The most popular one is the following:

Once there was a hunter living in the mountain regions of South India. He went hunting in the forest. After a whole day of searching, he could not find any animal. As he was returning home disappointed, he encountered a lion who began to run after him. He ran for his life and climbed a *bilva* tree (*Aegle Marmelos*, popularly known as the wood apple tree). The lion approached the tree and sat down under it waiting for the hunter to come down. The hunter began trying to chase the lion by throwing down leaves and twigs. It so happened that there was a stone in the shape of a *linga* under the tree, and as the leaves fell on it they turned into flowers. The night passed, but till the next morning the lion did not leave the place and the hunter could not come down. He stayed awake all night throwing the leaves.

In the morning, Siva appeared before the hunter and told him how pleased he was with him and blessed him with liberation (*moksha*). The hunter asked Siva why he was pleased with him. Siva said that the hunter had fasted the whole day and night and worshipped the *linga* with flowers.[12] That night happened to be the great night of Siva which falls on the 14th day during the dark half of the month of *Magha* (January–February).[13] On that day Siva is especially favourable to his devotees and showers blessings on those who observe a fast and perform his puja with *bilva* leaves. According to the *Isana Samhita*, Siva manifested himself as a luminous *linga* to establish his supremacy over both Brahma and Vishnu on the 14th day of the month of *Phalguna* (February). In the above mentioned text, Siva tells his wife about the significance of the day in destroying all the sins if it is observed with fasting. The difference in date is, perhaps, attributable to local custom in India. For instance, in South India, the festival begins on the 13th day of *Phalguna* (Wilson, 210–12).

During the festival of *Sivaratri*, in most South African temples, Siva is worshipped throughout the night. Devotees stay awake in the temple singing *bhajans* in praise of Siva. The next morning they go home and celebrate the festival with members of the family. In the recent times, many South Africans are beginning to go on a pilgrimage to Mauritius to witness the *Sivaratri* festival there. In Mauritius, *Sivaratri* is celebrated on a large scale analogous to the way it is done in Varanasi (Benares).

Ramanavami

Ramanavami literally means the ninth day of Rama. The birthday of Rama, the hero of the epic of *Ramayana*, is celebrated on the ninth day in the light half of the month of *Caitra* (April–May) (Monier-Williams, 877, col. 3). In South Africa, the festival has greater popularity among the North Indian communities than the Tamil community. The Telugus tend to celebrate the festival with the same amount of enthusiasm as the North Indians. The underlying theme of the festival of *Ramanavami* is traditionally associated with the Aryan and Dravidian conflict. The hero, Rama, is seen as the Aryan hero, avenging the abduction of his wife by a Dravidian king, Ravana. Perhaps, more for political reasons than religious ones, the Tamil community in South India exhibited historically less enthusiasm for the festival.[14] Besides, another significant factor is that the Tamil-speaking Hindus in South India are largely Saivite in their religious orientation, and *Ramanavami*, being a *Vaishnava* festival, is certainly not considered popular among the Tamils. But, the Telugus in Andhra Pradesh, in view of their greater assimilation of the Sanskrit culture, tend to celebrate the festival with the same enthusiasm as the North Indians. The same holds true of the South African situation.

The Tamil-speaking Hindus seem to have carried with them their early Indian sentiments into South Africa and perpetuated them here in a system that has been quite congenial for a separatist culture. The festival of *Ramanavami* and such other festivals reveal a gap in the cultural integration among different linguistic groups of Indian origin. This aspect of cultural integration or the lack of it among linguistic groups of Indian origin has been discussed in another subsequent chapter (see Chapter 7).

Quite apart from the Tamil perception of the festival, even among the North Indian groups, there are different ways in which the festival is celebrated. The Arya Samaj group celebrates the birth of Rama more as a historical figure and as an Aryan hero. Their interpretation of the story of Rama is more an allegorical one of the victory of good over evil. The Ramakrishna Centre of South Africa also follows an allegorical interpretation of the story of *Ramayana*. This is in line with the interpretation given by Swami Vivekananda. On the other hand, the Sanatanist Hindus in South Africa celebrate the birth of Rama as an incarnation of Vishnu to kill the demon king – Ravana.

Krishna Jayanti

The festival falls during the months of July–August.[15] The festival celebrates the birth of Krishna, one of the incarnations of Vishnu.

The story of the birth of Krishna is told in the mythological texts of the Hindus, such as *Bhagavata Purana, Matsya Purana* and *Padma Purana*. This festival is celebrated especially by the Hare Krishna followers in South Africa.

Krishna is said to have been born on the eighth day of the second half (i.e., the dark half) of the month of *Sravana*, and hence the other name of the festival, *Krishnajanmastami* (literally it means, the eighth day of Krishna's birth). According to the puranic story that is remembered in South Africa among the followers of the Hare Krishna sect, there was a wicked king by the name of Kamsa who ruled in the kingdom of Mathura. He had a cousin named, Devaki who was married to Vasudeva. On the wedding day as the procession was going, a voice from heaven declared that a child born to Devaki and Vasudeva would kill the king. So the king decided to kill the children born to Devaki. He managed to kill the first six children but the seventh and the eighth were rescued by divine intervention. The seventh one was named Balarama, and the eighth one was Krishna. When Krishna grew up, he killed Kamsa and established himself as king with Dwarka as his capital. In *Mahabharata*, Krishna played a major role between the two warring families, the Pandavas and the Kauravas.

For the devotees belonging to the Hare Krishna temple, Krishna is of particular importance. In South Africa, *Krishna Jayanti* is more popular among the North Indian groups and, to some extent, among the Telugus too. Some Tamil calendars do list the festival, but its popularity among Tamils seems to be less.

Divali or Dipavali

The popular Hindu festival of *Divali* is celebrated during October–November (on the 14th and 15th day in the asterism of Tula). *Divali* (*Dipavali*) literally means a row of lights. Both in North India and South India, the festival is celebrated with rows of lights. Various stories and myths are associated with this festival. In one of the later Hindu scriptures (*Srimad Bhagavatam*), the demon king, Narkasura, the son of the Goddess Earth (*Bhudevi*) stole the earrings of the mother of Indra (the lord of the gods) along with the umbrella of Varuna (the lord of the natural order). Indra approached Krishna for help. But Krishna had previously made a promise to the Goddess Earth that he would not kill her demonic son. This put him in a dilemma. The difficulty was overcome by casting Satyabhama, the consort of Lord Krishna, as a manifestation of the Goddess Earth. In the actual battle, Satyabhama gave her final consent to Krishna and enabled him to kill the demon king (in another popular account, it was Satyabhama herself who killed the demon king when Krishna suddenly fainted during the fight). The demon king is finally killed and the gods were vindicated once again. It is the victory of Krishna over the demon king Narkasura that is celebrated during *Divali*. Another variation of the story of *Divali* is its association with the return of Rama to Ayodhya with his wife, Sita and brother, after killing the demon king Ravana. In the final analysis, Ravana returned to the divine abode. In both stories, what is common is the triumph of good over evil.

The festival is popular both among South Indians and North Indians in South Africa. Most North Indians know about the association of the festival with the story of the *Ramayana* while the story according to the *Bhagavata Purana* is known by the South Indians, particularly the Telugu community in South Africa. The symbolic distinctions and different ways in which the festival is celebrated are described succinctly by a South African Hindu in the following way:

> The Tamils celebrate it a day earlier than the Telugus and the Hindis. They eat meat on that day. The Telugus and Hindis do not eat meat on the day on which they observe Dipavali. To the Hindis Dipavali is both sacred to Lakshmi, the Goddess of Wealth, and also honours the triumphant return of Rama and Sita from their exile [sic]. To the Tamil people, Dipavali marks the destruction of Narkasura, the Demon of the Nether Regions. They celebrate it on the day before the new moon of Kartika. For the Gujaratis, Dipavali has even more complicated [sic] significance. Two days before Dipavali they perform their adorations to Lakshmi, Goddess of Wealth and Prosperity; on the day preceding Dipavali they worship Kalka Mata, a manifestation of Kali. Then comes Dipavali, which is a day of general rejoicing and merriment. On the day after this the Gujarati New Year begins and is marked by prayer and worship. (Nowbath, Chotai and Lalla, 18)

Parattassi

According to the Sanskrit calendar, the festival is known as *Mahalaya Amavasya* (*mahalaya*—the great house; *ama*—together, *vasya*—living)—living together in the great house.[16] In the Hindu calendar, on the 14th day of every lunar month, the sun and the moon are said to live in one house. In other words, the moon is completely overshadowed by the sun thus causing the night to be the darkest. This cycle repeats itself every month. Nevertheless, when this happens as the sun enters the constellation of *Kanya* (Virgo) (September–October), the departed fathers are said to be released from the world of Yama to go to their respective homes on the earth (*kanya yate yatha surye pitras tistanti sve grihe*—"as Virgo (Kanya) emerges in the sun, the fathers dwell in their own homes") (quoted from Sastri, 15. Translation mine). While the deceased fathers dwell in their house, the living members of the family are supposed to offer food to them. According to the orthodox practice, the rituals should be offered everyday during the fortnight before the *Mahalaya Amavasya,* and the ceremonies are terminated on the day of *Mahalaya Amavasya.* The Hindu practice makes some concession to those who are unable to perform the rituals during the fortnight preceding the *Mahalaya Amavasya.* Those who are unable to perform the rituals during the fortnight before the *Mahalaya Amavasya* may perform them during the fortnight after the *Mahalaya Amavasya,* because the dead fathers continue to live in the house of their children during that fortnight after *Mahalaya Amavasya* in the hope that their children will offer ritual food to them. In the event that these rituals are not offered to them even during the fortnight after the *Mahalaya Amavasya,* the dead fathers are said to leave the house in disappointment with a curse for their children. In Sanskrit, it is said that the disappointed fathers leave upon seeing the scorpion (in the sun) (*vricchika darsanat yanti nirasa pitaro gatah*) (Sastri, 17). That is, when the sun enters the constellation of scorpio, the fathers are said to leave. If the fathers leave in disappointment, it is not an auspicious sign for the family. That is why, while the orthodox Hindus observe the traditional rituals meticulously every day of the fortnight before *Mahalaya Amavasya,* the average Hindu makes sure that the rituals are offered at least during the fortnight before the *Mahalaya Amavasya.* Thus, the practice of observing the festival for 30 days has come into vogue.

The festival is commonly known in South India and in South Africa (mainly among Tamilians) as *Parattassi. Parattassi* is the name of the month during which these rituals to the dead are offered. It is usually considered a Vaishnava festival. The rituals are offered to Krishna in his other name as "Govinda".[17] Within South Africa, the festival is understood to represent the harvest season. For the contemporary South African Hindus the idea of harvest season is not relevant as most of them are no longer involved in farming activities. When the indentured labourers came from South India (Tamil Nadu), they might have brought with them the local myth (*Purana*) which tells us about the famine that occurred at some distant past. According to the myth, when the farmers did not have rain for a long time, they prayed to their dead fathers that if it rained, they would make food offerings to them during a whole month. Accordingly, in response to their prayers there was rain, and during that month of *Parattassi* the people in the Tamil areas performed rituals to their dead fathers.[18]

The North Indians celebrate this festival as *Pitrpak* (Sanskrit—*Pitrpaksa*). *Parattassi* or *Pitrpak* is not to be mistaken for the ancestor worship that is found in other cultures. In this festival, the Hindus claim that the dead are not worshipped in any sense. The idea of the dead fathers returning to their earthly homes for a while must be understood in the context of the Hindu belief in reincarnation and the idea of transmigration of the soul. According to the orthodox Hindu belief, the soul of the dead person takes another birth depending on its accumulated merits and demerits. In other words, it is imperative for the soul to exhaust its *karma* before it is finally liberated from its bondage. So, until such time the soul is believed to be born again and again in the course of its attempt to exhaust its *karma*, both good and bad. In this process, it is imperative for the soul not to accumulate new *karma*, whether good or bad. That is why in the *Bhagavad Gita*, the idea of action without desire (*nishkama karma*) is emphasised. Taking rebirth in the empirical realm is the only way to exhaust one's accumulated *karma*. The soul goes to the realm of Yama, the god of death after leaving its body. Until the souls depart to the higher realms, they are released periodically to return to their earthly homes to exhaust their karmic bond with their earthly relatives. Thus, it is incumbent upon the relatives of the dead to provide an occasion for the dead to stay for a while in their ancestral homes so as to enable them to go through the karmic process. In other words, the offering of food to the dead is a symbolic way in which the sons and daughters of the dead prepare the way for the souls to go through their karmic process.

The two myths, namely, the North Indian myth of the dead fathers returning to their earthly homes and the agrarian myth of the South may have been intertwined in the later Hindu thought. Thus, the idea of the dead going through their karmic process is linked with the idea of food offered to the dead.

In South Africa, it is celebrated for 30 days (from September 17 to October 17). During this period, most Hindus (mostly Tamils) observe fasting, which means they do not eat any non-vegetarian foods.[19] During the same month, the North Indian Hindus observe *Pitrpak* that is offering food to the dead fathers.

Karttikaidipam

This festival is common mostly among the Tamils and Telugus. But its background is mainly drawn from the Tamil sources. As noted elsewhere, this festival has special significance for the followers of the Saiva Siddhanta philosophy. The most well remembered myth of the festival in South Africa is about the Arunacalam Hills of South India in the eastern ghats. The Tamils believe that this hill is the oldest hill on earth. Siva is said to have appeared in the form of a pillar of fire to test the powers of Vishnu and Brahma. The myth of this festival is based on the Hindu puranic texts, but is often modified to reflect the Tamil tradition. For instance, the classical myth does not mention the hills of the Tamil country. Although there are many Tamil variants of the myths related to the manifestation of Siva *linga,* (Shulman, 42) the myth of the festival of *Karttikaidipam* relates to the myth which is associated with Tiruvorriyur temple and comes from the Arunacalapuranam (Shulman, 42; also see f.n. 14). It seems to be based on the original in Sanskrit which occurs in *Skanda Purana* and *Siva Purana*. The myth as transmitted in South African Tamil circles goes as follows:

> Brahma and Vishnu quarrelled over who was superior. Siva appeared to them in a linga of fire. Vishnu tried to find its base by digging in the form of a boar, while Brahma became a goose and flew toward the top. Neither could find any limit to the linga. They recognised it as a form of Siva, who made the fiery linga into the mountain Tiruvannamalai. (Shulman, 42)

With some variations the South African Tamils remember the myth in the above details. They give great importance to the Tamil Tevaram hymns composed by the Tamil poets during the period between sixth and the ninth centuries C.E. Some of these ancient Tamil poets make reference to the linga of fire. For instance, Campantar (Sambandar), one of the ancient poet-singers of Tevaram sings:

> Parankunru is the shrine
> of the Lord who shares his body
> with the girl who plays with a ball,
> the god who rose
> as a splendid column of light. ...

Appar another Tamil poet-singer of the Tevaram sings:

> Ayan of the lotus flower
> and the god who dismembered Iraniyan
> sought to know him;
> but for all their seeking,
> they could not contain in their vision
> our Lord who was the great flame. (Peterson, 127)

The South African Tamils re-enact the festival myth of *Karttikaidipam* year after year by setting up a bonfire to symbolise the fire-linga of Siva. In another sense, the Tamils see this festival as their counterpart of *Divali* which is very dear to the North Indian Hindus in South Africa.

The various festivals observed by the Hindus in South Africa reflect the central role they have played in their lives from the time of their forefathers' arrival to the present. These festivals provided them with the atmosphere in which they could realise their Hindu identity and feel comfortable in the midst of different cultures. The festivals also offered them the opportunity to pass on the wealth of cultural and religious knowledge to the next generation. More importantly, the festivals offered the much needed avenue to forge closer bonds with one another often across linguistic barriers. Today, for instance, the festival of *Divali* is held on the beach front in Durban attended by all Hindus across narrow linguistic boundaries. As such, festivals have become bridges between different Hindu groups.

Notes

1. The *Bhagavad Gita*. 8: 24–25. "The six months that are the northward course of the sun, dying in these, go to Brahman. ... The six months that

are the southward course of the sun, in these (when he dies) to the moon's light attaining, the disciplined man returns". (Translation from F. Edgerton. *The Bhagavad Gita.* New York: Harper and Row Publishers, 1964, 44).

2. The Sri Lankan priest in the Siva Subramaniar and Mariamman temple (Pietermaritzburg) pointed out that in the context of Siva worship the pole, the *darbha* grass and the yellow string represent *Pati* (Lord), *Pasu* (animal) and *Pasam* (bond) respectively. These three categories are explained in some detail in the chapter on Saiva Siddhanta Sangam.
3. The festival image (*utsava murti*) is different from the permanent image placed in the sanctum sanctorum. It is consecrated specifically for the festival purposes and is transportable unlike the permanently fixed image. The transportable image is taken round the temple precincts in procession as devotees sing *bhajans* and chant *mantras*.
4. In South Africa, the elders are drawn from the community regardless of their caste background. In the temples in India, it is an exclusive privilege of the Brahmin community. In other words, both the officiating priest and the assistants are from the Brahmin community.
5. Elaboration of the meaning of each ritual activity is not common in the Hindu tradition. For instance, many commentaries are written on the metaphysical speculations in the Hindu theology but no commentaries explain each ritual activity. The Vedic texts and the Agama texts describe the long procedures of the ritual activity and provide rules and exceptions to the rules but no elaboration of the meaning of the ritual activity.
6. For instance, the festival of *Divali* has more than one myth in the South African context. For some, it is the celebration of Rama's victory over Ravana and his return to Ayodhya, for others the festival celebrates the victory of Krishna over Narkasura, the demon king.
7. At the cosmic level, the ritual process in which the presiding deity appears and disappears seems to enact the creation and dissolution of the universe. Both the Vaishnava and Saiva myths relate the process of creation and dissolution to the waking and sleeping of the deity. It is these cosmic activities of the deity, namely, his sleeping and waking which are ritualised in the context of the festival celebration.
8. *Kavadi* literally means a horizontal pole on which water is carried with pitchers on two ends of the pole, the practice still exists in rural India.
9. The *Kavadi* ceremony is also associated with other Tamil festivals, namely, *Citraparuvam*. It is also a ten day *Kavadi* festival which falls in the month of April. Technically, it is not a Brahminical festival, but within the context of South Africa no such distinction is maintained. Even in India, Brahmin participation in the ritual is common today.

10. The main *Kavadis* are three in number and represent Murugan and his two consorts.
11. Ritual bathing of the deity's image is a very lengthy and also costly process. In one temple where I witnessed the ritual, nearly 500 litres of milk (in addition to large amounts of honey, curd, *ghee*, etc.) was poured over the image.
12. In a similar myth found in *Siva Purana* (ch. 34) the hunter was killed by the tiger (not lion) in the morning. As Yama, (the Lord of death) came to take the soul of the hunter, Siva's servants also arrived to receive the hunter's soul. A dispute arose, and finally Siva's servants prevailed by arguing that the hunter observed fast and worshipped Siva with *bilva* leaves. See H.H. Wilson. *Religions of the Hindus*. New Delhi: Cosmo Publications, 1978, 218. A local myth which survived in South India, mentions some variations. In that myth, the hunter while sitting on a *bilva* tree next to a pond, encountered an antelope. As he was about to kill the animal, it begged for permission to go and visit its wife and child. Next, the mother antelope arrived and it also made a similar request. It was then followed by the baby antelope which also made the same request. The hunter waited for them through the four watches of the night. At dawn, as the three antelopes came towards him he saw on the other side his wife and child also coming in search of him. The hunter then realised the bond between the antelopes and decided to let them go. At that moment, Siva appeared and took all six (three antelopes, the hunter, his wife and child) to his realm. The constellation of Orion which appears with three stars in it, and stars in the shape of an antelope's head is considered a symbolic representation of the myth. See Pt. S.M. Natesa Sastri. *Hindu Feasts: fasts and ceremonies*, (New Delhi: Asian Educational Services, 89–96).
13. According to the lunar calendar of the Hindus, every 14th day of the dark half of the month is dedicated to the worship of Siva and is usually known as *Siva caturdasi* (literally the 14th of Siva). The 14th day of the month is usually the darkest night, and since Siva is associated with darkness, and dissolution of the universe, it is especially dedicated to his worship. The 14th day of the month of *Magha*, however, has special significance and is known as the great night of Siva (*Maha Sivaratri*). Cf. M. Monier-Williams. *A Sanskrit-English Dictionary*, 1075.
14. W.T. Elmore notes that in some places in South India the defeat of Rama is celebrated. It is recorded in the Manual of Administration of the Madras Presidency, I. 71. He says, "At one time I was watching the removal of a fallen Ramaswami shrine in a hamlet where his worship had ceased, and beneath the image were found shells and little pots used in Dravidian devil worship." See W.T. Elmore. *Dravidian Gods in Modern Hinduism*, (New Delhi: Asian Educational Services, 1984, first published in 1913), 8.

15. In India, it is generally the rainy season at this time, and farmers are busy. During this month, perhaps in light of the farming activity, it is customary for the newly married woman to stay in her parents' home, thus giving a chance for her husband to concentrate on his farming. From a religious point of view, therefore, it is considered inauspicious for newly married couple to stay together during the month of *Sravana*.
16. This is generally the meaning given by some Hindus in South Africa.
17. It is interesting that the name "Govinda" is specially associated with the death ceremonies. The name "Govinda" (same as Govendra = the Lord of the cows, see Monier-Williams, Sanskrit-English Dictionary, p. 366). is uttered repeatedly as the dead body is carried away to the burial place or crematorium. It seems to me that the idea of offering special rituals to Krishna in his name as 'Govinda' has to do with the dead ancestors since the name is associated with the death ceremony, and not so much the harvest season as no harvest is gathered at this time of the year in India or in South Africa.
18. It is possible that an independent non-Brahminical agrarian myth might have been in existence in the Tamil region, and the same might have been remembered among the non-Brahmin communities as part of *Parattassi*. It still does not explain why an agrarian myth has become associated with *Parattassi*. The only element that is common in both the Sanskrit and the non-Sanskrit myth is the idea of offering food to the dead fathers. It is difficult to say whether the Sanskrit tradition has appropriated the non-Sanskrit festival and its myth or the other way round. Either way, both the myths have survived to the present day, at least in the case of South Africa. I have not had the opportunity yet to verify if the agrarian myth still survives in Tamil Nadu in India.
19. In the parlance of the South African Hindus, fasting does not necessarily mean that one is literally not eating any food. It simply means that the non-vegetarian Hindus eat vegetarian meals.

6 Goddess Worship

In every religious tradition, there is an idea that provides space for mundane activities of life. For instance, people deal with natural disasters, such as famine, drought, cyclones, epidemics, ill-health, accidents, death, and so on by using religious rites. Unlike modern western secular societies, most traditional societies tend to deal with natural disasters like famine, drought, etc., and other threats to life like accidents, epidemics, etc., by relating them to something religious. Although many of the traditional societies today are part and parcel of modern technological worldviews, religious values of many of them still survive in a number of subtle ways, namely, through actions that are accepted as normative in a society. Sociologists view such actions as "predetermined". For instance, the Japanese society deals with death, and other crises of life by resorting to various religious activities which are predetermined. Ian Reader points out how young Japanese students participate in intense religious activity during the examinations (Reader, 20). He provides a useful example of how seriously people take to festive activities for purely mundane reasons. Referring to a famous Sumo wrestler in Japan, he says:

> [H]aving fought his way to the very highest levels of Sumo, an old back injury flared up again, putting him out of action for over eight months. During this time he missed three full tournaments and there were fears that he might never return to his previous prowess. At New Year 1989, just prior to his reappearance in the January wrestling tournament, he, along with most of the rest of Japan, took part in the custom of hatsumode (a shrine festival). Whereas, he later told reporters, he normally did not have much to pray for (in other words, normally he was just following the social custom), this year he did, and thus he made a special request to the Kami. One presumes that he asked for help in returning

successfully to the ring: as it happens, he did so, winning his comeback tournament in powerful style! (Reader, 21)

It is there kinds of supernatural and extraordinary results that are associated with the Hindu festivals of the non-vegetarian[1] goddesses in South Africa. In this chapter, by goddess festivals, I refer to the non-vegetarian goddesses. The close connection between the non-vegetarian goddesses and non-Brahmanism necessitates that we distinguish these rituals and practices from the Brahminical ones. Hindus from all walks of life and different linguistic backgrounds zealously participate in these goddess festivals. The popularity of these festivals even in modern times is attested by a micro study conducted by Alleyn Diesel (1990). It is also interesting that today the non-vegetarian goddess festival has become a tourist attraction in South Africa. When I attended the firewalking festival recently at the Ambika-Ambalavanavar temple (off Bellair Road, Durban), I was quite surprised by the presence of many western tourists and some local African men and women. Even more surprising was the participation of two European men in the ceremony. Given the past trend of exclusivistic life to which each ethnic community in South Africa is used, western participation in a Hindu ritual seems to indicate a growing influence of Hindu ritualistic life on the rest of society.

I have already alluded to the presence of non-Brahminical aspects of Hinduism in the previous chapters in relation to ritual. In this chapter, I shall provide a fuller account of non-Brahminical Hinduism vis-à-vis the non-vegetarian goddess festivals. It is mostly in relation to the non-vegetarian goddess worship that the non-Brahminical elements have been assimilated into the South African Hinduism. In fact, although the *Kavadi* ritual has also originated from the non-Brahminical Hinduism, both in South Africa and India certain aspects of the ritual are performed by Brahmin priests in the Brahminical temples. The main participants of the rituals, the bearers of *Kavadis,* and those who seem to experience trance are, however, non-Brahmins. On the other hand, the non-vegetarian goddess worship is clearly kept separate from the Brahminical priesthood. When I was attending the Draupadi Amman festival recently at the Second River temple (Durban), I noticed that the Sri Lankan Brahmin priest who performed rituals at the main Cato Manor Hindu temple was standing in the crowd and did not participate in the ritual in any manner. All the rituals were performed by local non-Brahmin elders of the community. It is the one ritual that enables the non-Brahmin lay persons to function as priests and perform rituals both inside and outside the temple. At the recently held Draupadi Amman festival at Sri Siva Subramaniar and Mariamman temple (Pietermaritzburg), the Sri Lankan Brahmin priest performed the ritual acts, such as washing the image of Draupadi and decorating it for the procession. But, the key rituals, namely, decoration of the *karakams* (vessels) and the related vessels rituals at the river were performed by the local lay elders.

In the traditional Hindu practice, in India, there are some festivals and religious ceremonies which are specific to certain caste groups. The non-vegetarian goddess worship reflects one such phenomenon. At these festivals the Brahmins honour the caste boundaries and participate in a passive manner.[2] In the South African context, although people are not aware of these distinctions, the fact that the local non-Brahmin elders perform all the core rituals, such as ritually bathing and decorating the *karakams* (kalasam/vessels) and ritually preparing the devotees who have taken vows to walk on the fire, reaffirms the age-old Indian practice of honouring the caste distinctions. In the present-day Hindu practice, both in India and South Africa, whatever the extent of participation by the Brahmin priests, it is very clear that the festivals of *Kavadi* and the non-vegetarian goddesses are mainly intended for non-Brahmin groups. Such distinctions, however obscure they may be, are important in the Hindu practice whether in India or in South Africa. One might argue that in the absence of a clear caste consciousness among the South African Hindus, such distinctions are insignificant. Such a point of view is, perhaps, well taken. But it is important to recognise the unconscious way in which the South African Hindus reaffirm their caste boundaries in the context of the ritual. However, in the absence of caste structures in South African Hindu society, to speak of caste boundaries is also misleading in the sense that there are no rigid expressions of them. The local Hindus do not necessarily operate along caste lines, as such boundaries could not be maintained even at the very beginning of their life in South Africa. It is more the newly appointed Sri Lankan Brahmin priests who tend to observe such distinctions.

Most certainly this phenomenon of maintaining caste boundaries, at least at the level of the ritual, was bound to come up in the wake of the increasing number of Brahmin priests arriving from India and Sri Lanka. Already one could see the difference in the ritual performance in many key temples. At one point, the rituals in the inner sanctum of most temples were performed by the local non-Brahmin Hindus. But now, at least in the major temples, the non-Brahmin laymen function merely as assistants to the Sri Lankan Brahmin priests. This shift is an important one as it prefaces the dawn of a new ritual order in the Hindu religious practice in South Africa. In the absence of a strong and visible Brahmin community, many non-Brahmin elders may continue to be involved in the ritual activities in the inner sanctum of the temple (a privilege exclusive to the Brahmins in the case of Hindu temples in India, except those belonging to the non-vegetarian goddesses).

Although caste consciousness and distinctions of Brahminical and non-Brahminical practices are maintained on a subtle level, unlike India the non-vegetarian goddess phenomenon has, undoubtedly, become integral to the Hindu life and practice. The goddess temples are built in the same complex as the Brahminical temples. In fact, the South African Hindu community has made deliberate attempts to integrate all forms of Hindu practice. One of my informants at the Tongaat South Vishnu temple (Tongaat is a suburb of Durban) told me that in view of the various backgrounds from which the Hindu community in South Africa came, they had to provide for all those groups. Building a non-vegetarian goddess temple or shrine in the same complex where temples for Brahminical gods and goddesses are built does not imply total integration of Brahminical and non-Brahminical elements of ritual. The fact that the shrines of the non-vegetarian goddesses are separate, albeit in the same complex, indicates that the difference is affirmed by the Hindus. Especially when non-vegetarian offerings are made to the goddesses, the community is certainly aware of the difference between vegetarian deities and non-vegetarian gods and goddesses.

Background of the Goddess Phenomenon

Goddess worship, in general, is a pan-Indian phenomenon. Its origins are traced all the way back to the Indus valley civilisation. In this chapter, I shall not attempt to trace the entire history of goddess worship, only among the Hindus in South Africa. Goddess worship exists in India among all linguistic groups in the rural and semi-urban areas. Nevertheless, the South African forms of goddess worship among Hindus seem to have come from distinctly Tamil- and Telugu-speaking areas in India.[3] Of the four dominant forms of the non-vegetarian goddess worship, two (Mariamman and Draupadi Amman) have a Tamil origin; the other two (Ankalesvari and Gangai Amman) have Telugu ones. All four of them exist in both Tamil- and Telugu-speaking areas in India. But, whereas the former two forms of the goddess worship are more dominant in Tamil-speaking areas, both the latter are more popular in Telugu-speaking areas. Thus, in South Africa, there are basically four forms of goddess worship among the Hindus. Although the four goddesses are popular in South Africa, only two goddesses have festivals that are quite popular, namely, the Mariamman festival and the Draupadi Amman festival. Two temples that are well known for the Draupadi Amman festival are: Second River temple in Durban, and Sri Siva Subramaniar and Mariamman temple in Pietermaritzburg. The Isipingo temple is, perhaps, the most well-known one for the Mariamman festival. The other two goddesses (Ankalesvari and Gangai Amman) are worshipped along with both Mariamman and Draupadi Amman, but do not have individual festivals in South Africa.

Draupadi Amman Festival

Firewalking is a major religious event in South Africa, mainly in the KwaZulu Natal province. It is associated with the goddess Draupadi. This event is so well known that it attracts not only hundreds of Hindu devotees, but also scores of tourists. For the devotees, it is a very powerful and visible manifestation of the presence of the goddess. For the tourists, it is a breathtaking moment. Presently, the festival of Draupadi takes place in South Africa in at least three major temples: The Draupadi Amman temple adjoining the Ambika-Ambalavanavar temple (popularly known as the Second River temple) in Durban, the Jacobs Road temple in Durban, and the Sri Siva Subramaniar and Mariamman temple in Pietermaritzburg.

The myth of Draupadi is traced to the original story from the *Mahabharata*. Speaking to the people one does not get a very clear picture of the events and characters in the myth. Often there are conflicting views about some details. For instance, some of my informants said that Draupadi had five brothers and not five husbands, as it is told in the *Mahabharata*. The firewalking myth, in general, is quite different from the story found in the Sanskrit version of the *Mahabharata*. The story in the *Mahabharata* (Sanskrit) mentions Draupadi having five husbands. In brief, the story goes as follows: The sons of Pandu and the sons of Dhritarastra were cousins. In the struggle for power, they played a game of dice in which the five sons of Pandu lost their kingdom along with their wife, Draupadi. The eldest and the second sons of Dhritarastra attempted to strip Draupadi in the open court and insulted her. Her honour was, however, protected by Krishna. At that time, the second son of Pandu vowed to avenge her shame by killing the two sons of Dhritarastra on the battle field and smear her hair with their blood. In the end the vow was fulfilled.

But, in the local version of the story, popular among the South African Hindus, it was Draupadi herself who killed the enemy and tore their stomach open and drank their blood. Then, she walked on fire to establish her purity and power. In this version, Draupadi is seen as an incarnation of the goddess, Sakti, whose characteristics are also attributed to Draupadi. Whether there existed such a variation of the myth in the South Indian context, especially in Tamil Nadu, is not certain. Hiltebeitel does not report any such variation in his book, *The Cult of Draupadi* (1988). In the version that he records in Tamil Nadu in India, it is Bhima who kills Duhsasana (the brother of the evil king Duryodana). This version follows the Villiparatam which is popular in Tamil Nadu (Hiltebeitel, 407). One of my informants suggested that she is the incarnation of Ankalesvari. According to him, during the day she lived with her five husbands and at night she transformed into Ankalesvari and went out into the burial grounds and fed on the dead bodies there. Many other fierce as well as auspicious characteristics are usually attributed to Draupadi by the devotees. Although these variations of events and themes do not always match the variations either in the Sanskrit or Tamil version, they reveal an interesting perception of Draupadi by the South African Hindus. One of the most important themes that is often emphasised in the South African Draupadi stories is the idea of her being a virgin. Although the original Sanskrit text does not contain such perceptions of Draupadi, it is her devotees who often define her nature. Nevertheless, these details have a basis in the myths that exist in Tamil Nadu in connection with the Draupadi cult.

Even there, different aspects of her are emphasised in different regions. Hiltebeitel points out:

> Elsewhere, however, in local temples within the core area (and beyond it), Draupadi's fierce character as protectress of a kingdom loses the precedence it has at Gingee and is in various ways muted and redefined. Though still often a goddess of village boundaries, she is not regularly connected with the pre-eminent dangers of the north. And though she is ever a virgin, she usually shares her garbhagriha (private chamber) with one or more of her husbands, most notably Yudhisthira or Dharma: an association that implies a dharmic regulation—re-enacted at each Draupadi festival—of her fierce form, rendering her locally benign in each village. (Hiltebeitel, 75)

The Tamil translation of the Sanskrit epic seems to depict Draupadi as a goddess. According to Hiltebeitel, the Tamil version of the Draupadi story is based on the *Mahaparatam* written by Villiputturar. It is popularly known as *Villiparatam* among the Indian Tamils. In the myths of the Draupadi cult, she is depicted as goddess, and identified with Durga and Kali.

The *Terukkuttam* (popularly known as "six-foot dance" with its story about the 18-day battle that the five Pandava brothers fought) dance-drama performed in South Africa in connection with Draupadi festival seems to be based on *Villiparatam*. The South African Hindus enact and relive the myth in two parts: first, in the enactment of the myth via the *Terukkuttam* dance[4] which is performed a night before the firewalking, and second, by walking the fire and thereby reliving the firewalking[5] experience of Draupadi.

The festival begins, like all other Hindu festivals in South Africa, with the hoisting of the flag that symbolises the Draupadi ritual. The flag bears the sign of a lion or a tiger[6] and is hoisted, in some temples for ten days and in others for eighteen days before the firewalking ceremony.

Diesel observes that "Jacobs Road temple seems to be the only temple which observes the full 18-day preparation period, with Pietermaritzburg and Second River keeping a ten-day period" (Diesel, 20). On the first day when the flag hoisting takes place, the shrines of the goddess and other related deities (the guardian deities et al.) are rededicated with elaborate rituals and the images of the deities (with the goddess at the prominent place) are taken out in procession. Thus, the shrines, the deities and the devotees are prepared for the beginning of a new ritual order. As the firewalking ritual approaches, the intensity of the ceremonies increase at the temple and the consciousness of the devotees is dominated by the thought of the goddess or even her presence vis-à-vis devotees in a trance. The final stages of preparation for the firewalking ritual may be identified by the following phases.[7]

On the penultimate day at about midnight, the *Mahabhishekam* (the great consecration), a ritual purification of the main image is performed in the inner sanctum with eighteen different elements. At about 8:00 p.m., the "six-foot dance" is performed which continues till the next morning. In some temples, the dance drama may begin before midnight and go on till the early hours of the morning.[8] Then, at about 8:00 a.m., the images in the inner sanctum (i.e., the images of Ganesa, Draupadi, Mariamman, and Ankalesvari) are decorated. At the same time, the festival images, which are kept separately outside the inner sanctum, are also decorated. The whole area, both inside and outside and the inner sanctum are covered with neem leaves. This is followed by the ritual *yajna/homa/havan* ceremony in front of the temple and the fire from there is taken out in procession to the fire pit to light the pile of logs placed there. At about 10:55 a.m. *arati* is offered to the deity (Draupadi) to the accompaniment of music and drum-beating. Women and men, especially those who have taken vows, sing and dance in ecstasy. A procession is then led to the flag post where *arati* is offered again and the devotees place their offerings (fruits, etc.) at the flag post. The procession then moves to the nearby ant hill which is located to the east of the temple, and is also associated with Gangai Amman. *Arati* and offerings of fruits, etc., are made to the deity (Gangai Amman) there. Part of the offerings are distributed among the people present. After this, people participate in a community meal.

In the mean time, while the fire pit is getting ready, at about 12:05 p.m., the devotees who have taken vows gather in the temple. *Kankanam* (a sacred thread smeared with turmeric powder, with a turmeric root tied to it) is given to the devotees and to those who have taken vows for a donation of three Rands (South African currency). They tie the *kankanam* to their wrist as a mark of their vows. The devotees receive blessings from some of the senior devotees who usually experience a trance. It is a way of passing on the trance to the other devotees who have ritually prepared themselves for the occasion. Then all the devotees circumambulate the temple while carrying the festival image of Draupadi and then circumambulate the fire pit, then proceed to the nearby Gangai Amman shrine where they make offerings to the goddess and then proceed to the open ground on which they decorate and consecrate the sacred vessel (*karakam* in Tamil).[9] At this point, the devotees gather as individual family groups and perform a *havan* in front of a trident (one of the symbols of the goddess). As the ritual continues, some of the devotees experience a trance whenever the drums are beaten. Some people tend to touch these devotees with a view to receive blessings from them. The decoration of *karakams* with flowers, and turmeric and *kumkum* powders, etc., takes a significant amount of time. Some of the devotees inflict severe pain on themselves, piercing sharp needles through their skin on the shoulders, through the tongue, cheek, and so on. No one, however, seems to experience any pain. Meanwhile, the fire pit is being levelled evenly to enable the devotees to run across the fire.

At about 4:30 p.m., the devotees congregate in front of the Gangai Amman shrine and offer prayers and then, carrying the *karakams*, proceed in procession to the fire pit. The procession is led by a senior devotee who carries a coconut on a sacred pot (*kalasam/karakam*). Along the way, some devotees offer coconuts and wash the feet of those devotees who are carrying the *karakams*. The devotees who have taken vows carry the *karakams* as they trample on the fire. The devotees finally approach the fire pit and the firewalking begins. At once the atmosphere turns tense and people become ecstatic as they witness the firewalking. The devotees who walk the fire start from one end, walk across the fire, enter the temple and prostrate themselves before the goddess. The priest in the temple gradually calms them down by offering *arati*. At the Second River temple only one devotee had minor burns. Such incidents are attributed to the devotee's weak faith, and lack of adequate spiritual preparation. As the firewalking comes to an end, the goddess is finally propitiated so as to bless the devotees, and is finally given a farewell and requested to return the next year. Although the firewalking ritual is exclusively associated with the Draupadi Amman festival in South Africa, traditionally in India it is also associated with the Mariamman festival. For the thousands of people witnessing it, it is walking on fire, but to the devotees it is said to be walking on a bed of flowers (Chettiar, 50). In the

Pietermaritzburg temple, a woman who acts as Draupadi carries a pot of hot coals from the fire pit in her lap. The devotees believe that her clothes do not burn. Carrying a pot of hot coals by women is a part of the Mariamman festival in Tamil Nadu, India. It is said:

> Carrying of *agni-cchatti* or fire-pot on heads and palms of women and girls, respectively, is another form of offering in Mariamman temples. For 21 days prior to the festival, the devotee eats just a single meal a day, sleeps on the ground, avoids sexual pleasures and if he/she gets a spiritual feeling, carries a pot of fire to the Mariamman temple during the festival. (Chettiar, 50)

Unlike India, the South African Hindus have associated the firewalking ceremony exclusively with the festival of Draupadi. As such, Draupadi in the South African context, acquires a special status. She is known as the firewalking goddess. The devotees who walk the fire not only demonstrate their own purity, but in a way, they also relive the experience of Draupadi. For devotees, it is the demonstration of the power of Draupadi.

Mariamman Festival

In India, the goddess Mariamman is associated with small-pox, cholera, and other contagious diseases (Chettiar, 49). She can bring about both disease and healing. Therefore, propitiating the goddess every year is very important for the well-being of the village. The Tamil Hindus have kept this tradition alive. The most well-known temple for the Mariamman festival is the Isipingo temple in Durban. The festival is usually celebrated in the month of April. The festivities go on for three days, beginning on a Friday and ending on a Sunday during the Easter week. On Friday and Saturday, the celebrations draw the biggest crowd of devotees. On Saturday, the goddess, Mariamman, is taken out in procession in the temple chariot. Prior to the procession, the goddess is bathed ritually and decorated in the temple and the devotees make their offerings. The ritual in the temple is much the same as in the case of the Draupadi festival. After the procession, the goddess is brought back to the temple and people line up to make their offerings and receive blessings from her.

Most of the devotees who participate in the festival are those who have taken vows. The mall devotees wear a garland of neem leaves around the neck and women wear the same around the waist. As in the case of the Draupadi festival, neem leaves are associated with the goddess, Mariamman. The leaves are supposed to have a healing effect on the devotees. In fulfilment of their vows, they bring offerings of fruits, vegetables, milk, coconuts, cooked food, etc. What makes this festival different from others is the non-vegetarian offerings, such as, live chicken and goats. The devotees circumambulate the temple with their offerings three times and then enter the temple to make their offerings. Those who offer chicken and goats take them to the back of the temple where they are slaughtered ritually. The meat is then cooked with rice and other curries and distributed to the devotees in the temple. Distribution of food to the devotees by other devotees in the temple is the most prominent feature of the festival. Some distribute vegetarian food and others non-vegetarian food depending on their vow they have made.

One of my informants told me that a few years ago some devotees used to offer liquors to the devotees, a practice still common in the non-vegetarian goddess festivals in India. But, in South Africa, those practices have been stopped in view of the social problems that it gave rise to in the past.

The devotees, along with their offerings, bring an image of the goddess made of aluminium foil and offer it. Those images are carried to their homes and installed in their *puja* rooms as a mark of the living presence of the goddess. Devotees also offer human images made of aluminium foil in a symbolic way to represent the person whose healing they were intended for.

Another important feature of the festival is that the devotees visit all the shrines of the goddess located in the precincts of the temple. The image of the goddess installed outside the temple (at Mt. Edgecomb temple) in the centre of a water tank draws a continuous flow of devotees. Almost every devotee who comes to the main temple visits this shrine also. The devotees throw money (mostly copper coins) into the tank in the hope of receiving prosperity from the goddess. Here, the image is that of Lakshmi who bestows wealth on her devotees. As they throw money into the tank, the devotees make a wish, and in fulfilment of that wish they return the next year to repeat their offerings and again to make new wishes. It is this unending cycle of vows and wishes which brings the devotees to the temple of the goddess year after year.

Some General Features of the Goddess Phenomenon

Myth and Ritual

Each one of the goddesses has a distinct tradition, myth and ritual. They are, however, mutually inclusive. The broader mythical and ritual elements are mutually interchangeable. All the non-vegetarian goddesses are associated with disease and death. All of them are periodically propitiated, failing which their wrath is said to strike the community. All of them are associated with Siringa or neem tree, the leaves of which are used in the ritual context for purification. Not all the individual myths of these goddesses are preserved in the South African context. The most well preserved myth is that of Draupadi Amman, enacted in the six-foot dance.[10]

In all the myths, the basic elements are similar: the goddess represents both life and death; she is associated with some male companions (Mathuraiviran, Poturaju, Kartavarayan and others) who are known as the guardian deities. They are usually located in the outskirts of a village. The ritual related to the goddess usually takes place in the outskirts of a village or on the bank of a river. In South Africa, tradition has it that in the early days the devotees used to take a procession to the nearby river (e.g., at the Umbilo temple). For instance, the Draupadi Amman festival takes place at the Draupadi Amman temple adjoining the Ambika-Ambalavanavar temple (popularly known as the Second River temple).[11] The procession goes to the nearby Gangai Amman temple on Bellair Road, instead of the river. It is at the site opposite the Gangai Amman temple that the preparations of *karakam*, etc., are carried out and the preparatory rituals are performed. At the Sri Siva Subramaniar and Mariamman temple (Pietermaritzburg), the procession of the Draupadi Amman festival goes to the nearby river on the East Street where the rituals are performed.

Drum and Trance

It is mainly in the case of Draupadi Amman festival that we come across drum-beating and see people going into a trance. At the Mariamman festival in Isipingo temple, no one is seen going into a trance. However, as mentioned in the chapter on festivals, the trance is also associated with the *Kavadi* ritual.

Beating of drums and the people going into a trance are integral parts of the goddess festival in South Africa. There seems to be a structural relation between the two. In other words, every time the drum-beating starts, the devotees become ecstatic, and those who go into a trance become uncontrollable. The intensity of the trance seems to depend on the intensity of the sound of the drum. The sound of the drum seems to enhance the devotee's emotional mood to go into a trance.

The trance is considered by the devotees to be a way of experiencing the goddess. It is believed that the power of the goddess is so great that the devotee cannot withstand it. Through the devotee she manifests herself to the people. It is to aid the devotee with additional power, as it were, the drums are beaten with a certain rhythm so that the devotee swings and dances to the beat. The devotee who is "taken possession" of by the goddess is further aided by the loud chanting of the name of the goddess by the rest of the devotees who stand around him/her. The drum-beating, the devotee getting into a trance and the rest chanting the name of the goddess loudly, are events that happen at the same time. The spontaneity of the unfolding events around entranced devotees lends itself to the credibility of the experience. There are no producers and directors, only actors and actresses who respond to their own inner convictions and feelings. The devotees seem to know spontaneously when the goddess "visits them". When she does, it is a moment of ecstasy, it is as though the devotee experiences total freedom from his/her own being. That moment is filled with a total lack of inhibition. Men and women, young and old, dance to the beat of the drum. It is as though the drum-beating invokes the goddess who descends on the devotees. In that sense, the drum seems to function as the sacred medium through which the power of the goddess is invoked into the lives of the devotees.

Devotee as an Embodiment of the Goddess

As the sound of the drum becomes synonymous with the power of the goddess, each devotee in a trance actually becomes the embodiment of the goddess. As the power of the goddess pervades the whole of the temple, devotees claim to have experienced her. They believe that during the ritual the goddess dwells not only in the image in the temple, but also in the devotees themselves. The goddess gives an audience to the devotees as her festival image is taken around in procession. But her most visible form of manifestation is the devotees themselves. As the devotee becomes the physical embodiment of the goddess, he or she is transformed into something different. It is expressed not only in their outward behaviour, but also in the way they feel within themselves. It is precisely in this context that one has to understand the extraordinary claims of the devotees, e.g., their claim not to have burned their feet when walking on the fire during the firewalking.

Goddess and Healing

One of the most significant aspects of the goddess phenomenon in South Africa is its association with healing. It is this therapeutic aspect what makes the goddess worship all the more important. In South Africa, there are many women who might be identified as therapeutic counsellors. They function as priestesses in shrines built in their backyards. Scores of devotees visit them seeking remedies for their illness, bad luck, etc. These priestesses perform rituals to the goddess on behalf of their clients and seek blessings for them. In the South African context, this phenomenon is not only pervasive among the South Indians, but also among other linguistic groups. It is certainly a growing phenomenon. It seems to appeal to people regardless of their educational and social background. Perhaps when calamity strikes, people tend to go anywhere for help. The priestesses of the goddess are most certainly the ones that attract such clients. In this sense, the goddess worship seems to impinge upon the very modernist view of life. A Hindu who wants healing, be it mental or physical, most certainly considers the goddess option. Call it superstition, or cultural conditioning, the goddess phenomenon seems to pervade the very centre of the Hindu life in South Africa.

Goddess: Affirming Multiplicity

Studying Hinduism one finds three basic models of understanding reality. Some Hindu philosophies present a radical oneness of reality; others present a radical dualism; and still others present a radical pluralism. It seems to me that the non-vegetarian goddess phenomenon presents a radical pluralism. Although one might attempt to synthesise the various non-vegetarian goddess phenomena, there is a certain sense of uniqueness in each of the goddesses, in that their myths, their manifestations, their relationship with the devotees, etc., is unique and distinctively different. For instance, witnessing the firewalking ritual no one would miss the unique personality of Draupadi Amman. Similarly, the Mariamman manifestation at Isipingo temple is distinctively different. I remember, while watching the Draupadi ritual at the Sri Siva Subramaniar and Mariamman temples (Pietermaritzburg), asking one of my colleagues who was also present with me, what I later thought was something obvious. I said, "I wonder why they don't sacrifice goats, rams and chicken to Draupadi" The instantaneous response was that "She is not Mariamman, you see!"[12] Somehow, the very ritual acts have distinguished the various goddesses. They all seem to serve the same purpose of saving the devotee from disease and death. Nevertheless, they all present a different dimension of reality. Naturally, the devotees do not offer the same thing to all the goddesses. Only Draupadi expects her devotees to walk on fire, at least in the South African context! Only Mariamman receives blood sacrifices. In the larger framework, all the non-vegetarian goddesses are related as sisters,[13] and their male companions are either brothers or husbands.

During the festival period, the goddess dwells in the devotees, and as such, she is experienced in her multiplicity. Each devotee experiences different facets of the goddess. And, accordingly, they act out their inner experiences which become expressed in their ecstatic dances and outward appearances. On the part of the goddess, she seems willing to be experienced, placated, and worshipped in the way the devotees wish. The devotees' different experiences and perceptions seem to be the simultaneous manifestations of the goddess. All these manifestations are nowhere better expressed than in the dance performances of the devotees. For instance, one devotee dances as the angry and ferocious goddess, and another dances in her more sober and calm appearance.

Thus, the goddess phenomenon in South Africa is unique. People from both educated and uneducated background are found to be part of the goddess worship. When it comes to healing, material prosperity, etc., there seem to be no inhibitions or distinctions on the part of the Hindus. Goddess worship effectively meets such needs of the devotees.

Notes

1. I am using non-vegetarian and non-Brahminical in some sense synonymously, although I am aware that not all Brahmins are vegetarian. In Maharashtra, Kashmir and Bengal and in other parts of India, some classes of Brahmins are found to be meat eaters of one kind or another.

Therefore, my use of these two terms (non-vegetarian and non-Brahminical) is confined for purposes of broader analysis.

2. W.T. Elmore observes, "Practically all of the people except the Brahmins join actively in the worship of these minor gods, and the Brahmins are by no means indifferent. Most of the sacrifices are of slaughtered animals, hence usually a Brahmin will not act as priest. An occasional exception, however, is found. The Brahmins quite commonly direct some parts of the worship, and often are present, usually standing at a distance." See W.T. Elmore. *Dravidian Gods in Modern Hinduism* (New Delhi, 1984, first published in 1913), p. 9. Also see f.n. 1 on the same page.
3. There are North Indian versions of goddess worship in South Africa, but they are mostly either Brahminical or less known non-vegetarian goddesses. I came across one Hindi family that mentioned the name of Sitala, a North Indian non-vegetarian goddess.
4. At present, the *Terukkuttam* dance (also known as "six-foot dance" is not regularly performed during the Draupadi festival due to the generation of dancers has faded away and the younger generation seem less interested in those dance performances.
5. In contemporary society, firewalking is adopted by many modern management gurus as a team-building exercise. Firewalking can be taught, according to Gordon Cooper, who is an instructor. See the website—"FireWalkInstructor.com". In South Africa, firewalking is mainly confined to Draupadi Amman worship. However, recently in Chennai (Saturday April 10, 2010) devotees of Mariamman and Kali Amman performed firewalking ritual (see *Hindustan Times*, April 10, 2010). The occurrence of the firewalking ritual was also reported in 2007 in Chennai (see *Hindustan Times*, April 9, 2007). For the most recent performance of this ritual in Durban at the Umbilo Shree Abbalavanaar Alayam temple in Bellair Road, Read more at: http://www.digitaljournal.com/article/290614#ixzz1A4IOXEN9
6. In the Sakta tradition, the female goddess is associated with the tiger as her vehicle. The lion does not appear in that tradition.
7. My description of the ritual details are based on my observation at the Second River temple, and the Pietermaritzburg temple. Some details may vary in other temples. For instance, the Pietermaritzburg temple does not have the *Terukkuttam* dance-drama.
8. As far as I know, the Second River temple and the Jacobs Road temple (both in Durban) used to perform the dance-drama until at least the early 1990s.
9. *Karakam* in Tamil means a pot with a spout. The word may be a corruption of the Sanskrit *kalasam* which also means a pot or a pitcher used in a ritual context. *Karakam* here refers to the sacred pot which is

ritually decorated. A coconut is placed on top of the pot. It is said to symbolize the presence of the goddess or mediates her power. It is carried on the head of the person who is consecrated ritually and walks on the fire. *Karakam* is not peculiar to the goddess rituals. It is also used in other temple rituals.

10. The six-foot dance is a folk drama enacted in the open-air theatre. In the Indian villages, such dramas still take place under a tree where usually the public gather for various meetings, festivals, etc. In South Africa, the drama associated with Draupadi Amman festival is known as six-foot dance because of the way the actors jump as high as six feet while singing and dancing during the play.
11. The First River temple was built in 1875 and later destroyed in floods in 1905 and subsequently the present highway was built on its location. Some of the idols are said to have been recovered. The present temple known as Second River temple was rebuilt in 1946 at the current site. However, some indicate that the First River temple referred to the Hindu temple in the corner of the Bellair Road before proceeding to the Ambalavanaar (Druapadi) temple. To me this explanation does not seem to be historically accurate.
12. However, it must be pointed out that Draupadi also has Brahminical roots vis-à-vis the epic narrative in the Sanskrit tradition. This distinguishes her from Mariamman who is fully non-Brahminical.
13. Draupadi is perhaps an exception to this, for she is not related as sister to all the other non-vegetarian goddesses. Perhaps this has to do with her Sanskrit origins. She, as such, stands alone.

7 Community Organisations, Schools, Rituals and Language

In the preceding chapters, we have noted the significant role that temples, rituals and festivals played in the lives of Hindus in South Africa in shaping their identity and nurturing their culture. In this chapter I wish to throw light on the ways in which their languages have survived on the back of community organisations, schools which functioned as places where rituals were performed and language was propagated. One of the questions that often perplexes scholars in the field of religions is the intrinsic relationship between ritual and language. The inseparability of ritual and language raises an interesting question for the philologists, on the one hand and the religionists on the other. The Indo-European philologist, for instance, is interested in the survival of Sanskrit phonetics which survived in the context of ritual. On the other hand, the religionists and other social scientists are interested in the overall structural relationship between ritual and language. It is not merely how language survives and what forms of syntax and phonetics have survived, but how ritual and language depend on each other mutually and how language takes a ritually sanctified role even when it is no longer a spoken medium.

The Vedic religion is, perhaps, a case in point. Despite the fact that Sanskrit has not been a common person's language and has not been a spoken language, it has survived for many centuries. Both religionists and Indo-European philologists would agree that it is largely due to its intrinsic relationship with Vedic ritual that Sanskrit is alive today. The orality of the Vedic tradition is of a different kind, in that the sacred *mantras* and rules of the ritual are committed to memory with great accuracy. It is not like remembering a story or legend, and passing it on to the next generation. In the process of passing on of such oral tradition, as stories and legends, each generation usually adds its own modifications. But the Vedic tradition passed on the sacred hymns and rules of ritual, etc., without any change whatsoever. That is why each book of the *Vedas* has an addendum at the end, which contains various phonetical rules as to how each *mantra*, hymn, etc., are pronounced. Accuracy in recitation of the hymns is directly related to the effectiveness of the ritual. As such, it is in the process of preserving the Vedic ritual that the Sanskrit language has survived over the years.

Although modern Hinduism is immensely different from the Vedic tradition, the Sanskrit language has survived in the Brahminical rituals to this day. Hindus living outside India have also been able to use Sanskrit in the context of rituals. It is the vernacular language, however, that seems to have occupied a more prominent place in the context of ritual. In the South African context, various linguistic groups use their regional languages in singing the *bhajans*, chants and prayers. What is interesting is that the situation of their vernacular language is analogous to Sanskrit. In other words, just as Sanskrit *mantras* are recited by devotees and priests regardless of whether or not they understand the meaning of those words, the South African Hindus also use their vernacular language in the context of ritual. It seems to me that a language can survive without having to be a medium of speech by occupying an important role in the context of ritual. It is in the context of the ritual that a language becomes reified and sanctified.[1] As such, ritual and language become two sides of the same coin, depend on each other and survive on mutual support. The devotees cannot perform a ritual without the aid of the language, and without the ritual, the particular language has no chance of survival since it is no longer the medium for their daily transactions. In the context of the ritual, the language becomes elevated to a sacred status, and is thus perpetuated. In this chapter, an attempt is made to demonstrate that the survival of ritual and language is mutual. The Hindu ritual has survived largely in the course of obtaining the material needs of people through religious means. It has become an integral part of the Hindus in South Africa. The Hindu identity depends on the ritual. In other words, the Hindus live in a worldview in which their empirical life is transacted through transcendental means. It is in the context of those ritual transactions that the vernacular languages of Indians have survived in South Africa. Every effective transaction needs specific linguistic categories. Similarly, the Hindu ritual transactions need specific categories that are provided by the Indian vernacular languages. Thus, it is in this economy of the Hindu worldview that their ritual and language survives.

Within South Africa, after the passing away of the first and second generations, a majority of the Hindus are unable to speak or use their mother tongue as a medium of communication. Nevertheless, most of them use their mother tongue in the context of ritual and to a certain extent, as the medium of family conversations mainly among the older generation. However, this usage in family conversations is essentially in broken sentences and twisted word formations that often sound strange to a native speaker of the language. Therefore, for the survival of their languages, we must look to the role that ritual played. Various chants, hymns and *bhajans* have been committed to memory and their oral recitation is far more accurate than the written form as found in many of their locally produced *bhajan* books. Many of their *mantras,* and hymns are misspelled, or have some syllables missing. But when they sing those *mantras* and *bhajans,* they tend to sing with greater accuracy. Thus, their oral tradition seems to be far more accurate than the written form for the simple reason that they know how to pronounce the words and use the correct intonations and accent, but do not have the ability to read and write.

I shall now attempt to show how the vernacular languages and rituals of the Hindus are intrinsically related and how the vernacular language is sanctified in ritual vis-à-vis the various community organisations built along the lines of linguistic identities. I shall also attempt to describe each one of the linguistic groups in terms of their religious activities, and highlight some of the important features that are either distinct from or similar to one another.

Types of Religious Orientation

Among the Hindus, there are largely four linguistic groups of India that live in South Africa: the Tamils, Telugus, Hindus, and the Gujaratis. In order to understand South African Hinduism, one has to understand these linguistic variations that have contributed to a significant variety of cultural distinctions. Within each linguistic group there are many different organisations in different locations. It is difficult to study every single organisation belonging to the various linguistic groups in the present study as it would be too unwieldy. I shall, therefore, take representative organisations in order to provide the general trends. These trends are by no means binding on all the people belonging to those respective groups. They do, nevertheless, provide us with some general perspective.

In South Africa, there are various associations and organisations that represent the different linguistic groups. Some of these are based on purely religious grounds and others are either for cultural or socio-political reasons. Often a linguistic organisation is closely tied up with a particular religious orientation. For instance, the Tamil Protective Association is, perhaps, one of the older organisations started in the 1900s primarily to protect the interests of the Tamil indentured labourers. Its members are mostly dedicated to the worship of Murugan, Ganesha and Siva. The Saiva Siddhanta Sangam of South Africa is a religious organisation drawing its members largely from the Tamil community. The Andhra Maha Sabha is a linguistic organisation but most of its activities might be termed religious. The Gujarati organisations and the Hindi organisations can also be treated as religious in orientation. The recently built Kendra Hall in Durban represents a cultural organisation of the Gujarati community. Almost all the linguistic organisations have weekly prayer meetings during which *bhajans* are sung or rituals performed, depending on their religious orientation.

Although there is in general some commonality of religious orientation among people of each linguistic group, there seems to be no unanimity about what particular worship pattern is to be followed. For instance, broadly speaking most Tamils would follow the South Indian form of Saivism. Nevertheless, within that broad spectrum there are traditional Saivites who are ritual oriented (e.g., those who worship in Murugan temples or Siva temples) and there are those who follow a reformed Saiva Siddhanta philosophy (e.g., Saiva Siddhanta Sangam).[2] Among the Telugus, some are oriented towards the worship of either Siva or Sakti, while some towards Vishnu worship. I have noticed that the members of the Andhra Maha Sabha in Pietermaritzburg seem to be following the worship of Sakti, within the larger Saiva tradition. During their weekly prayers, they sing *bhajans* which invoke all the other deities as well, but the picture of Durga and the symbol of *Aum* above it are the most striking features. The members of the Andhra Maha Sabha in Durban (Chatsworth area) seem to worship Vishnu. Besides, the Pietermaritzburg branch of the Andhra Maha Sabha follows the *bhajan* pattern, whereas the Durban group seems to follow a more ritualistic pattern. Let us now look at the linguistic groups individually.

The Gujarati Community

The Gujarati community in South Africa consists primarily of two groups: the Kathiawadis and the Suratis. In terms of their religious orientation, the Kathiawadis are predominantly Vaishnavites and the Suratis are Saivites. They seldom intermarry and claim superiority over each other in terms of their social status. However, such notions of superiority must be tempered with the modern trend of youth finding their own partners and seeking the consent of their parents. There are many sub-groupings within the Gujarati community in terms of caste. The most commonly known are: Sonis (Jewellers) and Vaniks (Traders). The Sonis are subdivided into Pattani Sonis and Girana Sonis. They also seldom intermarry in South Africa.

Although at present caste consciousness is gradually diminishing among the Gujaratis, it is certainly alive among them. In fact, in Cape Town, there are two Gujarati temples, one built by the members belonging to the *Mochi* (shoemakers) caste, and the other belonging to the Patel caste. Both the temples belong to the Vaishnava tradition, but there is no interaction between them.

The early stage of their presence in South Africa is clearly characterised by their strong caste consciousness. This may be seen in the way they formed their social and religious organisations at the beginning: The Kathiawad Arya Mandal (f. 1908), The Kathiawad Pattani Soni Association—mostly jewellers and goldsmiths (f. 1925), Saurashtra Hindu Association—a parallel body to the Kathiawad Arya Mandal (f. 1927/8), Sri Girana Soni Hitvardhak Mandal (date not known), South African Vanik Association (f. 1934) and Pattani Social Club (f. 1941). In 1943, an umbrella body was formed mainly for the Kathiawadi Gujaratis, namely, the Kathiawadi Hindu Seva Samaj (Durban). The organisation states its purpose in the following way: "In our case, the special purposes were almost invariably religious, the holding of festivals and of receptions to those leaving and to those arriving" (*The Souvenir Brochure of Kathiawad Hindu Seva Samaj*, 1943–1956, p. 67).

Undoubtedly, religion has been given the top priority by the Kathiawadi Gujarati organisation. The organisation sought to provide a means of preserving their religion and culture. In a very pragmatic way the organisation states:

> In a very real sense, like so many other Indians in South Africa, we, Kathiawadis live in two worlds, the world of our home, our home language, Gujarati, our religion of Hinduism and the world outside, where our very existence depends on knowledge of the world of trade and industry and of the context of English. (*The Souvenir Brochure of Kathiawad Hindu Seva Samaj*, 1943–1956, p. 67)

Thus, for all religious and cultural purposes they live in one world, and for the purpose of economic transaction they live in different world. Perhaps, this neat division of the two worlds and their boundaries enabled not only the Gujaratis but other Indian communities as well, to maintain their religion, culture and language.

At present, there are a number of Gujarati organisations in South Africa. They are: the Transvaal Gujarati Parishad, Natal Gujarati Parishad, Gujarati Mahila Mandal (Durban), and the Gujarati Vedic Society of Pietermaritzburg. It is clear from these names that the earlier parochial bodies gave way to larger bodies which seem to have larger concerns for the entire Gujarati community. Unlike the other Indian communities, the Gujarati community seems to preserve its consciousness of the various sub-castes and maintains marital alliances within those small groups.

In order to gain an insight into the religious dimension of these organisations, I have looked at one of them in Pietermaritzburg. Pietermaritzburg is known for the beginnings of the Gujarati community. Many stalwarts of this community, like M.K. Gandhi,[3] have been associated with this city. Many leading Gujarati families, such as the Bhoolas, the Sonis, the Lakhanis, to name just a few, have spread out from Pietermaritzburg.

The Gujarati Vedic Society of Pietermaritzburg

The establishment of the Gujarati Vedic Society is attributed to an informal meeting of four people that occurred in July 1947. They were: Damjee S. Vather, G.D. Soni, V. Raghavjee and J.M. Soni. They set out to establish an organisation "to promote the religious advancement of the Gujarati Community in Pietermaritzburg" (*Gujarati Vedic Society, Pietermaritzburg (1947–1988). Souvenir*

Brochure, 1988, p. 18). It is clear from the above statement that the organisation was primarily for religious purposes. Although it was intended for the members of the Gujarati community, the first organisers seem to have reached out to some influential members of the non-Gujarati community. This is clear from the fact that the president of the first official meeting on August 13, 1947 was a Tamil-speaking person, S. Muthray Pillay (*Gujarati Vedic Society, Pietermaritzburg (1947–1988). Souvenir Brochure*, 1988, p. 18). At this meeting, the organisation was named the Gujarati Vedic Society. Initially, the religious services were held at the Gujarati school which the society started in 1949 using the facilities of St. Anthony's English School.

One of the most pressing needs of the Indian community was that of education for their children. Naturally, the educational needs of the Gujarati community fell on the new society. In 1959, the Gujarati Vedic Society founded an English medium school for the Indian children. A youth organisation called the Gurjar Yuvak Mandal was established in 1968 under the leadership of Ishwarlal Ramdas Nathoo of Pietermaritzburg. In 1973, the society started a vernacular school to teach Gujarati to children.

Many of the activities of the society included bringing visiting lecturers from India, organising Hindu festivals in association with the Deepavali Cheer Society of Pietermaritzburg, and so on. The youth organisation seemed to have played a vital role in organising religious festivals, and cultural events, such as musical concerts.

The most important goal achieved by the society is the building of the Radha Krishna temple on Royston Road, Pietermaritzburg. A Gujarati priest was brought from India. He, however, left after a few months of his arrival because he could not get used to the South African society. The community had hoped that the new priest would be able to function not only as a priest but also as a teacher of the Gujarati language. In the absence of help from India, the community had to fall back on local Gujarati members to continue to help both with the rituals at the temple as well as the vernacular classes. The temple complex, however, continued to be used not only as a venue of religious activity, but also a place where their regional language flourished. One could not be done without the other. The most recent development is the building of Gujarati Hindu Sanskruti Kendra (1993) which has been established on Sydenham Road, Durban with the objective of promoting "the Hindu Religion and Culture and enriching the lives of all in the community through its social, cultural and educational activities" (see their website: www.kendra.org.za).

The Hindi Community

The Hindi-speaking Indians in South Africa are largely Sanatanist Hindus with about ten per cent of them belonging to the Arya Samaj. From the beginning, the preservation of their language, and through it the preservation of their religion and culture, was of utmost importance to the Hindi-speaking Hindus in South Africa. They still remember how their grandparents and great grand-parents gathered in the evenings and on Sundays "to learn to read and write Hindi, relate and hear scriptural stories, and reminisce about the motherland" (Shukla, 172). The Arya Samaj was largely instrumental in establishing many Hindi schools in South Africa. All the Hindi schools come under the umbrella body called the Hindi Shiksha Sangh. At present, the Veda Dharma Sabha of Pietermaritzburg alone runs five Hindi schools in Pietermaritzburg (*Souvenir Brochure of Veda Dharma Sabha, Pietermaritzburg 1909–1984*, p. 24). The Arya Pratinidhi Sabha also runs Hindi Schools in Durban and other parts of the country.

Both the Hindi-speaking Sanatanists and the Arya Samajists have realised the need to preserve their language through which they sought to spread their culture and religion. One of the main purposes of starting Hindi schools was to teach the correct way of reciting the chants and hymns. Hindi is essential for those who wish to become priests in the Arya Samaj tradition in South Africa. While the Arya Samajists rely for spiritual nurture on the literature produced by the Arya Pratinidhi Sabha, the Hindi-speaking Sanatanists draw their spiritual support, *inter alia*, from the *Ramacharitmanas* of Tulsidas. The importance of this religious text for Hindi community both for religious purposes and for spreading the Hindi language has been extensively studied (Chirkut, 1993).

U.D. Shukla points out that although they followed the Hindu almanac, the pattern of their worship was simpler. Shukla says, "The simplest home shrine ranged from a flower in a vessel of water placed in a clean corner of the room, or even the clean spot where scripture (sic) like the Ramacharitmanas was placed" (Shukla, 171). At present, many Hindi-speaking Hindus follow the practice of lighting a lamp. In a random sample survey that I conducted among various linguistic groups, many Hindi-speaking Hindus mentioned that they light a lamp every morning and evening.

The *Ramacharitmanas* is a Hindi rendering of the *Ramayana* of Valmiki. Tulsidas, a sixteenth century devotional poet rendered the *Ramayana* into the popular dialect of Hindi (Awadhi) so that common people would have access to the religious teachings of the text. It became so popular that many of the poems in the *Ramacharitmanas* have become part of the oral tradition of the Hindus in most parts of North India. The poems spread orally and have nourished millions of illiterate Hindus in North India. The Hindi-speaking Hindus that came to South Africa, though illiterate, brought with them their memories of the *Ramacharitmanas*. It is possible that some semi-educated Hindi-speaking Hindus might have brought with them a copy of the text. In November 2010, the local community newspaper, the *Rising Sun* carried an article that mentioned the family heirloom of the 120 year old "family Ramayana" ("Going back to her roots" in *Rising Sun 1860 Commemorative Supplement*, November 2010, p. 8). U.D. Shukla suggests that the Hindi-speaking Hindus brought with them the texts of *Ramacharitmanas* and the *Bhagavad Gita* (Shukla, 168). However, to a large extent, the influence of the Hindi *Ramayana* on the Hindi-speaking community in South Africa might be through oral tradition and by ritual participation.

The *Ramacharitmanas* had, and continues to have a significant influence on the lives of the Hindi-speaking Hindus in South Africa. Many of them can recite verses from it, often without knowing the meaning as such. The intensity of its impact can be noticed in the following statement of Shukla:

> It is interesting to note that one interviewee from Springfield (a suburb of Durban) indicated that his Kaki, father's brother's wife, actually worshipped the Ramacharitmanas itself and her reason for this practice was that the Ramacharitmanas contains everything that one needs, but most importantly, Sri Rama, the Supreme God permeates its pages and together with Him are found the many gods and goddesses of the Hindu pantheon. (Shukla, 171)

Such reverential attitude to their religious text often enabled the devotees to preserve their language so that they could pass on their traditions to the next generation. All attempts by the

Hindi-speaking community to teach their children Hindi stemmed from their desire to preserve their rituals and religious sources. Like the other linguistic groups among the Indians, the Hindi-speaking group also built some temples to perpetuate their forms of worship. The Sri Vishnu temple on Longmarket Street, Pietermaritzburg is one example of their efforts to preserve their religious orientation and linguistic tradition. The temple complex includes a school opened in 1922 to teach Hindi. The significance of teaching Hindi to the younger generation lies in the fact that many of the ceremonies (e.g., *katha*, which is recited in Hindi) could not be performed in English. Thus, both the study of their scriptures and observance of rituals presuppose the need for Hindi. At present, the Hindi Siksha Sangh, a Hindi language promoting organisation, is largely spearheading the teaching of Hindi to the younger generation. The recently established Hindi Radio Station called Hindvani Radio Station is another significant means to promote Hindi in South Africa.

The Tamil Community

Many of the Tamil language societies and organisations foster Tamil culture through their temples. There are many Tamil organisations in South Africa whose primary aim is to preserve the Hindu religion and Tamil language. The Tamil Vedic Society (Durban), the Tamil Protective Association (Pietermaritzburg), the Tamizh Manram (Chatsworth), Verulam Kalai Kazhagam, Verulam Siva Sabai, South African Tamil Institute (Verulam—teaches South Indian music), Saiva Vazhipattu Kazhagam (Verulam), Siva Nyana Sabha (Pietermaritzburg), Terukkuttam (Pietermaritzburg), Hindu Young Men's Association (Pietermaritzburg) and Saiva Siddhanta Sangam are some of the innumerable Tamil organisations in South Africa that continue to work for a distinctively Tamil culture. Their activities involve religious and cultural festivals, lectures on Saiva Siddhanta philosophy, South Indian music and dance, and so on. The teaching of Tamil is particularly encouraged by these organisations.

Among these Tamil organisations, the most widely recognised one is the Tamil Vedic Society which resulted as an amalgamation of two older organisations, namely, the Young Men's Vedic Society (YMVS) (f. 1912) and the Hindu Tamil Institute (f. 1914). The Young Men's Vedic Society was formed with the initiative of the visiting religious personality, Swami Shankaranad. The YMVS devoted its work to organising lectures and discourses on Hinduism, Saiva Siddhanta and conducting adult classes for Tamil. It was also instrumental in organising the Natal Tamil Conference in 1926 (Nowbath, Chotai and Lalla, 130). The Hindu Tamil Institute, on the other hand, concentrated mainly on the Tamil schools. After the arrival of Sir Srinivasa Sastri, the institute received greater encouragement. When Sir Sastri gave a call to the Indians to come forward to support the education of the Indian children, the Hindu Tamil Institute came forward. And this resulted in the Hindu Tamil Government-Aided Indian School in Durban in 1928 (Nowbath, Chotai and Lalla, 130).

Survival of Tamil in Temples

The most significant religious source of the Tamil people is the corpus of hymns (known as *Tevaram*) belonging to the ancient Tamil devotional singers. In the early days, these hymns and other basic religious forms, such as Murugan worship and Amman (goddess) worship sustained the Tamil people. Every Tamil family made concerted efforts to teach Tamil and Tamil hymns to their children. In fact, Tamil language survived in South Africa largely due to the Tamil hymns. Today, although many Tamil families make efforts to teach their children Tamil and Tamil hymns, the tradition is slowly dying. Many of the younger generation can sing the hymns and have memorised them from childhood, but they do not know the meaning of those hymns owing to the lack of knowledge of the language. This trend applies more or less to all the linguistic groups in South Africa.

In order to educate the Tamil Hindus, religious organisations, such as Verulam Kalai Kazhagam have begun to introduce a mini-sermon series which are paraphrases of the *Tevaram* hymns. I have incorporated a few sample ones here:

> 'White ashes cover His divine form. He is the Lord who showered His grace on me. The white ashes symbolize the purity attained through spiritual upliftment. If you pray with concentration and singleness of mind the bad effects of your past misdeeds will disappear and you will become pure' says Tirujnana Sambandar. (This hymn is a paraphrase of Sambandar's hymn called "todu daiyya seviyan.") (*Tevaram Mini Sermons*, n.d.)

The above hymn obviously refers to Siva.

Another hymn refers to the five syllabled *mantra* of siva (na mah si va ya):

> 'Whether you are awake or asleep, let the presence of the Lord be with you. Think of the Lord at all times by uttering NA MA SI VA YA. This *mantra* helped the great Markandan to fight against Yama, the Lord of death. Sing this hymn and be protected from fear,' says Tirujnana Sambandar. (*Tevaram Mini Sermons*, n.d.: 1)

In several hymns, Siva is praised as both the mother and the father:

> 'The truth is that you are the Mother and the Father, your true devotees enjoy your everlasting grace. The learned ones know that it is not enough to look after the physical body only. Even the celestials do what you bid. Pray for the grace of the Lord to protect us from the evils of the world,' sings Tirujnana Sambandar. (*Tevaram Mini Sermons*, n.d.: 1)

In the days of hard labour, coupled with political and economic uncertainty in South Africa, the Tamil Hindus seem to have derived their strength and support from these hymns.

> 'O Lord! You have the power to change poison into sweet nectar. I worship you even when I am worn out by troubles and tribulations. I do this because I know that your power can change suffering into joy. Grant me your great grace' sings Tirujnana Sambandar. (*Tevaram Mini Sermons*, n.d.: 2)

> 'Shankara is the giver of good. He is the supreme Lord who is subject to no other power. He is our Lord. We are not under any one else's control. He protects us. We do not fear death. We are always joyful' sings Tiru Navukkarasar. (*Tevaram Mini Sermons*, n.d.: 4)

Today, these and many other such hymns continue to provide not only a zest for life, but also tremendous spiritual power. Often the majority of the devotees do not understand the meaning of the hymns. But they seem to derive great spiritual satisfaction when they sing the Tamil hymns in the context of their rituals.

In almost all the rituals, the singing of the Tamil hymns is most important among the Tamil people. The Tamil hymns are common to both the Saiva Siddhanta Sangam of South Africa and the Tamil Hindus in general. The most commonly sung hymns of the Tevaram are selections from four Saivite poet-saints, namely Tirujnana Sambandar, Tim Navukkarasar, Sundaramurti, and Manikyavacakar.[4] The Gurupuja festival, which is dedicated to the sacred memory of the Nayannar poet saints of Tamil, provides an occasion for the singing of the Tamil hymns. On that day, the Tamil Hindus in South Africa celebrate especially the four poet saints mentioned above.

Another important religious source of the Tamils is the *Tirukkural*. The Tamil-speaking people, who have special appreciation for their language, derive inspiration from works, such as *Tirukkural*. *Tirukkural* is not only a religious book, but also a secular one because it deals with human ideals, moral issues, political philosophy and leads to an appreciation for the Tamil language. It is because of this special affinity for the Tamil language that it is also a source of Tamil patriotism. By Tamil patriotism, I mean a special and elevated zeal for the Tamil language and the Tamil land. Even after more than 150 years of their existence in South Africa, the Tamil-speaking people have special affinities and feelings for their homeland. This special appreciation for their language and the land is derived from the songs of the early Tamil saints. For instance, Tirujnana Sambandar treats the Tamil language "as the vehicle or depository laden with love for God". It is further noted that:

> [E]very letter of the Tamil alphabet is meant to be a praise, or veritable glorification of Lord Siva. Therefore, the saint's song and Tamil are virtually synonymous. Tirujnana Sambandar indicates the ultimate purpose of Tamil as being a means for divine glorification, much less petty quarrels for its vulgar and undignified use. (Saradananda, 1991: 21)

It is precisely because of their conviction that the very letter of the Tamil language conveys the glory of God, that they recite the Tamil hymns. This, perhaps, best illustrates how a particular language becomes associated with the sanctity and glory of the Divine. I shall provide a few examples from the *Tirukkural* to indicate the influence it has on the present Tamil community in South Africa.[5] The connection between language and God may be seen in the opening verse of *Tirukkural*:

> *akara mudala eluttellam adi*
> *pakavan mudarre ulaku*
> A is the starting point of the world of sound: even so the eternal God is the starting point of all that exists. (Saradananda, 1.1)[6]

The unwavering devotion to Lord Siva may be seen in the following verses:

malarmicai ekinan manadi cerndar
nilammicai niduval var
Those who find refuge in the great feet (of Him) who lives in the lotus of the heart (of the devotee) live eternally in heaven. (Saradananda, 1.3)

vendudal vendamai ilan adi cerndarkku
yandum idumbai ila
Those that take refuge at the feet of the Lord who has no likes or dislikes will be rid of all woes. (Saradananda, 1.4)

Some of the Tamil religious practices have been clearly articulated in the *Tirukkural*. For instance, the text speaks of the significance of worshipping the ancestors, gods, guests, etc.

tenpalattar teyvam virundu okkal tanenranku
aimpulattar ombal talai
It is the supreme virtue (of the householder) to fulfil his obligation to his ancestors, gods, guests, relatives and to himself. (Saradananda, 2.43)

The idea of an obedient wife is deeply rooted in the Tamil Hindu society in South Africa. The *Tirukkural* provides some basis for this kind of perception:

tarkattut tarkondan penit takaicanra
cokattuc corvilal pen
To the one who (faultlessly) preserves her chastity, who attends to her husbands comfort, who preserves the honour of her household and who never fails in her domestic duties, she is an ideal woman. (Saradananda, 2. 56)

The mutuality of father and son is mentioned in the following verses:

tandai makarkarrum nanri avaiyattu
mundi iruppac ceyal
The greatest boon that a father can bestow upon his son is to make him occupy the front seat in the councils of the wise (Saradananda, 2.67)

makan tandaik karrum udavi ivantandai
ennorran kolenun col
The best service that a grateful son could offer to his father, is to conduct himself so that men may wonder what meritorious deeds the father might have done to obtain such a son. (Saradananda, 2. 70)

These excerpts provide us with some insight into the kind of ideals and traditions that the Tamil-speaking Hindus in South Africa perpetuated. Among the Tamils, there are those who are purely Siva worshippers, others who worship Murugan and other deities and those who are followers of Saiva Siddhanta Sangam. The first and the third group are often known to avoid image representations of Siva except his manifestation in the form of Nataraja (the king of dance). The middle group, that is, the Murugan worshippers are oriented to image worship. Apart from temple worship they draw their religious inspiration from a variety of Tamil sources. In addition to the two sources mentioned above hymns of the Tamil poet-saints and the *Tirukkural*, one might also mention the *Sivajnana Bodham* of Meykandar, who elaborated the Saiva Siddhanta philosophy during the thirteenth century C.E. I shall deal with this material later in a separate chapter on the Saiva Siddhanta Sangam. The special relationship seen between God and the Tamil language, as illustrated above, kindles a deep interest in the language among the Tamil-speaking Hindus. In order to preserve and perpetuate their religious orientation, and observe their rituals both in the temples and at home, Tamil is fundamental to the Tamil-speaking Hindus in South Africa. Their traditional rituals and religious orientation hinge on their ancient language. This affinity for their language is an important marker of their identity, notwithstanding the fact that most of them cannot speak the language today. However, with the arrival of the Tamil films on a large scale, even the younger generation is beginning to appreciate their mother tongue through films, especially through film songs.

Telugu Community

The number of Telugu-speaking Hindus is relatively smaller in South Africa. Their cultural and religious activities are, nonetheless, quite significant. For a long time they have been hidden by their unassuming presence in South Africa. From the very beginning of their lives in South Africa, they tended to merge with the more dominant Tamil group. In fact, many Telugu-speaking Hindus who came from the border of Tamil Nadu have become very much a part of the Tamil community today. For instance, many Naidoos (not those who spell their last name as Naidu) and Reddys today tend to feel part of the Tamil community on their own.

In recent times, however, there is an awakening among the Telugus of their individual identity as a cultural group. This is evidenced by the Andhra Maha Sabhas emerging all over South Africa, more particularly in the Natal region. The Andhra Maha Sabha of South Africa is the umbrella body of all Telugu organisations. It is based in Durban, Pietermartizburg and other towns in Natal, and attempts to provide some direction to the fast diminishing Telugu culture and language in the country. Like the Tamil and the Hindi groups, the Telugus did have their own vernacular schools in spite of their small numbers. But, in the course of time, the younger generation did not seem to find any incentive to learn their mother tongue in the face of the pressures to learn English and become part of the mainstream society.

The beginnings of the Andhra Maha Sabha can be traced to the arrival of Sir Kurma Venkata Reddy, the second Agent General for the Government of India in 1929. Being a Telugu-speaking person, he naturally spoke in Telugu while delivering some of his public speeches. The Telugu community was inspired by his presence and began to organise themselves as a cultural group. Finally, a meeting was organised in Durban on May 14, 1931, under the patronage of Sir Kurma Venkata Reddy. At this meeting, the Andhra Maha Sabha was inaugurated. The objectives of the organisation are quite broad-based:

> The main objects and purposes of the Sabha are to bring the Telugus into closer unity, with the Sabha as the parent organisation; to aspire towards the ideals of an Andhra Brotherhood; to propagate the Telugu language; to spread the teachings of the Hindu Religion; to establish branch sabhas; to open Telugu *patasalas* (schools); to assist in such educational pursuits as are necessary in this country; to build schools or halls for these purposes, to encourage Andhras to live in peace and harmony with all sections of the Indian community, and to be good citizens of the Union of South Africa. (Nowbath, Chotai and Lalla, 115–116)

The Andhra Maha Sabha received encouragement from two distinguished visitors that followed Sir Reddy. These were: Sri Paramahamsa Sacchidananda Yogesvarar who visited South Africa on November 20, 1931 and Dr S. Radhakrishnan, then Vice-Chancellor of the Andhra University in India, who visited South Africa on April 7, 1939 (Nowbath, Chotai and Lalla, 116). Both of them inspired the Telugu community with their speeches in Telugu. By 1960, the number of branches exceeded twenty five within the Natal province. Separate programmes were developed for women and children. In

1939, they started organising the Andhra Eisteddfod to provide an occasion for children to participate in Telugu cultural programmes. The then Agent General of the Government of India, Mr Rama Rao and his wife (both of whom were also Telugu) inaugurated the first Eisteddfod in Durban (Nowbath, Chotai and Lalla, 116).

Efforts to introduce Telugu as a subject for the Junior Certificate and Matriculation Examination began in 1941, which finally resulted in accepting Telugu as a subject for the Social Science Degree of the University of Natal. The statement in Nowbath, Chotai and Lalla's book claims that "This was the first time in the history of South Africa that an Indian language was recognised and accepted for a University Examination" (Nowbath, Chotai and Lalla, 117).

At present, there are clear efforts to see that the language survives in the community. The establishment of Telugu in the department of Indian languages at the former University of Durban-Westville was one step toward the same goal. Locally each Andhra Maha Sabha branch is now introducing coaching classes for Telugu. There is a great need for teachers.

Survival of Telugu as a Language of Ritual

Like Tamil and other languages, Telugu has also survived largely through the *bhajans* and songs that are sung during Telugu religious ceremonies and festivals. I have attended the Andhra Maha Sabha weekly prayer meetings and festivals in Pietermaritzburg. They do not have a temple of their own as yet. Their prayers usually begin with a prayer to Ganesa, and an invocatory prayer to the goddess (in the form of Sarasvati). One of the most popular songs of the Telugus is the one sung to the praise of Rama:

> *paluke bangaramaye na, kodandarama*
> *pilacina palukavemi*
> *kalalona nama smarana maruva cakkani rama*
> *yenta vedina niku kontaina daya rada*
> *pantamu ceya ne nentati vadanu tandri*
> *saranagata tranambiru dhanakudavugada*
> *karunincu bhadracala vara ramadasa posa*

> O Kodanda pani (Rama), why are you silent? You do not answer even when I call upon you; O beautiful Rama, even in my dream I do not forget your name. Don't you have some consideration despite my appeals; O Father, for you to become so uptight, what am I? Are you not the giver to those who take your refuge; O

feeder of the devotees of Rama, the beloved of Bhadracala (a place of pilgrimage in Andhra Pradesh), please have mercy.[7]

Like any of the Sanatanists in South Africa, they worship all the deities and celebrate most of the Hindu festivals. The plurality of the deities that they worship does not, however, belittle their universal understanding of God and the world. The following *bhajan* provides an insight into their universal perception:

oke devudoke lokamu, oke devudoke lokamu
oke devudoke lokamu, oke devudoke lokamu
karunincu vega mammu kalusambu bova nimmu
dari dapu nive summa, daya toda brova rammu
ananda rupa rara mayavi rara

Only one God and one world, Only one God and one world,
Only one God and one world, Only one God and one world,
Hasten to bestow grace on us, remove the impurity (sin),
you are the way and the goal, through grace protect us,
O with the form of bliss, come, O trickster, come.[8]

This hymn sings the praise of Krishna and universalises his divinity. The word trickster (*mayavi*) is used with reference to Krishna. For a Hindu, every single deity at some level becomes universalised. The anthology of hymns compiled by the Pietermaritzburg Andhra Maha Sabha contains hymns for almost all the deities. The majority of them are attributed to Vishnu and his various *avataras*. Some hymns invoke the Hindu Trinity:

Bhaja siva omkara jaya jaya bhaja siva omkara
Brahma visnu, sadasiva hara hara hara hara madhava (sic) (mahadeva?)
Guru brahma sivananda hara hara hara hara sadasiva

Praise Siva, the maker of Aum, praise Siva, the maker of Aum.
Brahma, Vishnu, and Sadasiva—the destroyer, the Great God.
Brahma, the teacher, and Siva, the Joy, the destroyer, Sadasiva. (Siva, the existence)

Another song invokes all the Hindu gods:

brahma visnu, mahesvara sayi mahadeva
durga laksmi saravati sayi jaganmata
sayi jaganmata mam pahi jaganmata

Protect us, O Brahma, Vishnu, Siva, Satya Sai, Durga, Lakshmi, Sarasvati, Satya Sai, Jaganmata (Universal Mother), Satya Sai, Universal Mother.

This *bhajan* is obviously borrowed from the Satya Sai group. The repetition of the name of Sai Baba indicates it. The hymn invokes the Hindu Trinity, and all the popular goddesses. One of the interesting things about the Telugu Hindus is that their singing of the Telugu *bhajans* is very accurate with respect to pronunciation and intonation. But most of them do not know the meaning of these *bhajans*. The written versions of their songs are grossly inaccurate and I had to correct the spellings, accents, etc., while incorporating some of them in this book. Besides, unlike the other linguistic groups, the Telugus use the Roman script to transliterate their songs. This clearly indicates their inability to read the script. Nevertheless, when they sing, the accuracy of their pronunciation is very impressive. This is because most of them know their songs by heart. They have been passed on to them from generation to generation through the oral tradition. As such, the Telugu *bhajans*, which have been transmitted orally and sung during worship, have preserved the language. Whether or not they understand the meaning of the songs, it is fundamental for Telugus to sing *bhajans* during worship because it provides them with an identity of their own.

Language and Ritual: Their Survival Strategy

South Africa has become a crucible of all forms of Hindu worship. The different linguistic groups seem to have borrowed from one another quite freely. As a result, the surviving Hindu practice is a syncretic mixture of all the linguistic traditions. Nevertheless, the linguistic groups retained something of their own and still hold on to it as a mark of their identity. Individual traditions and practices are kept alive only through their individual languages. Therefore, survival of these individual traditions is dependent on the survival of these languages, at least in the context of worship. Perhaps, the possibility of regaining their ability to speak and write in their vernacular is remote in the wake of the rapid social changes in South Africa. But it seems possible that their languages will, undoubtedly, survive in the context of ritual for a sufficiently long time in the future. The intrinsic relationship between ritual practice and vernacular makes it possible that both ritual and language will survive on a mutual basis. In other words, one does not survive without the other. The languages will disappear only if Hindu rituals disappear from the lives of people, something that seems highly unlikely, Hindu ritual will survive as long as Hindu life is guided by those ritual activities. After all, ritual provides the structure and meaning of the Hindu worldview. In the context of the diasporic communities which are cut off from their original cultural roots, such use of their mother tongues in ritual in spite of not understanding the meaning is significant in many ways.

Notes

1. In India, Syriac is used among the Syrian Christians only in the context of their liturgy. Young people of that community simply commit the long prayers and chants to memory without any conscious attempt to understand the meaning of the words. Without Syriac their liturgy will have no significance. When I asked some of their members how they use Syriac without understanding the meaning, they said that they could survive without knowing the meaning of Syriac words, but they could not survive without using Syriac in their ritual. It gives them their identity and a sense of belonging.
2. In referring to the organisation in South Africa, I shall retain the name used locally for the organisation (i.e., Saiva Siddhanta Sangam). But while referring to the philosophy, I shall use the more commonly accepted name, i.e., Saiva Siddhanta.
3. It was in Pietermaritzburg that M.K. Gandhi was thrown out of the train when he was travelling in a first class compartment which was then an exclusive privilege of the whites. Now the local Indian community has installed the statue of Gandhi in the city centre.
4. Although Manikyavacakar is not counted as one of the 63 saints known as the Nayannar saints, the South African Tamils Hindus include him in the group of saints, and he occupies a place among the four favourite ones.
5. It is because of the popularity of the *Tirukkural* among Tamils in South Africa that the Ramakrishna Centre has brought out a special edition (cited above) with original text, transliteration and English translation.
6. I am following the translation offered in the text cited above (Swami Saradananda, 1991). References are to the chapter and the verse
7. Taken from the Telugu Bhajans compiled by the Pietermaritzburg Andhra Maha Sabha, 2.
8. Ibid., 4.

8 Some Reflections on the Major Neo-Hindu Organisations

The major neo-Hindu organisations in South Africa have emerged in an attempt to preserve the Hindu culture and religion in an alien land. Virtually all of them have been imported from India. As such, their emergence as "neo-Hindu movements" has to do with nineteenth century India and not so much with the South African context. Not all of them emerged in the nineteenth century. But the nineteenth century Indian climate certainly set the pace for the emergence of the neo-Hindu movements in India and elsewhere. The emergence of these movements continued up to the mid-seventies in the twentieth century. In order to understand as well as to contextualise these movements, we need to look at the nineteenth century developments in India.

Although the west had become aware of the religious and cultural heritage of India much earlier than the eighteenth century, the turning point for the Indian heritage came with the translation of the *Bhagavad Gita* in 1785[1] by Charles Wilkins. Initially the translation was received with less enthusiasm in England, though it was better received in Germany and France (Sharpe, 17–22). But, the number of copies printed was so few that some western orientalists found it hard to get a copy. By the mid-eighteenth century, there was a significant shift in the western outlook. On the one hand, the Romantics left their options open in their search for the truth. On the other, the Transcendentalists were beginning to react against evangelical Christianity in New England (USA). Both of them kept their minds open to the possibilities in the east. Naturally, the *Bhagavad Gita* attracted the attention of both of them. The Christian missionaries, however, were not positively disposed towards Indian religion and culture (Sharpe, 15–46). As Klostermaier puts it, "Foreign visitors (Christian missionaries) considered Hinduism a hopeless case and expected it to die of degeneration within a century" (Klostermaier, 385). The monumental work of translation of the Hindu scriptures by Max Mueller in the nineteenth century had a profound impact on western scholars. For more than the next one hundred and fifty years Indology became a major discipline in many western universities. As a result of the significant number of publications on Indian religions during the nineteenth century, the Western attitude towards Hinduism began to change. In the course of this interaction with the western world, Hindus began to look at their own religion from the western perspective. The fact that the Hindus accepted the term 'Hindu' to designate their religion is a case in point. Nowhere does the word 'Hindu' occur in any of the Hindu scriptures. Several scholars such as Smith and Klostermaier have already pointed out the alien origins of the word.[2]

By the eighteenth century we witness attempts of Indians to reform Hindu society in the light of western and other influences. Raja Ram Mohun Roy (1772/4–1833) certainly stands out in this regard. Roy launched Brahmo Samaj in 1828 on the basis of his idea of universal worship. Although he drew from the *Gita*, he seems to be more influenced by both Christian and Muslim ideas (Sharpe, 11). Nevertheless, it is not until the late nineteenth century that we see the emergence of a substantial number of Hindus making efforts to reform Hinduism from within. The educational policy adopted by the British (with their insistence on English as the medium of instruction) in India eventually gave rise to the so-called 'elite' who were well versed in English and were exposed to western ideas. It is this 'elite' that began reading the *Gita* that was translated into English by Edwin Arnold in 1885. Eric Sharpe points out the significant role played by the *Gita* in providing impetus to the cultural revolution in India when he says:

> [A]t first slowly, and after 1900 with the force of an avalanche, the *Gita* came to occupy a position (which in the popular mind it has since that day never lost) as the undisputed statement of all that is most central and most important in the Hindu world of ideas. (Sharpe, 69)

While the western world was slowly getting to know about the Indian religious and cultural heritage, the newly-emerging Hindu 'elite' within India was faced with the greatest challenge they had ever faced, namely, the preservation of their religion and culture. On the one hand, English education in India was gradually influencing the educated Indians and swaying them towards western ideas and values. On the other, Christian missionaries in India began making significant inroads into Hindu society during the nineteenth century. Especially among the underprivileged classes, there were a large number of conversions to Christianity. The emerging Hindu elite took notice of it and began to rally round to withstand the western influence in general, and the impact of Christianity, in particular. Besides, there was already a significant Muslim population in India by this time and the Hindu community had to interact with them as well. In the face of two highly monotheistic faiths (Christianity and Islam), Hinduism felt a special need to redefine and re-organise itself to meet the new challenges.

One of the most dominant needs was to reinterpret Hinduism in order to spell out more clearly its 'monotheistic'[3] and universalistic aspects.

In 1875 two major societies were founded in India which revived not only the Hindu society, but also provided a fillip to the emerging nationalist movement in the country. These were the Arya Samaj and the Theosophical Society. Under the leadership of Dayanand Saraswati, the Arya Samaj claimed that only a return to the original *Vedas* would restore India to its former pristine glory. But the Theosophical Society (1883) began exploring the teachings of the *Gita* and became an ardent supporter of Indian values. There is, perhaps, reason to believe that in a sense the Theosophists helped to remove the inferiority complex from India's educated classes, a complex produced by modern European culture (Sharpe, 88–89). However, the two movements have played a significant role both in the Indian national movement as well as in reforming Hinduism.

Another significant movement that provided Hinduism with not only a new dimension, but also a universal appeal is the one centred on Ramakrishna Paramahamsa. Subsequently, through the efforts of Swami Vivekananda this movement played an important role in bringing Hinduism out of its traditional mode and making it acceptable in the west. People like Bal Gangadhar Tilak and Mahatma Gandhi addressed themselves to the political issues and derived their inspiration from the Hindu religious texts. Tilak reinterpreted the *Gita* in the context of the nationalist movement and argued in favour of a militant approach toward the British. On the other hand, Gandhi reinterpreted the *Gita* in terms of a spiritual struggle. The text, as a fact of history, did not appeal to him as much as its spiritual message. For him the text was a product of its own history and must be reinterpreted in the light of the new circumstances of his time. For this reason, he interpreted the message of the *Gita* to be non-violent action despite the fact that the text is set in the context of a battle field. In that sense, his hermeneutics included historical consciousness and the need to apply the text to his contemporary struggle against the British. As Sharpe points out, the interpretation of Gandhi made a strong impact on the west (Sharpe, 119) in the context of the First World War. Another important figure who responded to the western ideas and the British presence in India was Aurobindo Ghosh (1872–1950). Although his earlier interpretation of the *Gita* was to inspire more militant attitude among the Indians, his later interpretation was more in search of the universal principle or what he called "the *sanatana dharma*".

The South African Scene

As a result of all these various Hindu responses, there were a number of reforms that were carried out within the Hindu society both in terms of religious teachings and social values. Most of these major movements succeeded in reaching far beyond the Indian boundaries, mainly to countries where Indians emigrated. Most major neo-Hindu movements found their way into South Africa. The most popular ones that one comes across today in South Africa are the following: the Arya Samaj, the Divine Life Society, Ramakrishna Centre (later modified the name as Ramakrishna Mission in line with the Indian organisation), Chinmaya Mission, the Saiva Siddhanta Sangam, the International Society for Krishna Consciousness (ISKCON popularly known as Hare Krishna movement), Satya Sai Baba, etc. Those that belonged to the nineteenth century developments in India are the Arya Samaj, and the Ramakrishna Centre. The Arya Samaj appeared on the South African scene very early during the first decade of the twentieth century and the Saiva Siddhanta Sangam was founded in 1937, whereas the other movements had to wait for a significantly long time before they arrived in South Africa. Although the Ramakrishna Mission started its activities in India during the nineteenth century, it was brought to South Africa only in 1942 through the efforts of a self-motivated South African Indian who came to be known to his followers as Swami Nischalananda. The Divine Life was introduced in 1949, while the Chinmaya Mission arrived in 1979. All these organisations originated in India in an effort to provide what they considered the "right" kind of interpretation of Hinduism. Nevertheless, the question is whether these movements, after having arrived in South Africa, remained as movements, or whether they consolidated themselves as individual Hindu organisations along sectarian lines.

From a religious point of view, the conditions in which the South African Hindus found themselves were similar to those in India during the nineteenth century. Firstly, the South African Hindus had to rely heavily on western education and the English language in order to survive in an alien land. Secondly, although they were able to practise their religion through the observance of the rituals they had brought with them, they did not have the advantage of knowing the philosophical background of Hinduism. This was due to the fact that the majority came as illiterate people not only in the sense of western education, but also in the sense of the Indian tradition. They came from a social background that did not have the privilege of learning the elite-based religious traditions, such as Sanskrit-based knowledge and Tamil religious literature. Thirdly, by the second generation, they began to lose even those oral traditions that they had brought with them. Finally, the Indian families, being constantly exposed to a western culture, began assimilating many social values which were often seen as contrary to the traditional Hindu values (e.g., drinking, divorce, gambling). This, coupled with the lower economic status of the Indian community, was an advantage to the missionaries in spreading Christianity among the Hindus in South Africa during the latter part of the nineteenth century and the early part of the twentieth century. At the beginning, the only means of education for the Indians in South Africa was the missionary schools, since neither the government nor their employers were keen to provide them with such opportunities. Nor did the Indians have the financial resources to establish their own schools.[4] So, the missionary schools were the only option for the Indian families. But, the missionaries combined their educational programmes with a rather heavy commitment to convert Indians. This tendency became a serious concern for the Hindus, and they began exploring the possibilities of protecting their own Hindu culture. To redirect Hindus to "their roots" many serious Indians brought visiting lecturers from India to educate the Hindus in South Africa. Some people with a religious inclination even went to India, got initiated into various monastic orders and lived there to acquire greater knowledge of Hinduism. They eventually returned to South Africa with a mission to revitalise and transform Hinduism and its followers. They hoped to give the Hindus what they considered a "higher" form of Hinduism. These new religious organisations began to perceive the popular Hindu rituals as the preoccupation of the ignorant person. They did not condemn the popular' rituals, such as firewalking, and *kavadi,* but began to attract Hindus toward a more philosophically sophisticated Hinduism.

Emergence of Denominationalism

Within the South African context, the neo-Hindu organisations emerged gradually as what one might call "denominations", and ceased to function as movements of significant social and religious force. That is, the neo-Hindu organisations could no longer be considered as movements in the sense of their nineteenth century character in India where they had campaigned vigorously against both westernisation and Christianisation. Today in South Africa, they operate largely as organisations with specific doctrinal leanings. However, they continue to have strong ties with their Indian headquarters. Let us examine the reasons why they cannot be seen today as movements, but rather as organisations along denominational lines.

The neo-Hindu movements that have their offshoots in South Africa (the Arya Samaj, the Ramakrishna Centre, Divine Life Society, Satya Sai Baba, Hare Krishna Movement, Saiva Siddhanta Sangam) originated in India. While the Arya Samaj, the Ramakrishna and the Divine Life Society were mainly the result of conditions in nineteenth century India, the Saiva Siddhanta,[5] Satya Sai and the Hare Krishna[6] movements have emerged as significant Hindu forces in India during the later part of the twentieth century. As soon as these movements were launched on the Indian soil, they spread far and wide to other countries where they became mainly denominational branches of various forms of Hinduism. In other words, these movements were not the direct result of South African history, but rather they were, in a sense, brought to deal with the Hindu situation in South Africa. Having arrived in South Africa they helped to spread Hinduism in their respective ways. Each one of them has attempted to emphasise their particular doctrines and begun to organise themselves as denominational groups with a membership. For instance, the Arya Samaj placed heavy emphasis on the *havan*-based ritual, not encouraging image worship. The Ramakrishna Centre, Divine Life Society and the Chinmaya Mission, even the Satya Sai Baba tradition, among others, have tended to emphasise a somewhat watered down form of the non-dualist neo-Vedanta tradition. The Hare Krishna group, while emphasising the traditional Vedanta tradition, claims for itself traditional Hindu practice.[7] Nevertheless, they all seem to have their individual activities of worship and tend to project the image of the founder or leader in the forefront in an attempt to project their distinct identities. But the result of this is to manifest themselves along denominational lines with faithful followers. As such, today many Hindus associate themselves with one or more of these organisations, often, with a sense of belonging and perhaps with some serious consideration for the specific teachings of the organisation. Many of the organisations have committed followers who subscribe to their teachings and contribute financially to their activities.

Over the years, not all of the organisations have been able to keep up their momentum in the work they do. Some of them have become virtual non-entities. For instance, the Saiva Siddhanta Sangam lacks its former dynamism, perhaps due to the lack of a charismatic leader. The Chinmaya Mission is not so much known beyond Chatsworth (Durban). The Divine Life does a great deal of publishing of religious and semi-religious material, mostly produced by Swami Sivananda.[8] The Satya Sai, the Ramakrishna Mission, and the Hare Krishna groups seem to have greater popularity. Nevertheless, it is hard to measure the activities of any organisations against their popularity. All of them seem to have a fixed membership. Occasionally, non-members attend some of their major activities in large numbers, such as the chariot festival organised by the Hare Krishna group.

There seems to be no attempt on the part of the various organisations to put themselves together with some degree of unity. Also, there seems to be some sense of isolation among all of them. They tend to operate more or less separately, often duplicating the programmes (especially in the area of social work) and fail to come together for any particular occasion. In 1986, however, there was an attempt by some of them to organise themselves as a Hindu Alliance. The organisations that came together were: Chinmaya Mission, Ramakrishna Centre, Saiva Siddhanta Sangam, and the Divine Life Society. The other groups did not join. These four came together in an effort to "initiate a programme of cultural unity". In a journal called *Hindu Dharma*, which they intended to be their official organ of communication, they made the following statement: "The formation recently of the Hindu Alliance of South Africa has been hailed as one of the most significant moves made in South Africa in recent years to revitalise interest in religious and cultural affairs within the Hindu community in this country."[9] The Alliance did not seem to have lasted beyond the first meeting. The enthusiasm that was expressed to come together was, nonetheless, great. The journal was meant to initiate a dialogue among the various Hindu groups. But its initiative never saw light as the journal disappeared along with the alliance. It would, however, be preposterous to suggest that such an alliance can never take place again. But some understanding of why the alliance failed might help us to gain an insight into the Hindu phenomenon in South Africa.

One of the things that we need to remember is that almost all the Hindu organisations in South Africa seem to project a fairly strong sense of self-identity. As a result, they tend to isolate themselves from the others. Secondly, the leaders seem to project a strong sense of their presence resulting in a sort of guru culture. Some people are loyal to some gurus and others to other gurus. Within the same organisation, the loyalty of devotees is directed to different gurus, or leaders. A case in point is the Ramakrishna Centre where devotees show loyalty to different gurus. This is not seen as a negative aspect, but rather as something that is essential in the process of spiritual growth. Thus, both the devotees as well as the gurus seem to enjoy and encourage it. Furthermore, this tendency seems to be an outcome of the emergent elite in the Hindu society in South Africa. From the time the western educated elite emerged on the scene they tended to develop a greater degree of individualism which seemed to be absent in the first generation Hindus who came together as a group much more easily than the present generation. In spite of the fact that the first generation

Hindus in South Africa came from a wide variety of cultural backgrounds, they tended to cooperate with one another and celebrated one another's festivals and ceremonies with greater ease. The emergence of the Hindu elite and various Hindu organisations seem to have happened simultaneously in South African Hindu history. The emergence of the Hindu elite also coincides with the leadership that looked for loyal followers. It is from the time of the emergence of these organisations that we witness the Hindu community becoming more and more sectionalised along denominational lines.

The various Hindu organisations have, undoubtedly, contributed to a greater degree of Hindu cultural and religious awareness and interest. On the other hand, they seem to present the problem of sectionalism in Hindu society. That is, their presence is needed to preserve Hindu culture. But their highly individualised activities that are without coordination by a single body seems to be conducive for gradual division of the Hindu society along denominational lines. The only umbrella body of all the Hindus is the Hindu Maha Sabha of South Africa. But, the Sabha does not seem to have any direct control over the various organisations. Neither the heads of the various organisations nor the common Hindus seem to consider the Hindu Maha Sabha in any sense a controlling body. In fact, the Hindu Maha Sabha seems to have its own activities, that of hosting lectures of any visiting lecturer from abroad. Although it sends out invitations to various groups, the response is invariably not very significant because they do not have a membership of their own. The Hindu Maha Sabha's is generally seen as loose representative body that sometimes mediates with the government on certain issues of communal concern.

The sectionalism that has emerged within the Hindu community in South Africa is due not only to the emergence of various new religious organisations, but also to the fact that the Hindu community in general operates along linguistic lines. I have pointed out this tendency in a previous chapter (*Vide* Chapter 7).

Some Distinctive Features

In the next few chapters, I shall explore the functioning of the various Hindu organisations to highlight not only their distinctive teachings, but also to understand their work in the total context of the Hindu society in South Africa. These Hindu organisations include those that emerged during the nineteenth century and the twentieth century India as those promoting reformed Hinduism. The Saiva Siddhanta is also included here. Although in the Indian context Saiva Siddhanta belongs to the older (medieval) Siva bhakti tradition of Tamil Nadu, the Saiva Siddhanta Sangam in South Africa claims that it is a reformed Hindu tradition and tends to identify itself with the other branches of Hindu reform groups which emphasised the idea of one God.

In the context of South Africa, different Hindu organisations have developed their own programmes and strategies which they intend to implement. In the process, they have developed their own characteristic features. For instance, the Ramakrishna Centre and the Divine Life Society may be characterised by their social work not only among the Hindus, but also among the African blacks. Both tend not to promote conversion to Hinduism, but instead concentrate on the development of spiritual and human aspects within a broad and open framework which might be characterised by their universalistic outlook. The Hare Krishnas and the Arya Samajists, however, are known for their unmitigated stance on conversion and both expect to convert non-Hindus to Hindu tradition. The two organisations have developed their own strategies to pursue their goals. The Hare Krishnas have become more of a charismatic group which uses evangelistic out-reach strategies along the lines of the Christian missions to expand their influence in South Africa. On the other hand, the Arya Samajists have tended to become more education oriented, especially in promoting Hindi as a language. As such, they have tended to operate more within a linguistic group, namely, the Hindi-speaking people. At the initial stages they did have a strong conversion campaign, but in recent times their work is more related to education in the field of language, religion and culture. Within South Africa, the Arya Samajists have perhaps the largest network of educational programmes. The development of Hindi language programmes in South Africa is largely due to them. The Saiva Siddhanta Sangam of South Africa stands mainly for its commitment to Tamil-oriented Saiva tradition. As such, it has concentrated on spreading the Saiva doctrine. It is not oriented towards either ritual or social work. It's main commitment seems to be to the Tamil Hindus, mainly in educating them in the Saiva Siddhanta teachings. The Satya Sai Baba organisation tends to be more a cult group which is drawn by the charisma of Sai Baba, the cult figure, whose claim to be the incarnation of God is accepted as fundamental by his followers. Sharing among themselves their personal experiences of Sai Baba seems to be the binding factor for the group. Their experiences of Sal Baba have to do largely with the miraculous and mysterious ways in which he manifests himself to his devotees. The fundamental qualification to be part of this cult group is to experience Sai Baba personally. Since everyone seems to have a personal encounter with Sai Baba in a mysterious way, the number of such miraculous experiences of devotees tends to become multiplied on a daily basis. Almost every other devotee tends to come up with a new miracle that s/he has experienced. One refers to seeing Sai Baba in a drop of honey, and another speaks of the falling of sacred ash from the ceiling. Thus, the number of miracles grows infinitely. The devotees seem to pay a great deal of attention to the miraculous experiences. One of the first things they ask a new member is to say how s/he has experienced Sai Baba. It is these accounts of miracles which tend to draw new members to their fold.

Thus, each organisation or group develops its own strategies to survive and expand. The members belonging to these organisations have a clear identity of their own. Different people tend to be attracted to different groups depending, not only on their personal convictions, but also on how they wish to see themselves within the Hindu community. In other words, different people are looking for different things from these organisations. Thus, different strategies of the organisations or groups work for different people. Additionally, there are theological or philosophical differences as well as agreements that need to be taken into account. The Arya Samajists and the Ramakrishna Mission do not necessarily share a common philosophical view. But they seem to agree on their view on the epic depictions of Rama and Krishna. Both regard the epics as human compositions and Rama and Krishna at best as historical persons and not divine figures. On the other hand, the Divine Life Society and the Satya Sai may not agree with their overall philosophical views, but they do agree with the view that epic heroes, viz., Rama and Krishna are indeed the incarnations of Vishnu. While in some sense Swami Sivananda, founder of the Divine Life Society in India, is considered a divine incarnation, the Satya Sai followers see Satya Sai Baba as a divine incarnation. With such agreements and disagreements it is not easy to divide them into neat groups.

Fulfilling Social and Religious Need

All the major Hindu organisations seem to fulfil an important need within the Hindu community. As society in South Africa continues to change rapidly, Hindus in general are beginning to face a sense of loss of identity. Especially, with the breakdown of the "group areas" and the Hindus beginning to live freely among other racial, cultural and religious groups, the older generation today experiences a sense of loss with regard to the religious orientation of future generations. These days, many families are beginning to send their children to one or the other Hindu organisation regularly so that they would eventually be grounded in some form of Hinduism. In many of my interviews, Hindu parents, expressed a need to belong to an organisation and raise their children with some Hindu orientation.

It is this need that will continue to provide the various Hindu organisations the opportunity to grow. Perhaps, this would be the most positive contribution that there organisations could make to the Hindus in South Africa. Their individual orientations will, perhaps, cater to the different spiritual, social, cultural, and linguistic needs of the Hindus in South Africa. Besides, if not all, at least some organisations seem to have better inter-faith relations. Also, it would be essential in the multireligious context of South Africa that there be some Hindu organisations which would enter into dialogue with other faiths in order to foster an attitude of mutual respect. The need for this attitude within the South African society does not need to be emphasised any more than it is obvious from the general sociopolitical climate that exists there at the moment. More importantly, Hindu-Muslim relations in this country have still to be clarified. Although the Hindus and Muslims in this country do not have any local disputes to settle, they have a history of animosity and misgivings which they seem to have carried over from India. What happens to Hindu-Muslim relations in India seems to affect the two groups here invariably. In 1993, a Hindu temple in Pretoria was bombed. Though no Muslim group claimed the responsibility and both Hindus and Muslims unequivocally condemned the incident, it would be naive to assume that Hindu-Muslim relations are completely free from any tension.

This means, both Hindus and Muslims have a lot to discuss in this country and in this regard the neo-Hindu organisations can, perhaps, provide initiative for dialogue. The Ramakrishna Centre used to have an annual programme of inter-faith dialogue. But in recent years, no such activity has been undertaken by this organisation. Although the various Hindu organisations have created some sectionalism within the Hindu community, they seem to fulfill important social needs, like providing religious orientation to the younger generation. Also, the responsibility to foster social harmony, especially between the Hindus and Muslims also seems to be vested in them. In that sense, neo-Hindu organisations, like the Ramakrishna Centre, and the Divine Life have the potential to enter into dialogue with the Muslims. It must be noted, however, that the overall percentage of Hindus affiliated to various neo-Hindu organisations is still negligible, and a majority of the Hindus claim to be traditionalists (Sanatanists) who worship either in the temples or at home or at both places. This means, since the various neo-Hindu organisations cannot claim to represent the majority of Hindus, they need to develop strategies that would not require people to become members in order to spread their message of unity and harmony with other religions.

Notes

1. Prior to this date in 1780, the first copy of a manuscript of the Vedic hymns was acquired by western orientalists after a great deal of effort to coax the orthodox Brahmins in Calcutta to give these to them. Once they acquired copies of the Vedic hymns from other parts of the country, they compared them and found to their surprise that the hymns were preserved with great accuracy right from Kashmir to Tamil Nadu country in the south (see Basham, 1989).
2. The word "Hindu" is derived from a corruption of the word "Sindhu" which referred to the land around the Indus river. Both the orthodox Brahminical scholars in India and some Sanskrit scholars in the west tend to suggest the word "dharma" as an alternative, but it seems to me that even that term will not convey adequately the highly differentiated nature of the Hindu tradition. What one calls Hinduism today is the result of a synthesis of the traditions of the original inhabitants (*adivasis*), the Indus civilisation, the Dravidian culture and the Sanskrit-based Brahminical culture over a long period in Indian history.
3. The term "monotheism" is, perhaps, misleading with reference to the Hindu tradition. Although there is, in general, a strong idea of the one ultimate reality that emerges from the *Upanishads*, it is not to be equated with the term "monotheism" which carries a heavy load of

Judaeo-Christian and Islamic connotation. In fact, Hindu thinkers became obsessed with the idea of "monotheism" as a result of the constant criticism levelled against Hinduism by the nineteenth century Christian missionaries. One of the early Christian missionary efforts to propagate Christianity in India resulted in a book published by the Christian Literature Society in India in 1900. The title of the book is quite provocative: *India Hindu and India Christian or, What Hinduism Has Done for India and What Christianity Would Do for It: An Appeal to Thoughtful Hindus.* The author sets out to list a few items for Hindus to consider in order to reform their faith. One of the things suggested was the following: "Reformed Hinduism should be neither polytheistic nor pantheistic, but monotheistic. All intelligent men now believe in the existence of only one true God. There are no such beings as Vishnu, Siva, Sarasvati, Durga, or the thirty-three crores of the Hindu Pantheon. The Vishnu bhakti, the Siva bhakti, etc., would all come to an end. No sectarian marks would be worn. The blasphemous assertion, aham brahmasmi, I am Brahman, would no longer be made" (Klostermaier, 386). Hindu reformers of the nineteenth century India seem to have taken serious notice of such criticism by western Christian missionaries. The idea of one God appealed especially to them. Ever since then, the idea of one God became the most dominant concept for the Hindu reformers.

4. Subsequently, Indians did start their own schools, especially after the Arya Samaj came on the scene. Prior to 1925, however, we have no concrete evidence of any schools run purely by the Indians. This is not to underestimate the enormous contributions to education that the temple-based language schools made to the evolution of the educational needs of the Indian community.
5. The Saiva Siddhanta movement in India traces its origins all the way back to medieval India, and is clearly a sectarian Hindu tradition, with its leanings to the worship of Siva as the universal God.
6. The Hare Krishna or Krishna Consciousness movement, having taken off from the American soil, has its small beginnings in West Bengal in India. It also has a definite sectarian interest with its leanings towards the worship of Krishna as the universal God.
7. During an interview with the author in 1993, Raghuvir Prabhu of Hare Krishna temple in Chatsworth clarified that the Hare Krishna movement is not based on neo-Vedanta but traditional Vedanta which follows the traditional Brahmin culture (Brahmin sampradaya).
8. Since the death of Swami Sahajananda the founder of the South African Divine Life Society in 2009, the organisation is run mostly by lay members without a spiritual head.
9. *Hindu Dharma* (A Journal of the Hindu Alliance of South Africa), August, 1986, 1.

9 The Arya Samajists

This chapter deals with the emergence of the Arya Samajists in South Africa and the extent to which they have been able to contribute to Hinduism in South Africa. Among other things, I shall explore their contribution to the promotion of Hindi in South Africa, their contribution to South African Indian politics, and their relationship with the Sanatana Hindu followers.

The Arya Samajists claim that they have initiated a religious awakening among South African Hindus, especially at the beginning of the century. Pandit Nardev Vedalankar describes the condition of the Hindus at that time as follows:

> They were steeped in orthodoxy, ignorance, bigotry, superstition, blind faith and witchcraft. The feeling of high and low emanating from the pernicious caste system had a grip on them. The system under which they had come to this country and the degrading treatment that they received at the hands of their masters had a demoralising effect on them, so much so, that their basic social and religious principles were destroyed. (Vedalankar, 14)

It is to change such conditions of the Hindus and instil in them a longing for higher spiritual values that the Arya Samaj began its task by sending two of its prominent ambassadors to South Africa. On August 5, 1905, Bhai Paramanand visited South Africa, and stayed there for about five months. During this time he started a Hindu Reform Society, and Hindu Young Men's Associations[1] at several places in South Africa. His main commitment was to spread Vedic religion, culture and philosophy. In retrospect, he was seen as "the first messenger of Aryan culture" and a "saviour of Hindus in this country" (Vedalankar, 14).

Bhai Paramanand was followed by Swami Shankaranand in 1908. He was not only committed to the awakening of "religious consciousness", among the Hindus in South Africa, but also to prevent them from converting to Christianity and Islam. In this regard, his efforts to introduce the *Divali* celebration in place of Mohrrum (a Muslim festival which the Hindus also celebrated), and organise the procession of Rama's chariot need to be seen as clear attempts not only to keep the people within the Hindu fold, but also to attract converts back to Hinduism (Vedalankar, 18). In order to attract both the Tamil- and the Hindi-speaking persons, he used the name 'Veda Dharma Sabha' instead of the Arya Samaj when he established his organisational network in 1909. Nevertheless in actual practice, the Veda Dharma Sabhas were designed and run along the lines of the Arya Samaj. As Vedalankar points out, most of the Veda Dharma Sabhas that he established became defunct by 1950 with the exception of the Pietermaritzburg branch (Vedalankar, 20).

One of the main achievements of his work was to introduce the *havan* ceremony in place of the usual temple-based worship. His work was received with great enthusiasm not only by the Hindus, but also by some prominent whites who were members of the Theosophical Society (Vedalankar, 19). He left South Africa for a while and returned in 1912 and found the South African Hindu Maha Sabha. This was the result of a conference on Hinduism that he organised (Vedalankar, 20).[2] Swami Shankaranand attracted many people through his lectures. One of those important figures was Gandhi himself who at that time was involved in his movement of passive resistance in South Africa. It is suggested that Gandhi's programme of passive resistance received indirect benefit from the lectures of Swami Shankaranand. Nevertheless, it is important to note that the two leaders differed radically on the question of Hindu-Muslim relations. While Gandhi's policy on this question was characterised by his liberal and tolerant attitude, Swami Shankaranand's programme was clearly directed to keep Hindus within the original fold and oppose conversion (Vedalankar, 22).

The work of Swami Shankaranand was carried out by a South African born, Pandit Bhavani Dayal Sanyasi. He went to India at the age of twelve and returned to South Africa in 1912. On his return, he participated eagerly in the Satyagraha movement of Gandhi for which he was imprisoned. Subsequently, he spent more time working for the Arya Samaj. Three important aspects characterised his programme: (i) teachings of the Arya Samaj, (ii) teaching of

Hindi, and (iii) arousing a sense of national pride in Indians (Vedalankar, 24). Under his guidance, many Hindi Pracharini Sabhas (Organisation for the Propagation of Hindi) and Hindi schools were established throughout Natal and Transvaal. In 1916, he organised a Hindi literary conference in Ladysmith. Through weekly newspapers, such as *Dharma Vir*, and *Hindi*, he popularised the study of Hindi. He placed special emphasis on the performing of many Hindu ceremonies associated with birth, marriage and death according to the Vedic rites. He introduced ceremonies, such as *upanayana* (sacred thread ceremony), and *antyeshti* (funeral rites). He also introduced the *suddhi* (cleansing) ceremony to receive those who reconverted from Islam to Hinduism. This ceremony, undoubtedly, became the target of attack by the Muslims in South Africa, because it was seen as a counter proselytisation programme. Upon the death of his wife, Bhavani Dayal Sanyasi returned to India where he took up *sanyasa* (ascetic life) and came back to South Africa with the special task of a missionary of the Sarvadeshik Arya Pratinidhi Sabha of India (Vedalankar, 26). His religious work in South Africa, however, was not isolated from the political happenings of the time. Being patriotic, proud of being an Indian, he plunged again into the political field. He became a member of the South African Indian Congress, and served as its President in 1938 (Vedalankar, 26).

Several other important leaders of the Arya Samaj followed after Bhavani Dayal Sanyasi. Swami Mangalanand Pun, Pandit Ishwaradutt Vedalankar, Pandit Pravinsingh, Pandit Karamchand, and Dr Bhagatram Sahagal are some of the prominent ones who served the cause of the Arya Samaj in South Africa. It was Dr Bhagatram Sahagal who actually initiated the idea of establishing the Arya Samaj organisations in 1929. Until that time, the numerous organisations that were established to serve the cause of the Arya Samaj by the various leaders did not use the name Arya Samaj. He also established women's organisations to cater to the needs of women in the Arya Samaj group (Vedalankar, 28). The work of the Arya Samaj did not go unopposed from within the Hindu community. In 1929, another Hindu leader, Pandit Ramgovind Trivedi, with Sanatanist leanings, came from Mauritius to establish the Sanatana practice of Hinduism in South Africa. This resulted in the division of the Hindi-speaking community into two groups, one loyal to the Sanatanist practice of Hinduism, and the other to the Arya Samaj. Obviously the two approaches did not have mutual support, although initially the Arya Samaj welcomed and arranged receptions for the Sanatanist leader (Vedalankar, 29). In February 1925, the birth centenary celebrations of Swami Dayanand Saraswati were organised, which became an occasion for the many important future activities of the organisation to be launched. One of the most important activities launched was the establishment of the Arya Pratinidhi Sabha (APS) in Natal which became the chief instrument for propagating the Arya Samaj ideals and religious practices. Subsequently, in 1927, it was affiliated with its parent body, the Sarvadeshik Arya Pratinidhi Sabha in India (Vedalankar, 32–33). Within South Africa, the APS saw its chief goals as follows:

> The aims and objects of the Sabha are to foster the Arya Samaj movement; to disseminate the Vedic Religion and Philosophy; to promote the art, culture and civilisation of India; to encourage the study of Hindi and other Indian languages, to protect and defend the rights of Hindus and concern itself with the spiritual, moral and social advancement; and to co-operate with other Hindu organisations in matters affecting the Hindu community. (Nowbath, Chotai and Lalla, 120)

In pursuit of its goal of propagating the Arya Samaj faith, the Arya Pratinidhi Sabha (APS) organised at least six Vedic conferences between 1925 and 1947. Two other important conferences that were organised by the APS were the Priests' Conference in 1944 and the Hindi Conference in 1948. The result of the Priests' Conference was the regularising of certain priestly activities, such as the procedures regarding the various ceremonies. The Hindi Conference brought all the Hindi schools together so that a common syllabi could evolve. The present activities of the APS are mainly that of propagating the Arya Samaj faith, training priests for the Arya Samaj temples through its organisation called Purohit Mandal (Priests' Academy), looking after the Hindi schools, publication of various Arya Samaj related literature and providing social welfare services through its subsidiary body called the Aryan Benevolent Home located in Chatsworth township, Durban.

Contribution to Religious Awareness

The Arya Samaj is largely responsible for propagating some of the Hindu religious ceremonies in South Africa. For instance, the Arya

Samaj members claim that they have made systematic efforts to spread the practice of the sixteen sacraments (*samskaras*) that are usually followed by the orthodox Hindus in India, in South Africa. Although the Arya Samaj is not ritualistic, it is not against rituals that are considered useful. One of my informants commented that in the eyes of an Arya Samajist the sixteen sacraments are seen as a way of life rather than as ritual activities. The Arya Samaj makes the observance of these sacraments according to the Vedic ritual practice an obligation on its members. The APS reiterates in one of its reports:

> It is obligatory for members of the Sabha to have weddings and other samskars performed according to Vedic rites, that is, by the use of the Samskar Vidhi, written by Rishi Dayanand (Dayananda Saraswati). (Nowbath, Chotai and Lalla, 122. Parenthesis mine)

The Arya Samajists also claim that they were responsible for propagating the *havan* as a ritual. It is the most central activity of the Arya Samajists. It is around the *havan* that all the Arya Samaj activities revolve. For the first time in South Africa, the Arya Samaj introduced the system of properly trained priests. The Purohit Mandal, which was formed in 1944 after a Priests' conference, oversees the work of Arya Samaj priests in South Africa. Members of the Arya Samaj are selected for the training of priesthood and are carefully trained in Vedic rites, and in Sanskrit and Hindi languages. At the end of the training, a certificate of competence called Siddhanta Ratna is awarded which qualifies the priests to officiate at the Arya Samaj ceremonies. The first batch of nine priests was trained in 1958. The Arya Samaj priests, like the Christian priests, are licensed to issue marriage certificates. In South Africa, only the Muslim and the Christian priests are licensed by the government to issue marriage certificates. This seems to have been the case until 1950 as per Pt. Vedalankar's book *Religious Awakening in South Africa* (1950). However, in 1960 Nowbath, Chotai and Lalla, record in their book *The Hindu Heritage in South Africa* (1960) that the Arya Samaj priests are licensed to issue marriage certificates (Nowbath, Chotai and Lalla, 122). The priests, unlike the traditional Hindu priests, wear a gown given by the Purohit Mandal as a mark of their authority. The priests are expected to follow "the daily recital of the *Sandhya*,[3] performance of *havan*, the sixteen *samskaras* and attendance at the *Saptahik Satsanghs* (weekly services)" (Nowbath, Chotai and Lalla, 122). The Arya Samaj also trains women priests.

As regards the Hindu myths, the Arya Samajists do not believe in them as such, but rather attempt to rationalise and provide reasonable explanations in order to make sense of them. For instance, the Arya Samajists in South Africa, like their counterparts in India, do not believe in the literal facts of the story of the *Ramayana*. For them Rama was a folk hero and not an incarnation of God. Thus Krishna and Rama are not gods, but historical persons who lived exemplary lives. However, both in their worship services and in their ordinary conversations they refer to Rama and Krishna as "Lord' almost in a worshipful manner, and most lay members of the Arya Samaj accept Rama and Krishna as incarnations of Vishnu. While the message of the *Bhagavad Gita* is accepted as a valid guide for the Hindus, its references to Krishna as the supreme Lord, (cf. *Bhagavad Gita* 6: 14) etc., are not accepted by them. The Arya Samaj also claims to have introduced important Hindu festivals, such as *Divali, Ramanavami,* and *Krishnajanmastami* (Vedalankar, 46).

The Teachings of the Arya Samaj

The teaching of the Aryan Samaj is based on the ten cardinal principles that are taught to all its adherents (Nowbath, Chotai and Lalla, 120–121). First, they believe in "the Primordial Root, the Eternal Unseen Sustainer of all true knowledge and of objects made known by true knowledge." The second principle deals with the attributes of God and his worship. God is described as a "Personification of Existence, Intelligence, and Bliss. He is formless, Almighty, Just and Benevolent, Unborn, Endless, and Infinite, Unchangeable, Beginningless, Incomparable, Support of All, All-pervading, Omniscient, and Controller of all from within, Undecaying, Imperishable, Fearless, Eternal, Holy and Maker of the Universe. To Him alone worship is due".[4] The third principle deals with the *Vedas*. It says, "The Veda is the scripture of true knowledge. It is the paramount duty of every Arya to learn and teach the Veda, to hear it read and to recite it to others". The fourth, fifth, sixth and the seventh deal with ethical categories of truth, righteousness, benevolence, love and justice. The eighth principle deals with "nescience and science". The Vedic idea of *vidya* (knowledge) is understood as science in the modern sense of the term. However, it includes both the physical and spiritual. The ninth principle relates to the notion of individualism with altruism thereby giving a corporate sense to the idea of the individual. In other words, the individual "should look for his good in promoting the good of all". The tenth principle speaks of "subordination and liberty" in the context of the laws of the society. Subordination to the laws of the society and at the same time freedom to promote one's own well-being are seen as co-relative concepts.

Although the Vedic tradition in general presents reality in pluralistic terms, for the Arya Samajists, as in the case of the Vedantists, the ultimate reality is one. Their notion is based on the Vedic statement "They say many, but reality is one" (*ekam sad vipra bahuda vadanti*—RV. 1.164.46c, AV. 9.10.28c). Almost all the reformed Hindus quote this verse in defence of a "monotheistic" notion of reality. Like some Vedantists, the Arya Samajists believe in God-realisation via the three paths: (ritual) action, knowledge, and devotion. It is a combination of the three that leads one to ultimate communion with God. Unlike the Advaitins, the Arya Samajists affirm that an individual will retain his/her identity in God and does not become God (Vedalankar, 8–9). Again, unlike the Advaita Vedantists, the Arya Samajists do not consider the world and its pleasures as illusory and unreal. In that sense, they are a world-affirming group. They reject the popular view that the west is materialistic and the east is spiritualistic. Vedalankar points out, "Both these tendencies are in existence in both the East and the West to a greater or lesser extent. The Easterners are also in pursuit of worldly pleasures. Even in ancient times this tendency was prevalent among the people" (Vedalankar, 12). Thus, the aim of the Arya Samaj is to combine both viewpoints. The Arya Samajists believe that following the four stages of life is the best way to achieve one's final liberation. These four stages enable one to pursue not only material prosperity, but also to detach oneself from those worldly things and pursue higher goals in life. They also instil a heightened social consciousness. They believe that when one becomes detached from material benefits, she or he can engage in selfless service.

One of the most important ideals of the Arya Samaj is universal brotherhood (*vasudha eva kutumbakam*). They believe that it is the only way to respond to the narrow nationalism of today (Vedalankar, 21–22). In order to develop such universal brotherhood, one has to look upon the entire earth as one's mother. For the Arya Samajists, such a view is based on the Vedic affirmation "The earth is my mother, and I am her child" (*mata bhumih putro aham prthivyah—Atharva Veda* 12. 1. 12d) (Vedalankar, 23).

Contributions to Politics in South Africa

One of the most distinguishing contributions of the Arya Samaj is in the area of politics in South Africa. Unlike the rest of the Hindu religious bodies within South Africa, the Arya Samaj, became involved in politics from the very beginning mainly through the Veda Dharma Sabha (VDS) of Pietermaritzburg.[5]

The Arya Pratinidhi Sabha (APS) as such, however, seems to have maintained a safe distance from politics. The political involvement of VDS began with the passive resistance at the time of Gandhi. In 1972, the VDS organised mass prayer meetings and boycotted the Tricameral parliamentary elections[6] in the country. In 1982, the VDS held a Peace Conference to which a prominent Muslim lawyer was invited as the chief guest.[7] In 1984, VDS put up an advertisement in the *Sunday Times* newspaper to boycott the elections. It became an important ally of the African National Congress (ANC) and many of its youth were arrested during the 1980s. During 1985–86, when sixteen members of the ANC were tried for treason at the Alexandra Road Supreme Court (Pietermaritzburg), the VDS gave its moral support to them secretly. Some of the members who were tried included Indians. In 1986, when six members of the Natal Indian Congress-ANC were held in the British Embassy, the VDS again provided moral support secretly. In 1989, some of its own youth were arrested by the government of South Africa. In 1989, VDS was part of a delegation sent to India to seek the lifting of religious and cultural sanctions on South Africa. Although the APS leadership is ambiguous on the question of Rama's birth place in India, the VDS is unequivocally against the idea of Hindu-Muslim conflict on the basis of an age old religious dispute.[8]

Within the context of South Africa, the Arya Samaj seeks peace and harmony among all sections of people. The Arya Samaj leaders in the country were opposed to apartheid and the Group Areas Act of 1950. They clearly affirmed equality in the new South Africa. Although the Arya Samaj does not seem to have any particular political leaning, they seem to recognise the Black political leaders with some enthusiasm. While it is difficult to interpret the honours they confer on political leaders, it may be worth noting that in 1983 the Arya Samaj, at its Dayanand Nirvan (death) Centenary Commemoration, conferred on the then KwaZulu chief minister Mr M.G. Buthelezi the honour of "Apostle of Peace."[9] In one of my interviews, a prominent Arya Samaj leader interpreted the release of

Nelson Mandela (the present ANC President) from prison as the return of Rama from his exile.

Contribution to Social Welfare

The most conspicuous witness to the involvement of Arya Samaj in social work is its organisation, namely, the Aryan Benevolent Home (ABH). It is in line with the principle of "benevolence" (one of the ten principles of the Arya Samaj) that the Arya Samaj upholds its commitment to social work. The ABH was established in 1918 initially for the homeless, and the aged. However, in 1926, it began catering to the needs of the orphans. It began receiving a government grant from 1921 onwards, a remarkable achievement for an Indian organisation at that time. The ABH admits a child from any religious background and the children are kept until they are 18 years old. The ABH also takes the responsibility to arrange for the marriages of the girls.

Over the years, the ABH claims to have enjoyed the support of Hindus, Muslims, Christians, Europeans, and non-Europeans. Funding is drawn, aside from the government, from many businesses and private individuals.

Conflict between Arya Samaj and Sanatana Group

From a South African perspective, it is important to understand the Arya Samaj and Sanatana division in Hindu society. As a result of the work of the Arya Samaj, not just the Hindi-speaking Hindus, but those in general are divided into two major groups. Within the Hindi-speaking group the Arya Samaj enjoys greater patronage, although the percentage of people who belong to it is not as great as the Sanatana (traditional Hindus) group. In other words, although the Arya Samaj is better received among the Hindi-speaking Hindus, it would be unrealistic to claim that it represents the majority of the Hindi-speaking Hindus. Although exact statistical figures are not available from speaking to people at random one gets the idea that the Sanatanist Hindus are in majority even within the Hindi-speaking group.

While there is this uncomfortable division within the Hindi-speaking group, within the larger Hindu community there is also a division that marks the Arya Samaj group as a separatist one. In fact, T. Naidoo points out that "the two terms 'Samajists' and 'Sanatanis' came into vogue to distinguish representatives of the two factions" (Naidoo, 79). Naidoo draws attention to three areas of controversy between the Arya Samajists and the Sanatanists. They are: the question of caste, the mode of worship and the scripture. On the question of caste, there was a controversy at the turn of the century between a Sanatanist Pandit S. Dube and Swami Bhavani Dayal Sanyasi of the Arya Samaj. The former claimed that caste "as a religious and social phenomenon of the Hindu society" is found in many Vedic *mantras,* while the latter rejected that such a claim has any basis in the *vedas* (Naidoo, 96). But today, the caste question does not seem to be as important as it was at the beginning of the twentieth century. Caste consciousness is more conspicuous among the Sanatanist Gujaratis than in any other group. After discussions with the Hindi-speaking groups, it is obvious that there seems to be some caste consciousness among families that have Singh and Maharaj as last names. On the question of mode of worship, members of the Arya Samaj reject worship of image whereas the Sanatanists focus on image worship. Contrasting the two modes of worship Naidoo comments, "But a temple filled with artefacts and images represents a cultural and religious tradition that is richly blessed with the symbol of love and cultural splendour. An Arya Samaj temple is known for its emptiness and even coldness, and many worshippers have difficulty in placing it into a specific cultural milieu" (Naidoo, 93). Perhaps his comments, namely, the words "emptiness" and "coldness" might be a little too strong, it is true, that the traditional temple worship is certainly eye-catching and full of vibrant activity. The third area of difference between the Arya Samajists and the Sanatanists concerns the scriptures. The Arya Samaj accepts only the *Vedas* and the Vedic tradition as valid scriptures which were revealed directly to the ancient sages. They do not accept the later Hindu scriptures, namely, the *Puranas* (mythological texts), epics (e.g., the *Ramayana* and the *Mahabharata*). They reject the idea of incarnation which pervades most of these texts. Naturally, they do not accept Rama and Krishna as incarnations of God. They treat them as historical personages who made great contributions to the religious understanding of the Hindus. For the Sanatanists, however, the *Puranas* and the epics are equally important because it is through them that the common Hindu is able to participate in the Hindu tradition. Moreover, for them Rama and Krishna are not just folk heroes but incarnations of the god Vishnu. Although there has never been any open controversy on these matters between the Arya Samajists and the Sanatanists in South

Africa, the intellectual leadership among the two groups disagree radically with each other on these issues.

Although it is possible to say that the presence of the Arya Samaj occasioned the division that exists within the Hindu community, it would be unfair to place the blame solely on them. They believe that they have contributed greatly to the preservation of the Hindu culture in South Africa. Twenty-five years after coming into existence, the APS staked its claim to bringing religious awakening among the South African Hindus. Vedalankar asserts:

> [T]he credit of protecting Aryan culture and Indian civilisation overseas must go to the Arya Samaj. Not only in South Africa but in other lands populated by Indians, the existence and maintenance of Eastern culture and traditions have been made possible singularly through the efforts of the Arya Samaj and by the acceptance of the line of thought expounded by Rishi Dayanand. The orthodox Hindu religion based on superstitions and a mythological conception of God cannot hold its ground in an environment where there is the impact of different religions, cultures, nationalities and races. The prestige of Hinduism both in India and elsewhere can be enhanced only on the basis of the scientific and logical interpretation of the Vedas given by the religious reformer, Rishi Dayanand. It is because of this that those Indians who desired to protect Hinduism in these remote parts of the world had to seek the assistance of the Arya Samaj and the "Light of Truth". (Vedalankar, 45)

On completing sixty years, the APS reiterated the need for its role in South Africa. The APS president wrote in the Golden Jubilee brochure, 1925–1975:

> [A]t a time when the world is in the throes of strife, wars and struggle for freedom and liberty; and when the destruction of property and violence are looked upon as the order of the day, it behoves people of a strong spiritual outlook to play their part toward restoring sanity and rekindling the spirit of brotherhood. This can be done by starting within the immediate circles and reaching out to the limit of one's capacity to the outer realms of society at large.

It is with this lofty thought that the APS in close cooperation with the Sarvadeshik Arya Pratinidhi Sabha (International Aryan League), took the pledge to contribute towards world peace in the thought that mankind is part of one family.[10]

While the statement of Vedalankar makes it clear that the role of the Arya Samaj in South Africa is seen not only as the harbinger of Hindu religious tradition but also as a corrective to prevailing Hindu practices, the statement of the APS president seeks to extend its role beyond narrow parochialism to world peace. Whereas its critics see the Arya Samaj as catering primarily to the needs of the Hindi-speaking community in South Africa, especially with its programme of language propagation, the Arya Samajists themselves feel they are contributing to the entire human community in South Africa.

Notes

1. Maureen Swan points out in her study on Gandhi and his South African experience that the initial impetus for Hindus to organise themselves as a group was a political one and it was largely in response to the 'old elite' who were drawn mainly from the Muslim community and were interested in their commercial interests rather than in the welfare of the indentured labourers. Thus, in order to address the issues of the indentured labourers, the newly emerging elite, who were mostly from the Tamil-speaking group, formed the Hindu Young Men Association (HYMA) under the leadership of Bhai Paramanand. However, in view of its religious character, it seems to have alienated the Christian group. But the Tamil-speaking Hindus and Tamil-speaking Christians seemed to have worked together in the Colonial Born Indian Association, and other organisations that emerged after the HYMA. See Swan, 10–19, and also see Chapter 5.
2. It is interesting to note that the South African Hindu Maha Sabha was started three years earlier than its counterpart in India.
3. Worship of the sun both in the morning and in the evening is called *sandhya*.
4. It is interesting to note that although the Arya Samaj speaks of the four *Vedas* as the only source of religious understanding, much of the attributes and qualities of God listed above are drawn from the Upanishadic texts. Attributes, such as "Almighty, Just and Benevolent" and "Holy and Maker of the Universe" seem to conjure up Christian texts. There is no doubt that the Hindu reformers of the nineteenth century borrowed quite openly from the content and language of the scriptures in restating Hindu theology.
5. My information on the political activities of the VDS is drawn from my interviews with the VDS leader in Pietermaritzburg during early 1990s. I

had no written records to verify the information. However, I chose to incorporate the information since it provides a dimension of the Arya Samaj that is crucial within the context of South Africa.

6. During the apartheid government, South Africa had three representative parliamentary bodies for the three race groups, namely, Whites, coloureds, and Indians. Blacks never had any such representative body since they were confined to homelands administered by traditional chiefs.
7. It is unusual for the Arya Samaj members to allow a Muslim to preside over a conference in which fifty *havan* fires were lit.
8. There has been some debate among Hindus and Muslims within South Africa on the question of Rama's birthplace on which the Hindus and Muslims in India have, during the recent times, fought bitterly, and it continues to affect the politics in India. The debate among the South African Hindus and Muslims has been mainly at the intellectual level. In 1991, I attended a conference of the Association for the Study of Religion in South Africa. A Hindu scholar presented a paper on the question of Rama's birthplace which resulted in a heated discussion between that Hindu scholar and other Muslim scholars. It was clear that the question of Rama's birthplace was important for the Hindu-Muslim relations in South Africa, at least during the early 1990s. In January 1993, a Hindu temple in Pretoria was bombed. Although no one claimed responsibility for the act, both the Hindu and the Muslim leaders condemned the incident. In spite of the speculation that a "third force" might have been involved in destabilising the Hindu-Muslim relations, the fact remains that Hindu-Muslim relations are visibly affected. However, by and large the issue of Rama's birth place has not become a major one among the common folk. At the present time, it seems a non-issue for the Hindu-Muslim relations in South Africa.
9. For a picture of the ceremony honouring Mr Buthelezi, see Arya Pratinidhi Sabha, South Africa: Souvenir 1985, 89.
10. Arya Pratinidhi Sabha, South Africa: Souvenir, 1985, 9.

10 The Saiva Siddhantists

Within South Africa, Saivism is manifested in many different ways. We can identify at least three ways in which it is expressed. There are those who consider themselves traditional Hindus and worship all the Hindu deities, but Siva is the most preferred object of their devotion and worship. Their worship is characterised by the presence of images of not only Siva, but all the other related deities, such as Murugan and Ganesha. They also consider the Nayannar poet-saints as significant. Gurupuja is an occasion for these worshippers of Siva, especially the Tamil Saivites, to venerate the Nayannar poet-saints. Temples, such as Siva Subrahmanya Alayam in Longmarket Street (Pietermaritzburg) and the Cato Manor Siva temple (Durban), reflect this phenomenon. It is largely associated with the Tamil community, although there are other linguistic groups who consider the worship of Siva as something special. Secondly, there are those who consider themselves as purely Siva worshippers and believe that he is the ultimate reality. They worship Siva not in his personified iconic representation, but in the form of a *linga*. This distinguishes them from the Sanatana Hindus who worship Siva in his various *murtis*, along with the other deities. There is a Siva temple in Palmridge (Johannesburg) which reflects this phenomenon. Then, thirdly, there are those who belong to the Saiva Siddhanta Sungam, who also worship Siva in his iconic form. While the second group is a combination of ritualistic and philosophical in its orientation, the third group is more pronouncedly non-ritualistic. Usually, a small *havan* takes place in their worship of Siva. It is this third group that traces its origins more systematically to the medieval Saiva Siddhanta tradition in South India. Nevertheless, it must be noted that within South Africa they think of themselves as a neo-Hindu movement rather than the traditional Saiva Siddhanta School. It is this third group that we shall consider more elaborately in this chapter. It is, perhaps, useful to consider some of the general historical and theological background of Saiva Siddhanta before we consider the South African phenomenon.

Saiva Siddhanta in Historical Perspective

The Saiva Siddhanta of South India is one of the most popular sects of the larger Saiva tradition in India. The others are: Pasupata sect in North India, Saiva-Advaita of Kashmir (popularly known as Kashmir Saivism), and Virasaivism of Karnataka in South India. All of them trace their origins to the Indus Valley civilisation in some way and subsequently to the Vedic god, Rudra. The Saiva sect flourished relatively better in the south, especially in Tamil Nadu as well as in Andhra Pradesh. Many kings in the south were known to have patronised the Saiva faith and imposed it on their subjects. For instance, during the medieval period, the Chola kings of the south were known to have persecuted the non-Saiva worshippers. Ramanuja, a medieval Vaishnava teacher, fled from the Tamil region to the neighbouring state to escape the persecution of the Chola king. It must be noted, however, that this kind of internecine feuds between the Saivites and the Vaishnavites, especially during the medieval period, were quite a common phenomenon in India. Many vernacular and Sanskrit puranic texts, commentaries and ritual manuals belonging to this period reflect these tensions.

Between the sixth and the ninth century (C.E.) there was a resurgence of Saiva faith in the south. A group of singers known as Nayannar poet-saints[1] emerged during this period. They went from temple to temple singing the glories of Lord Siva. By the end of the ninth century, the tradition became consolidated as Saiva Siddhanta (the Doctrine of Siva). The most significant person who provided the philosophical foundation for the Saiva Siddhanta was Manikkavacakar (seventh century C.E.) who wrote the text, *Tiruvacakam* (The Sacred Word) which became one of the foundational texts for Tamil Saivism. The other classical text for Saiva Siddhanta is the *Sivajnana Bodham* (The Teaching of the Knowledge of Siva) by Meykandar (thirteenth century C.E.). The Saiva ritual tradition is based on a genre of texts called the *Agamas* which they consider are on par with the *Vedas*. There are different *Agamas* pertaining to the worship of Vishnu, Siva and Sakti. The Saiva Agamas deal with the procedure of daily worship in the Saiva temples and homes. They also deal with Saiva theology. The Saiva *Agamas, Tiruvacakam,* and *Sivajnana Bodham,* together with the hymns composed by the Nayannar singers form the basis of the

Saiva Siddhanta doctrines. Though the Tamil Saivites regard the sixty three traditional devotees known as the Nayannar poet-saints, only a few are remembered to this day. Appar, Sambandar, Tirumular, and Sundaramurti are, perhaps, the most well known among the sixty three poet-saints. Their hymns continue to guide the Tamil-speaking Hindus to this day.

Saiva Siddhanta Teaching

The Saiva Siddhanta teaching developed in various stages. The Saiva Siddhanta follows a four stage development. First, there were the Saiva *Agamas* which provided information not only on the procedures regarding rituals, but also on the philosophical ideas; second, there were the hymns of the Nayannar singers; third, there were the Sanskrit theologians who wrote systematic theological treatises; and finally there were the Tamil theologians who wrote not only commentaries but also systematic works on Saiva Siddhanta. *Sivajnana Bodham* (written by Meykandar), *Tiruvacakam* (written by Manikkavacakar) and *Tirumantiram* (written by Tirumular) stand out as the most systematic works of the Tamil commentators. According to Dunuwila, the first phase is dated around the seventh century C.E., the second phase between seventh and tenth centuries C.E., the third phase around the eleventh century C.E., and the final phase is dated between the thirteenth and the eighteenth centuries C.E. (Dunuwila, 47–48).

The most significant period in the history of Saiva Siddhanta is the period of the Nayannar singers. It is during this phase that the seeds of Saiva theology are sown in Tamil Nadu. Subsequently, during the period of the Tamil commentators, these seminal ideas have been systematically developed. Nevertheless, in developing these ideas, the most fundamental guides are the *Agamas*. All the Saiva Siddhanta writings are judged by their standards.

Although, in general, Saiva theology elsewhere tended to follow the non-dualist model, the Saiva Siddhanta in the south developed a dualist theology. This is largely due to a Sanskrit commentator, Aghorasiva, who lived during the time of the Chola king, Kulottunga I (eleventh century C.E.) (Dunuwila, [illegible]). The Saiva tradition generally developed three models of theology: theology of 'Identity'—that "all reality to be one and identical with the transcendent", theology of 'Difference-in-Identity' ("identifying the contingent individuality with the eternal subsistence—without obliterating the contingency, but allowing it a lower degree of reality") and the theology of 'Difference' ("This solution supposes reality's supreme mode to be not Identity or Difference-in Identity, but Difference, denying universal reality to be entitatively unique") (Dunuwila, 1). The Saiva Siddhanta of South India developed the 'Difference' or dualist model under the influence of Aghorasiva. The Tamil Saiva theologians followed the same model. But the unique feature of the Tamil theologians is that they adopted Tamil as their theological language. About the same time the Virasaiva theologians in Karnataka (India) also adopted Kannada. Dunuwila attributes this trend to two important factors: first, the impact of Muslim invasions, second, the surging devotional movement of the Vaishnavas (Dunuwila, 71). It is suggested that both these factors posed a threat to the Saiva faith, and unless the Saiva theologians adopted the local languages they would not have succeeded in appealing to the common people.

The Saiva theology affirms three important principles, namely, *pati* (Lord), *pasu* (bound souls) and *pasa* (fetters). The universe is composed of these three ontological principles. In the actual ritual process, the Lord (*pati*) is Siva, the bound souls (*pasu*) are the human beings who are bound by their karmic bonds, and the fetters (*pasa*) are, thus, the karmic bonds. The Lord, Siva rules over the entire universe and the lesser deities. He has five main functions, namely, creation, maintenance, dissolution, concealment and grace.[2] Davis points out that underlying these three ontological principles are two basic dichotomies. On the one hand, the universe is made of consciousness, and on the other, it is made of unconsciousness. The fetters (*pasa*) belong to the category of the unconscious, whereas the bound souls (*pasu*) belong to both the conscious and the unconscious. But Lord Siva is fully and completely conscious. There is no limitation in Siva. Whereas Siva always has only one condition, namely, that of "liberated without beginning" (*anadimukta*), the human beings are characterised by two conditions, namely, bondage (*bandhatva*) and liberation (*muktaman*). In other words, souls of human beings are bound before liberation (Davis, 22ff). Furthermore, Dunuwila points out, "According to the degree of their bondage, the souls are classed as Intelligence-Deconditioned, Dissoulution-Deconditioned, and Conditioned" (Davis, 27).

In the Saiva Siddhanta teaching, human beings are considered as having innate powers. Nevertheless, it emphasises the grace of Siva in the process of the ultimate liberation of the soul. Moreover, the Saiva Siddhanta also emphasises the grace of Siva in obtaining worldly pleasures. The notion of divine grace, however, does not make the human beings totally inactive. Davis points out:

> [S]trict adherence to a doctrine of divine grace could easily lead to an attitude of quietism, while Saiva Siddhanta texts always prescribe a rigorously active program of study, proper conduct, yogic discipline, and ritual action. (Davis, 85)

By following the four-fold observances, namely, pursuing the knowledge of Siva (*jnana*), ritual action (*kriya*), meditation (*yoga*), and proper conduct (*carya*) human beings develop latent spiritual powers. It is not that human effort alone is a sufficient condition for liberation, but it is an important step which helps the individual in the direction of Siva's grace.

Although it is a dualist theology, the Saiva Siddhanta conceives liberation of the soul in a different way from those of the other Hindu theologies. It presupposes that the souls have an inherent Siva-ness in them. At liberation that inherent Siva-ness is brought to manifestation. In that sense, the highest goal of the soul is to attain equality with Siva by virtue of having the Siva-ness in it. Davis points out:

> In liberation a double transformation of the soul's condition takes place: the fetters that constrain it are completely eliminated, and its inherent 'Siva-ness" slowly emerges. This alteration constitutes "becoming a Siva" in the broadest sense. Achieving final liberation means, precisely, that the soul leaves behind its previous bondage and attains a permanent state parallel to that of Siva. (Davis, 83)

Thus, the dualism that exists before the liberation of the soul becomes meaningless at liberation. It does not mean that the soul has become one with Siva. Davis suggests that the nature of that liberation is such that the liberated soul takes "a form identical to that of Siva. The idea of "equality" and "a form identical" does not in any way suggest that the soul loses its own identity. But rather, as Davis puts it, it is seen "as an autonomous theomorphic entity" (Davis, 14).

Thus, it is not synonymous with the non-dualist assertion that the soul/self is ultimately the same as Brahman. In other words, in the non-dualist Vedanta the individual self is the same as Brahman. It is due to the ignorance of the individual self that it thinks of itself as different from Brahman. But in the Saiva Siddhanta theology, the individual self becomes a kind of a minor Siva, as it were, in the sense that it becomes part of the universal Siva-ness. In other words, the relationship between the individual self and Siva is characterised as part and the whole. In that sense, the individual self which is a minute part of Siva finally joins him at liberation. Thus, it is a kind of non-dualism analogous to that of the qualified non-dualism (*visistadvaita*) of Ramanuja's tradition. Again, there are fundamental differences between the Saiva Siddhanta view of the individual self's status at liberation and the view of the qualified non-dualism. In the case of the qualified non-dualism, the individual self becomes one with Brahman in the sense of eternal communion with the divine. In that sense, there is a continuation of the identity of the individual self in that final stage of liberation. The Saiva Siddhanta, on the other hand, posits a different kind of oneness with Siva. It means that the individual self occupies the status of equality with Siva except in its capacity to create the universe. It shares the bliss of Siva, but not his creative qualities. This theological discussion on Saiva Siddhanta is useful in order to assess how much of these philosophical ideas are really preserved in the South African context.

Background of Saiva Siddhanta in South Africa

In the light of the above, I shall look at the South African situation of the followers of Saiva Siddhanta. The Saiva Siddhanta Sangam of South Africa was founded in 1937 by a South African born Indian, who became a monk adopting the name, Siva Subrahmanya Swamigal. He was succeeded by Karunananda Swamigal. The organisation was later led by Swami Sivananda Navalar. He translated many Tamil prayers and hymns into English. He visited India twice and made further contacts for the spiritual support of the Sangam. Subsequently, in 1970, Maharshi Sudhananda Bharati was invited from India to strengthen the religious foundations of the organisation. He was mainly instrumental in removing most of the rituals and food offerings in the Saiva temples. He emphasised the use of the Tamil hymns from the *Tevaram, Tirukkural,* and *Tiruvacakam.* He also introduced meditation and yoga for the followers of Saiva Siddhanta. Many of his books are quite popular not only among the followers of Saiva Siddhanta, but also among the Tamils, in general.

The present head of the organisation is Swami Arjunananda who joined the organisation at the age of eighteen. He was, however, initiated at the age of forty eight by his predecessor, Swami Sivananda Navalar. Swami Arjunananda, unlike other heads of the South African Hindu organisations, is a householder. He still lives with his family occasionally, but most of his time is dedicated to the service of the organisation. Under his leadership, the organisation also has some social welfare programmes, such as, feeding of the poor children in the schools. It is part of their theological outlook that service to human beings is service to God. Swami Arjunananda believes that people should live a good life, dress well, raise good families, send their children to schools, and help the poor. All this is seen as part of the service rendered to Siva.

Saiva Siddhanta Sangam rituals in South Africa are fairly simple. They meet every Sunday for congregational worship which is led by the local guru. Most of their worship is in the form of devotional singing, and ends with *arati* (offering of the divine lamp). Their wedding ceremonies are also very simple and very brief. They celebrate most of the Hindu festivals. Sivaratri and Karttikaidipam, however, are the most important festivals. Their main emphasis seems to be on their doctrinal outlook and right religious attitude to Siva, rather than on rituals and ceremonies. They accept the basic teachings of Saiva Siddhanta like pursuing right knowledge (*jnana*), ritual action (*kriya*), meditation (*yoga*), and proper conduct (*carya*).

Doctrinal Outlook of Swami Arjunananda[3]

Swami Arjunananda never claimed to be a scholar in Saiva Siddhanta doctrine, but he expresses his religious convictions in very simple terms. He says that Siva is the spirit who pervades the entire universe. He creates, maintains and destroys the universe periodically. It is his divine play. Siva is also conceived as full of compassion and love. The most important means of obtaining Siva's grace is by uttering his *mantra*, namely, "namah sivaya." Siva is worshipped along with his consort Sakti in the form of Parvati. The two are always together, and without them there is no universe. For Swami Arjunananda, every woman is an embodiment of Siva's Sakti, and man is an embodiment of Siva. He points out that an ordinary man does not realise that he is part of Siva. In order to emphasise the two aspects of reality, namely, Siva and Sakti, he gives more importance to the celebration of the Mahasakti ritual which occurs in the Tamil month of Adi (July–August). It is in this ritual that both Siva and Sakti are worshipped.

Swami Arjunananda further points out that *karma* (action) is two-fold—good and bad. Human beings should detach themselves completely from both types of action. The divine grace becomes available only when one reaches the right stage. In that sense, human beings have a role to play in obtaining the grace of Siva. Although they emphasise the idea of selfless action, he suggests that it is not based on the teachings of the *Bhagavad Gita*, but on the Saiva Siddhanta itself. In other words, although for other Hindus the *Gita* provides the basis for such teachings as selfless action, for Swami Arjunananda it is derived from the teachings of the Saiva Siddhanta teachers.

Swami Arjunananda considers four gurus most important within the Saiva Siddhanta tradition—Tirujnana Sambandar, Tiru Navukkarasar, Sundaramurti, and Manikkavacakar. Their hymns and theological writings are the most crucial guidelines for those who follow the Saiva Siddhanta tradition. Even at present, the idea of the guru is very important, because the teachings of the Siddhanta are expounded by him, and the people look to him for spiritual guidance.

Influence of Saiva Siddhanta among South African Tamils

In South Africa, most of the Saiva Siddhanta Sangam branches are in Natal. Although their theological outlook and their hymns are quite pervasive among most of the Tamil-speaking Hindus, the Sangam does not seem to have as much following as the other Hindu organisations. While most Tamil-speaking Hindus are influenced by the Saiva Siddhanta teachings, most of them are not formal members of the Sangam.

The Nayannar poet-saints are venerated by Tamil Hindus, in general. Like the Saiva Siddhanta followers, they also observe Gurupuja to signify the importance of the Siddhanta teachers, namely, Tirujnana Sambandar, Tiru Navukkarasar, Sundaramurti, and Manikkavacakar. Most Tamil Hindus sing the *Tevaram* hymns in their temples and attend discourses on the Siddhanta teachings. Since most Tamil Hindus are worshippers of Siva and Murugan, they do not have any difficulty in accepting the Saiva Siddhanta teachings, in general. During my interviews with many Tamil devotees, it became clear that not only the Tamil Hindus in general but also the members of the Saiva Siddhanta Sangam are not so familiar with the subtle doctrines of the Siddhanta. Mostly, it is the Nayannar hymns that provide them with spiritual nourishment.

The Saiva Siddhanta Sangam is also unable to transmit the Siddhanta teachings systematically because of the lack of such knowledge among the leadership. In other words, the hymns of the Nayannar have become synonymous with the Siddhanta teachings. *Sivajnana Bodham* is often discussed among some intellectually-oriented Tamil Hindus. In some Tamil Hindu temples, some of those teachings are circulated in written form as sermons. For instance, in some temples in Verulam area a mimeographed text entitled "mini-sermon series" is often read during their prayer meetings. These sermons are based on the teachings of the Saiva Siddhanta. Some of those are actually paraphrases of Tevaram hymns. Thus, the influence of Saiva Siddhanta is rather implicit among the Tamil Hindus.

The Saiva Siddhanta Sangam in South Africa illustrates the important social phenomenon among Indian diaspora in general, namely, their desire to adhere to the original traditions in India on the one hand, and their inability to maintain those traditions in the face of not only generational gap, but also the urbanisation and modernisation in the societies in which they reside.

Notes

1. They are perhaps better described as Saiva devotees (*bhaktas*) rather than as saints.
2. The first three are considered cosmological functions, and the latter two are Siva's soteriological functions. See Dunuwila, 102–103. In the Vaishnava theology, only three functions are attributed to Vishnu, namely, creation, maintenance and dissolution. Although Vishnu also bestows his grace on human beings, the Vaishnava theology does not list it as a separate function. Concealment, of course, is not seen as the function of Vishnu. In this sense, the Saiva Siddhanta has a distinct theological position. It is also important to note that the puranic view of Hindu theology is that creation, maintenance and dissolution are functions which are distributed among the Hindu trinity, namely, Brahma, Vishnu and Siva respectively.
3. Much of the information on Swami Arjunananda's views was based on my interviews with him during 1991–1993.

11 The Ramakrishnaites

In this chapter, we shall deal with the work of the Ramakrishna Centre of South Africa focusing primarily on the founder's life and work. Perhaps, an understanding of Swami Nischalananda, the founder of the Ramakrishna Centre, might give us an insight into its overall functioning and the core of its character. It also helps us to understand how an organisation survives and copes in the absence of its founder. However, at the very outset it is important to clarify why the Ramakrishna Centre in South Africa was initially not known as the Ramakrishna Mission as it is known in India and other parts of the world. First, when the Ramakrishna Centre in South Africa was established it was not directly under the international body known as the Ramakrishna Mission. Second, the founder of the Centre, though committed to the teachings of the Ramakrishna Mission, did not feel that he was commissioned to start a branch of the Ramakrishna Mission in South Africa. As I discuss later in this chapter, he started spreading the message of Ramakrishna in an informal setting and made use of a local temple as his initial starting point. Of course, the Divine Life Society also began its work from the same temple in Durban. But the founder of the Divine Life Society in South Africa had a clear mandate from Swami Sivananda, the main spiritual head of the Society in India, to start a branch in South Africa.

At the time when the Ramakrishna Centre in South Africa had celebrated its golden jubilee in 1992, it was still called a Centre. Although recently the organisation changed its relationship to the Ramakrishna Mission in India, I shall use the older name in the context of the account of the founder. During its presence in South Africa for more than sixty years, one major way in which it attempted to contribute to Hindu spirituality has been by passing on the message of both Ramakrishna Paramhansa and Swami

Vivekananda. Perhaps, while the credit of proposing the idea of a universal religion goes to Ramakrishna Paramhansa, the credit of spreading that message in the west and making that message practical goes to Swami Vivekananda. The history of religions and its academic study has been deeply influenced by the World Parliament of Religions (1893) where Swami Vivekananda gave his first lecture to a western audience in a western country. In the aftermath of his profound speech, many common people in the west began taking deep interest in eastern spirituality as conceptualised in the east. This had led to serious academic study of eastern religions in western universities. Although the Ramakrishna Mission[1] became popular in the west at the turn of the century, South Africa had to wait a long while for its influence to be felt among the Hindus who have been isolated from their motherland and its culture.

The beginnings of the Ramakrishna Centre were quite different from the other organisations, such as the Arya Samaj which brought Hindu missionaries to campaign vigorously for its teachings. A young man by the name of D.C. Naidoo formed a group of young people in 1942[2] to study Indian philosophy and religion. He was born on July 22, 1925, and at an early age became deeply interested in religion. He was gradually drawn by the teachings of Ramakrishna. In 1946, a group of young people started an organisation called the Ramakrishna Centre of South Africa under his leadership.

In 1947, a monk of the Ramakrishna Mission visited South Africa. Having been encouraged by the visiting monk, D.C. Naidoo decided to go to India and learn more about Hinduism. On February 4, 1948, he left for India where he stayed for the next six years studying and meditating in the company of many senior monks. On his arrival in India, Swami Virajananda initiated him into bachelorhood (*brahmacarya*) with a new name, Jairam. From then on Jairam concentrated on his spiritual growth. In the middle of his struggle for spiritual growth and development, he had to give up his attachment for his family. Nevertheless, his attachment to South Africa and the Hindu community living there did not cease. In retrospect, he remembered the support and affection that he had received from his teacher, Swami Virajananda.[3]

After spending his initial preparatory period with his teacher, he moved gradually on to a more arduous path. He began his spiritual explorations in the Himalayan mountains in the company of monks who had severed their ties completely with the mundane activities of life. It was at this time that he had come into contact with Swami Purushottamananda who was at the time living in one of the caves in the Himalayas. That cave is identified with the name of an ancient sage, Vasishta. Swami Purushottamananda initiated Jairam on August 17, 1949 into asceticism (*sanyasa*) in the Ramakrishna Order of monks.[4] Thus, Jairam Brahmchari became Swami Nischalananda and remained with his teacher for sometime mainly learning from the silence of his teacher. It is said that the teacher, Swami Purushottamananda, did not engage in any verbal teaching, but through his silence he made his disciples understand the higher truths.

Having spent those formative years with his teacher, Swami Nischalananda began touring India, visiting many sacred places from the north to the south. It was pointed out to me by Swami Saradananda of the Ramakrishna Centre at Durban that after six years of stay in India Swami Nischalananda did not yet feel ready to return to South Africa. But his spiritual teacher told him that he was ready to take up the task in South Africa. He returned to South Africa on October 4, 1953. He started his work initially at Sri Vaithianatha Isvarar Alayam (Vishnu temple on Umgeni Road, Durban). Subsequently in 1959, the organisation was transferred to Avoca (a suburb of Durban) where its headquarters is today.

Work of Swami Nischalananda

Swami Nischalananda began his activities in Durban with a strong commitment to Hindu ideals and the teachings of the Ramakrishna Mission. He prepared a format for congregational worship and began organising weekly *satsanghs* (congregational devotions) at the Ashram. In order to appeal to all the linguistic groups in South Africa, he incorporated hymns, *bhajans*, songs, and prayers from all linguistic sources. The Prayer Book that Swami Nischalananda brought out in 1960 bears testimony to an inclusive attitude that he fostered among Hindus in South Africa. Meditations and discourses were based not only on Sanskrit texts, such as the *Upanishads*, the *Bhagavad Gita*, and the *Ramayana*, but also Tamil sources, such as *Tirukkural* and *Tiruvacakam*.

In an effort to spread the teachings of Ramakrishna Paramhansa he undertook tours throughout South Africa. The thrust of his message was the oneness of humanity and universality of religion. His concern was also to remove the ignorance of people both within the Hindu fold as well as outside it, regarding the mode of Hindu worship. In other words, his commitment was to restore Hindus to a "higher" spiritual pursuit. In order to achieve this, he organised many educational programmes via public lectures and publications.[5] One of his successes is recognising the fact that spiritual growth must begin at an early age. So, he started many programmes for children. He started a Ramakrishna Children's Club which has a membership of nearly 20,000 children today with nearly 60 branches all over South Africa.[6]

In order to bring together the Hindus of various denominational affiliations, he started a Mass Prayer Rally along the lines of Kumbha Mela.[7] In the context of South Africa where the majority of the people are Christians, Swami Nischalananda started a new way of celebrating Christmas and Easter with Yoga camps so that people could make use of such vacations for spiritual progress rather than spending their time in worldly pursuits. Thus, "[T]he holiday periods of the materialist were converted to a religious retreat for the seeker after enlightenment."[8]

Swami Nischalananda's work includes not only religious activities but also social welfare programmes. He realised that in a country where the majority of the population was below the poverty line, it was only natural that their physical well-being took precedence in thinking. So, he dedicated much of his time starting programmes related to education and other welfare activities for the African people in the Natal region. Many of these programmes are still continued by the Ramakrishna Centre. The 1991 report of the Centre includes welfare programmes, namely, meals in schools, Operation Survival (distribution of groceries and food grains), supplying tools and equipment for schools, building of classrooms, supply of school uniforms, and so on.[9] In addition to this, Swami Nischalananda began medical relief work among the poorer sections of the society. Today, the Ramakrishna Centre provides medical care to the needy not only in allopathic treatment, but also in the other alternative systems of medicine, such as, Reflexology, Homoeopathy, Ayurveda, and so on. A mobile clinic provides medical care to the African communities living in the rural and semi urban areas.

Swami Nischalananda was deeply interested in harmonising the various religious communities. He, thus extended his work to the field of inter-faith dialogue as well as that of politics. In an effort to bring all the different religious communities together, he started a programme called "Quest", an inter-faith dialogue meeting, mostly at the level of academic discourse. However, at the level of the community, he patronised the Inanda African Women's

Christian Association. As part of the commitment to political freedom, he became a member of the Natal Indian Congress and opposed the system of apartheid.[10] He saw religion and politics as closely linked because human beings are not only religious but also secular in their day to day activities. His political involvement and radical departure from the orthodox ways seemed to have raised some eyebrows within the Hindu community. Nevertheless, the Ramakrishna Centre, in retrospect, claims that its ideals are both "universal and non-political" (Nowbath, Chotai and Lalla, 182). Therefore, the leadership of the Centre argues that there was little reason for the orthodox Hindu community to have felt threatened by Swami Nischalananda's ideas and the actual implementation of those ideas. However, the present leadership and the organisation are not involved in political debates or issues.

Some of the ideals that Swami Nischalananda pursued which the Centre is still committed to, include (i) promoting the study of religion and philosophy in line with Vedantic principles, (ii) training men and women to spread those teachings, (iii) creating a fellowship of religious workers, (iv) organising lectures on spiritual matters, (v) establishing branches of the Ramakrishna Centre, (vi) inviting religious preachers and teachers to give lectures, and (vii) establishing hospitals, clinics, schools, libraries, and orphanages, etc. (Nowbath, Chotai and Lalla, 182). It was with these ideals that the Ramakrishna Centre made a considerable impact among the youth and women. In 1956, the Centre organised a Youth League under the leadership of Swami Nischalananda. In 1960, it was set up in Rhodesia (the present Zimbabwe) (Nowbath, Chotai and Lalla, 182). In order to encourage women in the field of religion, "Ramakrishna Women's Circle" was formed.

Although in the 1960s, the work of the Ramakrishna Centre was affected by an internal crisis due to the sudden death of Swami Nischalananda, the Centre came out of it with a renewed vigour. On February 11, 1965, Swami Nischalananda died under mysterious circumstances. Before his death, he fortuitously initiated Swami Shivapadananda who could quickly take over the leadership. After Swami Shivapadananda became the head of the Centre, he initiated Swami Saradananda, Swami Premananda, Parivrajika Atmaprana[11] (who has passed away) and Brahmacarini Gargi. In retrospect it must be noted that Swami Nischalananda prepared the ground for the future of the organisations. Although many rumours surrounded his death, no reliable explanation for his alleged suicide is proffered. At that point in its history, the organisation did collapse. The Ramakrishna Centre admits:

> By the time of his Mahasamadhi on 11.02.65 the membership of the Centre had dwindled from the thousands to a few pockets of stalwarts through the country. All the Branches of the Centre in the Transvaal and a few in Natal disaffiliated from the Centre. Many of these are still functioning under their original founding name given by Swami Nischalananda: "Ramakrishna Children's Club" or under a similar name linking them to the Ramakrishna Movement. A very few changed their names completely but have retained the original core membership.[12]

Nevertheless, Swami Shivapadananda who succeeded Swami Nischalananda in 1965 was able to revive the Centre and extend its activities to many parts of South Africa by inviting the branches not only in Natal but also in Transvaal area back into the fold. Today, within Natal there are branches in New Castle, Pietermaritzburg, and Chatsworth. The Asherville branch serves as the women's wing of the Centre. The Ramakrishna Centre in Avoca still assists in the work of the branch in Transvaal area. Swami Shivapadananda died in 1994 and was succeeded by Swami Saradananda. In 1994, the Ramakrishna Centre under the leadership of Swami Saradananda became affiliated with the global organisation, the Ramakrishna Mission. This meant that in 2007 the organisation formally came under the global body which controls the appointment of the head of the various national heads. As such, the new Ramakrishna Mission of South Africa is now headed by a Swami sent from its Indian headquarters. The new leadership is optimistic as it enters another important phase in its development.

Swami Nischalananda as a Mystic and a Social Worker

It is useful to outline the ideals and philosophical views of the founder in order to place his contribution in perspective. Swami Nischalananda seems to have projected a multidimensional personality throughout his life. Those who lived with him, or shared a few moments with him seem to have been influenced by his charismatic personality. Commemorating the work of Swami Nischalananda on the occasion of its golden jubilee, the Ramakrishna Centre records in its souvenir journal, "To those who knew him intimately, Swami Nichalananda was a Karma Yogi, a Bhakta, a Jnani, an adept in Raja Yoga and yet more than these."[13] In order to understand the man behind all his activities, I have interviewed many of his followers and those who in some way or the other had some familiarity with him. Whether they liked him or not, most persons expressed a certain amount of amazement at his accomplishments at such a young age. When he died, he was hardly forty. Perhaps, the man who was known to the outside world was only a fraction of what he had within him. It is this unknown dimension that I hope to present here as much as I can. Unfortunately, he did not write very much, although he was known for his oratory and poetic skills. Those few words that he wrote are imbued with deeper meaning, and express the depth of his inner struggle. In a poem entitled "Footprints in the Sand" he expresses his inner spiritual struggle. He appears a mystic who is on an inward journey. He says:

> I followed the footprints in the sand. Each step, I thought, drew me closer. It was a long and tedious walk and I was exhausted. Yet I moved on, with the expectation that I would soon be united with my beloved. (Nischalananda, n.d.: 1)

He was a man in love with the divine. Like his teachers, he felt the divine presence around him. He saw the divine in the entire universe around him. Like a painter he tried to visualise it and commit it permanently to his mental canvas. But he admitted that the divine was beyond his grasp. He says:

> A skilful painter I thought I was and tried to capture Thee on my canvas, but behold I find Thee splashed in myriad hues everywhere.[14]

It seems his own admission of his limitation in not being able to fully grasp the divine is indicative of his realisation of the divine, though it might be partial. Nevertheless, in his spiritual quest, he seems to have journeyed much farther. On the one hand, he admits that he is unable to capture the divine in his vision, but on the other, he does visualise the divine in its all-pervasiveness. It, perhaps, reflects his dialectical vision of the divine, namely, that the divine is visualised both within and without. In his mystical visualisations, he realises that:

> [T]here is nowhere that Thou art not I feel Thy consciousness in the vastness of the universe. I feel Thy eternal vibration ever within and without me.[15]

His experience of the divine seems to border between a non-dualist and a dualist idea. In so far as he makes the distinction between himself and the divine outside of him, he lives in a dualist world. But he also enters that non-dualist world where he finds the divine within himself. Nevertheless, it is not clear if his non-dual experience had reached the stage where he identified himself with the divine. Even if he did reach that stage, perhaps it would have been difficult to express it in linguistic categories.

For all practical purposes he did live and engage himself vigorously in the dualist world of joy and sorrow, life and death, the divine and the devotee. He seems to have identified with the plight of the people in the middle of their material as well as spiritual poverty. As a man progressing in his spiritual quest, he sought to share that divine experience with ordinary people. However, as a human being found in the middle of suffering, sorrow and poverty, he sought to provide a way out to those who were caught in material battles. Thus, his social work programmes reflect a combination of the material and spiritual life.

Sources of Swami Nischalananda's Spiritual and Social Life

Swami Nischalananda seems to have drawn heavily not only from his spiritual teachers with whom he lived in India, but also from the two towering figures of the Ramakrishna Mission, namely, Ramakrishna Paramhansa and Swami Vivekananda. His own quest for the divine bears close resemblance to that of Ramakrishna Paramhansa who also in his formative years sought to see the divine in the image of Kali. And when Ramakrishna Paramhansa received the vision of the divine in the Kali temple, it was a realisation that the divine was simply beyond his grasp. It is possible that Swami Nischalananda was constructing his spiritual experience along the lines of the experience of Ramakrishna. But it seems to have been passed on to him through his own spiritual teachers, especially Swami Purushottamananda with whom he lived in the Himalayas. His mystical experience is, perhaps, grounded in the experience of Swami Purushottamananda as it had been in front of that silent master where he spent nearly six full years. It was in the silence of his teacher that he was shaping and grounding his own mystical experience. Nevertheless, his social action programmes seem to have been drawn mainly from Swami Vivekananda. In his quest to combine his spiritual life with his social life around him, he seems to combine the examples of both Ramakrishna Paramhansa and Swami Vivekananda.

Whereas Ramakrishna Paramhansa revelled in his mystical union with the divine, Swami Vivekananda continually sought the divine in the living and the personal forms. It is in his hands that the non-dualist Vedanta truly became practical. It is worthwhile to note Swami Vivekananda's idea of practical Vedanta as it seems to impact on Swami Nischalananda:

> The Non-personal God is a living God, a principle. The difference between personal and non-personal is this that the personal is only a man, and the non-personal idea is that He is the angel, the man, the animal, and yet something more which we cannot see, because Non-personality includes all personalities, is the sum-total of everything in the universe, and infinitely more besides. (Vivekananda, 41–42)

For Swami Vivekananda, worshipping the living God is important. This means the divine is mediated through the images and symbols in the temples which provide a means to reach the divine. He, however, goes beyond that, and says that seeing the divine in one's own heart is far more important. In that sense, the non-personal idea of the divine is fundamental to him because he sees everything in it. Thus, for Swami Vivekananda, the divine is both personal and non-personal at the same time (Vivekananda, 49). In so far as he stresses the personal form, he sees the divine in all human beings. Resonating with the sayings of Jesus, Swami Vivekananda points out, "If you cannot love your brother whom you have seen, how can you love God whom you have not seen" (Vivekananda, 51). Elsewhere he says:

> Look upon every man and woman and everyone as God. You cannot help anyone, you can only serve: serve the children of the Lord, serve the Lord Himself; if you have the privilege. (Vivekananda, 160)

It is this message of Swami Vivekananda that seems to have become the guiding pole for Swami Nischalananda throughout his life. The work that he rendered for the society bears testimony to that. Resonating with Swami Vivekananda, Swami Nischalananda says:

> Providence has placed us here, we have a mission in South Africa. This is a human laboratory. Here we have the spirit of the West—technology, the soul of the East—peace; and a new South Africa raising its head. We must mingle and produce a new culture and force, a new balance. We have to start a great spiritual campaign. This campaign must continue and never cease. We have to balance this force of hatred. Mere talk is not enough. You have to grow spiritually and prepare.[16]

Ramakrishna Centre Beyond Swami Nischalananda

The work of Swami Nischalananda is being continued by his disciples under the leadership of Swami Shivapadananda. One of the factors that contributed to the success of the organisation beyond its founder is the idea of maintaining the tradition of the teacher. As elsewhere, the monks of the Ramakrishna Paramhansa Centre trace the lineage of their teachers (guru parampara) to Ramakrishna Paramhansa himself via Swami Nischalananda and Swami Purushottamananda. It is claimed that Swami Purushottamananda was initiated directly by Ramakrishna Paramhansa. In that sense, a direct line of continuity of the guruship was maintained.[17] While Swami Nischalananda was alive, he maintained a strong teacher-disciple relationship which is continued by the succeeding spiritual heads of the Centre. In other words, loyalty to the spiritual teacher is seen as part of the successful functioning of the organisation. It is through the immediate teacher that one is in touch with the first teacher, Ramakrishna Paramhansa. In that sense, the role of the teacher is to forge a link between the disciple and his supreme teacher, Ramakrishna Paramhansa. Swami Saradananda of the Centre (back in 1992 when it was still called 'Centre') suggested during my interviews with him that ultimately Ramakrishna is no longer a person, but becomes a principle to which any future devotee submits. He says that it is loyalty to that principle which enables the organisation to survive any crisis. In his lifetime, Swami Nischalananda is said to have done precisely the same thing, that is to become a link between the principle, namely, Ramakrishna Paramhansa and the devotee. The leaders of the Ramakrishna Centre claim that even after Swami Nischalananda had passed away leaving the organisation in a crisis, the devotees returned to the original Centre because their loyalty was established not merely to Swami Nischalananda, but to the principle, namely, Ramakrishna Paramhansa. The example of their founder monk seems to be emulated by the present monks of the organisation. They see their role as facilitators. Although in general, ordinary devotees tend to become attached to one monk or another from whom they receive their spiritual guidance, it remains the responsibility of the monks to make sure that they remain unattached to the devotees and also to ensure that the latter grow in spiritual strength and become independent. The monks maintain that the sole loyalty of the devotees is to the principle, Ramakrishna Paramhansa. It is, perhaps, in view of that commitment that the previous spiritual head, Swami

Shivapadananda recalled the message that Swami Nischalananda wrote in 1948:

> Never for a moment think that the Centre would be crippled without you or me. ... Remember, you are not working, it is the Lord in you who works; you are His instruments only. ... It is through Him that the sun shines, the wind blows, it rains, fire burns, the whole world exists. Never deny Him. Never be under the false notion that the Centre would collapse if you are not there, or I die, or some leave it—the Lord shall find a worthy person for it.[18]

The credit of building the ashrams at Pietermaritzburg, Chatsworth and Ladysmith including the Saradadevi Ashram at Asherville (Durban) goes to Swami Shivapadananda. The headquarters at Avoca in Durban was expanded under the leadership of Swami Saradananda. Currently, due to its changed relationship to the Indian mother body, the Ramakrishna Mission, though it continues to retain the older name, it formally refers to itself as a "Branch of the Ramakrishna Mission, Belur Math, West Bengal, India." It is now headed by Swami Vimokshananda, who has been appointed from the headquarters in India. The centre now has seven sub-centres—Chatsworth (Durban), Phoẹnix (Durban), Pietermaritzburg, Dundee, Ladysmith, Newcastle—all in KwaZulu Natal province. The seventh one is in Lenesia of Gauteng province and there are none in Western Cape and other provinces. They conduct *satsanghs* in all these centres for local devotees. Additionally they also have smaller *satsangh* groups largely in the greater Durban area—Durban Central, Glencoe, Red Hill, Sydenham, Tongaat, and Verulam; and another two in Escort, and Etete in KwaZulu Natal region.

Doctrinal Outlook of the Ramakrishna Centre

The Centre states publicly on its website (http://www.ramakrishna-sa.org.za) that its work is based on the Vedantic principles. It emphasises both religious and humanitarian work as significant for its engagement in South Africa. The general doctrinal outlook is based on the Vedantic teachings expounded by Ramakrishna Paramhansa and applied to practical life by Swami Vivekananda. In his own experience, Ramakrishna Paramhansa progressed from a dualist world to a non-dualist world. Thus, his ultimate experience of the divine is rooted in the non-dual Vedantic philosophy. It is in the writings of Swami Vivekananda that this non-dualist experience of Ramakrishna Paramhansa is best explained. As seen above, Swami Nischalananda subscribed to the very same views but in more simple terms. It might be useful to recall Swami Vivekananda's views on the Vedanta to provide an anchor to his views. The post-Nischalananda Ramakrishna Mission today draws more directly from the writings to the founding teachers of the Ramakrishna Mission in India in view of the fact that the leadership of the South African branch is headed by the Swamis sent from India.

Swami Vivekananda's conception of God is ultimately non-personal. The universe is the expression of that ultimate non-personal reality. In other words, God is the universe itself. Elaborating on the idea of God as the universe, he says:

> It is that idea, God immanent in the universe, the very essence, the heart, the soul of things. He manifests himself, as it were, in this universe. You and I are little bits, little points, little channels, little expressions, all living inside of that infinite ocean of Existence, Knowledge, and Bliss. (Vivekananda, 374)

Although he sees no distinction between God and the universe, he points out that God is not matter. However, he says, "whatever is real in matter is He (God)" (Vivekananda, 378).[19] Thus, God is beyond all conceptions or name and form. Nevertheless, Swami Vivekananda sees God in personal terms also. He says:

> Personal God is true as much as this chair is true, as much as this world is true, but no more. It is not absolute truth. That is to say, the Personal is that very Non-personal God and, therefore, it is true, just as I, as a human being, am true and not true at the same time. (Vivekananda, 376)

It is only in a relative sense that he accepts the idea of a personal God. For him the idea of a personal God cannot be accommodated in the highest generalisation. The idea of a personal God cannot be said to be all encompassing by its limited scope. In thinking of God as non-personal who is the universe itself, Swami Vivekananda makes sure that there is no limitation attached to such non-dualist conception. One of the questions that he raises in relation to the non-personal God is the relation of the universe to such a God. Does the non-personal God become the universe? He affirms that the non-personal God is unchangeable and infinite. If that is the case, how does the unchangeable, infinite and pure

Being become the universe? In response to such questions, he says that the universe that we see and experience is ultimately unreal and does not exist at all. It is the product of maya or illusion (Vivekananda, 118ff). The universe or the things in it, such as humans, trees and so on, have never been born or never will be. All that exists is Brahman. In that sense, the ultimate purpose of our life is to obtain that higher knowledge of Brahman. When one attains that knowledge she or he realises one's identity as Brahman. Swami Vivekananda admits that such higher knowledge is not possible for ordinary human beings. Therefore, he suggests the steps of yoga to be followed in order to control one's body and mind. It must also be noted that in addition to following the Vedantic philosophical principles, the Centre in line with their mother body also elevates the three key individuals associated with the Ramakrishna Mission—Ramakrishna Paramhansa, Smt Sarada Devi, and Swami Vivekananda—as the "holy trinity".

The above position of Vedanta, as expounded by Swami Vivekananda, is closely followed by the monks of the Ramakrishna Mission in South Africa. Swami Saradananda of the Ramakrishna Mission in South Africa pointed out during the interviews that for all practical purposes they do not compel their members to follow the non-dualist path. On a daily basis they operate with a dualist worldview. In fact the passage that I referred to by Swami Nischalananda, does indicate a dualist worldview. Nevertheless, as Swami Saradananda states, the ideal is always to go beyond the dualist worldview to the non-dualist realisation of Brahman. Swami Nischalananda expressed it in a poetic language:

> [H]ave you ever tried to merge into the beauty of a rose? The same molecules and beauty and consciousness are in your body too. There is a process of constant unification and merging.[20]

It is this unification and merging with the divine that is seen as the ultimate goal of human life. It is to achieve this final merging that one has to keep in mind in whatever one does. In a practical way Swami Nischalananda suggests:

> [W]e must bring joy into our lives and dedication to whatever we do. It must be a continuous merging and becoming. There is something great in us that must be awakened, through which Divine Realisation comes.[21]

The doctrinal outlook of the Ramakrishna Centre is noted for its inclusiveness. They see their aim as making people better in whatever religious persuasion they might be involved. This general attitude is expressed in the words of Swami Nischalananda:

> Every city and every village will be swept with spiritual change. But this cannot be done if you only create an impression. We have to change OURSELVES. Ours is the peaceful path of perfecting all races and all religious groups. We are destined to strive in every possible way to help make a Hindu a better Hindu, a Jew a better Jew, a Christian a better Christian, a Moslem a better Moslem.[22]

Within the context of South Africa, this message has particular relevance in light of its tolerant outlook. Thus, the Ramakrishna Centre can play a vital role in inter-faith dialogue in addressing community issues and forging better relations between all religious groups in South Africa.

General Activities of the Centre

Some of the general activities of the Centre include both religious/spiritual as well as developmental ones. In addition to many humanitarian activities, the Centre organises activities such as Desmond Tutu Peace Lecture, visits to local senior citizens, and Karate classes for children. On the religious front, they organise Hindu festivals such as *Divali, Navaratri,* and *Gita Jayanti*. They regularly conduct medical clinics in areas that are poor. As part of their Nutrition Programme they feed school children, orphans, senior citizens and HIV-AIDS patients. In an attempt to spread the Hindu ideals and religious values, they organise conferences on Hinduism periodically, Vedanta retreats and other major festivals. In line with their broader philosophical approach they engage in inter faith dialogues with other religions periodically and also organise events such as Christmas Eve. In their commitment to developing youth they also conduct events such as National Youth Day and facilitate retreats for young people. By dividing their activities into five categories—spiritual, medical, veterinary, educational and welfare—the organisation tries to cater to the entire society including the animals.

Notes

1. The Ramakrishna Mission refers to the organisation known in India and the Ramakrishna Centre refers to the organisation known in South Africa.

2. The 50 years celebration of the organisation in South Africa is based on this date, although the formal setting up of the Ramakrishna Centre was only after he had returned from India in 1953. In 1946, it was simply a loosely organised centre.
3. *Golden Jubilee Souvenir of Ramakrishna Centre of South Africa* (1942–1992), 12.
4. It is alleged that Swami Purushottamananda had left the Ramakrishna Mission and thus his initiation of Jairam could not be considered as authentic as far as the Ramakrishna Mission in India is concerned. This, perhaps, explains why there is no direct link between the Ramakrishna Centre of South Africa and the Ramakrishna Mission in India.
5. Ibid., 16.
6. Loc. cit.
7. Kumbha Mela is a major festival in India. It is the occasion for large-scale consecration of deities, and is mainly associated with Siva worship.
8. Ibid., 17.
9. Report of the Ramakrishna Centre, 1991 (a published pamphlet).
10. Loc. cit.
11. Atmaprana became the head of the women's branch of the organisation and after her death, she was succeeded by Gargi.
12. Golden Jubilee Souvenir, 18.
13. Ibid., 19.
14. Ibid., 35.
15. Ibid., 36–37.
16. Quoted from a pamphlet titled "Dedication", published by the Ramakrishna Centre of South Africa, Durban, n.d., 1.
17. Golden Jubilee Souvenir, 22.
18. Ibid., 25.
19. Also see *Complete Works of Vivekananda*. Vol. 2 (Calcutta: Advaita Ashrama, 1987), 38ff.
20. Quoted from a pamphlet titled "Dedication", published by the Ramakrishna Centre of South Africa, Durban, n.d., 2.
21. Ibid.
22. Ibid., 1.

12 The Divine Life Society

In the present chapter, I shall discuss the role of the Divine Life Society in advancing Hindu culture in South Africa. I shall not only highlight some of their activities, but also discuss their doctrinal convictions. The Divine Life Society of South Africa was established in 1949 in Durban by a local Indian, V. Srinivasen. He was a school teacher and interested in spirituality. His spiritual quest is said to have taken a new turn after he read a book, *Practice of Karma Yoga*. Influenced by the book, he took a trip to India hoping to meet some spiritual people and monks. In 1948, he visited Rishikesh where he met Swami Sivananda, the founder of the Divine Life Society in India. He returned to South Africa in 1949 having undergone a significant change in his personal life. He was trying to cope with the spiritual change that was beginning to occur in him and was in a dilemma for a long time deciding whether or not he should devote his life fully to spiritual development.

It was during this time that he received three letters in quick succession from Swami Sivananda asking him to start a branch of the Divine Life Society in Durban. Srinivasen was unable to decide and kept silent about the letters. Finally, towards the later part of 1949, his thoughts started crystallising and convictions gradually took shape. Finally, that very year he opened a branch of the Divine Life Society in Durban, and started a journal called *Light of Power and Wisdom*. Subsequently, the name of the journal was changed to *Path to God-Realisation* and presently is called *Divine Life* (Singh, 101).

Srinivasen started *satsanghs* (meeting of devotees) and discourses on religious topics at the Umgeni temple.[1] Gradually, he began attracting followers to the organisation. In 1956, Srinivasen took a second trip to India and this time he went to the Sivananda

Ashram where he was initiated by Swami Sivananda. He returned to South Africa this time as Swami Sahajananda. Taking *sanyas* seems to be the most effective way a person becomes involved in religious activities fully without any distractions from the family or society. With new vigour and enthusiasm, Swami Sahajananda registered the society in 1958 with the Registrar of Companies under the Companies Act of 1926. Six years later in 1964, a new constitution was drafted which made it a society and not a company. Thereafter, the society was able to have a membership and trustees. Subsequently, several branches were opened within Natal, especially in the greater Durban Metropolitan area. In 1959, the head office was shifted to the Reservoir Hill area in Durban. During 1954 and 1970 at least six more branches were opened in Natal. In 1950, a printing press was started to publish literature of the society. Today, publishing of popular religious literature seems to be the main activity of the society. The printing activity is directly controlled by Swami Sahajananda.

During all those formative years and until his recent death, Swami Sahajananda seems to have functioned as the sole authority of the society with every transaction under his direct control. Perhaps, he is able to do this under the guise of "traditional authority." In other words, in traditional Hindu society, the guru has more or less full control on his followers and their activities. Religious heads of present day Hindu organisations also seem to be drawn by that mode of operation. Singh points out the decisive authority which Swami Sahajananda had on his organisation and its activities: "As spiritual head, Swami Sahajananda represents traditional authority, all decisions and activities of the ashram must first receive his sanction and blessings" (Singh, 108).

Activities and Programmes

There are two types of activities that are generally undertaken at the Divine Life Society. First, the ashram activities provide for the spiritual development of the devotees. Second, the social welfare activities of the society give expression to its commitment to the holistic life of the individual. Ashram life is obviously of great importance to Swami Sahajananda given its commitment to the spiritual development of the people that associate themselves with the society. Singh points out that there are two types of members at the ashram: those who live at the ashram on a full time basis and those who are householders and visit occasionally (Singh, 112). The first group of devotees live directly under the spiritual guidance of Swami Sahajananda, whereas the second group tends to have greater independence in their lives, although they do consult the spiritual head on crucial matters of their life. Those who live at the ashram on full time basis follow a set pattern of life and observe more rigourous spiritual practices.

The organisation is fairly independent in terms of spiritual and other activities, although it depends on its devotees and other patrons for financial support. Most of their welfare activities are furthered on the basis of their fundamental commitment to a holistic development of the society. Singh observes:

> Social work is the means to develop the Sadhaka to achieve purity, compassion and spiritual virtues and attributes. Service should not be stripped of selflessness, but be performed with the pure spirit of karma yoga, i.e., selfless service. All activity must be viewed as worship and must be accompanied by the correct behaviour and attitude. (Singh, 202–203)

Most of their social welfare programmes are targeted mainly towards the African communities in South Africa, though they do cater to the poorer sections of the Indian community as well. Equipping Africans in skilled training, building classrooms for African schools, distributing food to the school children, medical relief, family planning, feeding the poor and so on, are some of their social welfare programmes. They emphasise the ideal of humanity which is drawn from the teachings of Swami Sivananda in India. Their social welfare activities are, however, seen as spiritual acts. It is through their publication activities that they aim at disseminating spiritual knowledge to the society at large. In order to demonstrate the spiritual dimension of their activities, they usually observe *satsanghs* in the homes of the recipients of the help given by the Society. The Divine Life Society emphasises that the observance of *satsanghs* in the homes of recipients is not to influence them to convert to Hinduism, but rather to emphasise the spiritual dimension of their lives. That is why their prayers tend to be more universalistic and general in an attempt to accommodate those who are not necessarily Hindu.

Sanatanist Tendencies

Their doctrinal outlook is fairly universal, in that they tend to consider all Hindu deities as important. Singh, however, points out that worship plays an important role in the life of the Divine Life Society members (Singh, 135). She also notes that worship is offered to Swami Sivananda. His image is placed in the shrine (Singh, 152). Their general philosophical outlook is drawn from Vedantic sources. Singh points out that the idea of God dwelling in human beings is quite significant for the members (Singh, 158). In other words, some diluted notion of Brahman as the basis of the whole universe is part of their worldview. Members may not be able to express such intricate philosophical views, but in their own way they seem to share a worldview that is characteristic of Vedantic thought.

At the same time, their usual religious life is expressed through their ceremonies and devotional singing at the *satsanghs*. They celebrate Katha, Jhanda, Navaratri, Pitripak, Gurupuja, Mariamman festival, Sarasvati Puja, Hanuman Jayanti, and Gangai Amman festival, *inter alia*. The festivals they celebrate are representative of all the linguistic groups within the Hindu fold in South Africa. Besides, they also observe most of the domestic rituals, such as birth, marriage and death ceremonies. In this sense, although they consider themselves neo-Hindu, their general practice seems to be Sanatanist.

Thus, the Divine Life Society members follow a modified form of traditional (*sanatana*) Hinduism despite their emphasis on Vedantic teachings. That is to say, they have played down the elaborateness of rituals that one sees in the traditional temples, while celebrating at the same time almost all the Hindu ceremonies. The average member of the society may not give up his/her ritual orientation so strongly, but the key members of the society and the monks in particular, place less emphasis on the rituals. For the head of the Divine Life Society in Durban and for those who consider themselves as serious members of the society, the various ceremonies and festivals are used as occasions for meditation and reflection. But the same attitude does not seem to be reflected among the ordinary members. Of course, this situation is not peculiar to the Divine Life Society as such. This difference in attitude between the ordinary members and the key members has been noticed among other groups as well, e.g., the Ramakrishna Mission of South Africa.

Sakti Puja

In view of the fact that the Divine Life Society in South Africa places significant emphasis on the worship of the goddess, it would be useful to explore some of the background of the same and how it is incorporated into their religious world. Perhaps, their philosophical views on the goddess worship are well-expressed in a book *The Philosophy of Sakti Worship* (1960), written by Swami Chidananda of the Divine Life Society in India. It seems to have a wide circulation in South Africa among the followers of the Society.

Swami Chidananda seeks to identify the goddess (Divine Mother, as he calls her), with the principle of Maya which the non-dualistic Vedantists see as an unexplainable aspect within the Vedantic framework. Nevertheless, in some dualist Vedantic framework Maya and the goddess are seen as identical and furthermore identified as the creative power of God. For instance, Madhva's dualistic Vedanta and also the recent Hare Krishna movement identify the goddess as the principle Maya and the creative power of the Supreme God. In a similar way, Swami Chidananda of the Divine Life Society speaks of the goddess as being identical to the Brahman of the Upanishads. She is the supreme power of the transcendent Brahman. Speaking of the relationship between the supreme Brahman and the Divine Mother he says:

> Para Brahman and His mysterious power of World illusion, called Maya or Devi, are, in fact, one and the same in essence. Though they are apparently different, yet they are one. It is a distinction without a difference. In fact, they represent the obverse and the reverse of the self-same coin. One cannot conceive of Para Brahman without at the same time conceiving of the Devi; and the conception of the Devi automatically presupposes the conception of Para Brahman. (Chidananda, 35)

Furthermore, the goddess is seen as the link between the material universe and the Divine Being. Using modern analogies, Swami Chidananda tries to explain how this relationship can make sense. He suggests that it is like electricity in the battery. In its motionless state, the goddess is Para Brahman, and in its active force, she is the goddess. The followers of Divine Life Society worship the goddess in various forms, such as Kali, Durga, Lakshmi, Sarasvati and so on. In that sense, it combines popular goddess worship with Vedantic philosophy.

Doctrinal Convictions

The Vedantic view of the Divine Life Society is largely syncretistic. It tries to accommodate many popular theological views within the framework of neo-Vedanta. While they dwell on the philosophical speculations regarding the idea of Brahman, etc., they also indulge in theological discussions on the puranic and epic views of God. For them, therefore, both the *Ramayana* and the *Mahabharata* are part of the sacred scriptures and Rama and Krishna are the two most important divine incarnations. Thus, their neo-Vedantic thought is a recast of the traditionalist (Sanatanist) Hindu idea of God. There is no radical departure from the traditionalist view as such, but it is blended with the neo-Vedantic thought.

Although they affirm a kind of non-dualist model of Vedanta, in the sense of seeking an identity between the power (*Maya*) of the supreme reality and the supreme reality itself, their ideas tend to be theistic. In other words, the formless, impersonal Brahman is seen as the personal Lord. Thus, when they speak of Rama as an incarnation of the Lord Hari (Vishnu) (Sivananda, 139) that same God is further seen as none other than the supreme Brahman. The traditional Vaishnava theology, of course, does the same. Swami Sivananda affirms this in no uncertain terms when he says, "[T]o a devotee, Rama is not simply a good and great person, but God Himself. Rama was the son of King Dasaratha, as well as the divine, omnipresent God, Self, Atman or Brahman" (Sivananda, 238).

In the same vein, Swami Sivananda speaks of Krishna as an incarnation of the supreme Lord Vishnu who is further seen as the impersonal Brahman. He says that Lord Krishna is:

> [T]he Supreme Lord who is the Indweller of our hearts, Who is Existence Absolute, Knowledge Absolute, Who is the Soul of this universe, Who bestows immortality on His devotees, Who is the source for everything and Who took a human form to please gods and His devotees and to destroy wickedness and establish righteousness. (Sivananda, 23)

It is clear from the above passage that they tend to use a language which resonates with the language of the *Upanishads*. It declares an identity of Krishna with the supreme Brahman in no uncertain terms. Furthermore, what seems clear in the theological assertions of the Divine Life Society is that for all practical purposes they affirm a truly theistic view despite their affirmations of a non-personal supreme Brahman. To draw a comparison, whereas the Ramakrishna Mission tends to dwell primarily on the Upanishadic teachings of Vedanta, the Divine Life Society seems to focus mainly on the puranic and epic material which provides for a highly theistic view of God. In other words, whereas the Vedantic philosophy is applied to practical life by Vivekananda via the affirmation that ultimately Brahman and the individual self are one and the same, the Divine Life Society seems to seek a different model to apply the Vedantic philosophy to practical life. They choose to seek a theistic model to appeal to the lay person's imagination. In that sense, their Vedantic approach is not really a non-personalist neo-Vedantic model, but rather fits into the traditional Hindu view in which God is understood in personal terms and the worship of all the deities is fully affirmed. It is precisely in the context of affirming the personal deity that the Divine Life Society incorporates the worship of God as the Divine Mother (*Sakti*) into its overall philosophical and ritualistic framework.

Moreover, what is significant about the Divine Life Society is that unlike the other neo-Vedantic reformers (e.g., Ramakrishna Paramhansa), Swami Sivananda is perceived by his followers as the incarnation of God. The biography (hagiography?) of Swami Sivananda clearly speaks of him as the incarnation of God. Swami Venkatesananda, the author of the biography, writes about the birth of Swami Sivananda, "[T]he day that was to usher into the world this glorious child who was none other than the Lord Himself, arrived. It was the 8th of September, 1887" (Venkatesananda, 36). It is not certain whether reference to Swami Sivananda in such divine terms is understood as a hyperbole or meant to be in a literal sense. The idea of Swami Sivananda being an incarnation of God is justified by the local devotees on the basis of the fact that the infinite God is able to manifest in a form, and it is only through a form that ordinary human beings can approach the divine. To support their idea of guru, they invoke the popular Hindu sayings, such as:

> *gurur brahma, gurur visnu, gurur devo mahesvarah,*
> *guru saksat para brahma tasmai guruve namah!*
> (Guru is Brahma, Guru is Vishnu, Guru is the God Mahesvara; Guru is truly the supreme Brahman; therefore, we bow to the Guru). (Venkatesananda, 8)

Furthermore, the followers of Swami Sivananda in South Africa defend the idea of their guru's divinity by quoting the following statement:

> [L]et us not forget, therefore, that when we refer to Bhagavan Sivananda, it is not to his body that we refer but to the divinity in him. This is true of all of us: it is more so, in his case, and that makes all the difference. For, we live in body-consciousness: but he lives in body, conscious of the existence of God. He is God conscious of the body. He is a man: and we are men too. But, there is just this little difference—he descended into this earth from God, and we have been struggling to ascend to this human birth, from lower orders of creation. (Venkatesananda, 11–12)

In other words, the followers of Sivananda seem to be looking upon their guru on the one hand as an incarnation of God,[2] and on the other hand as a fully realised soul. There seems to be no contradiction in their mind, but clearly the two perceptions are based on two different modes of thinking: the former is based on a dualistic theism, whereas the latter perception seems to be invoking a non-dualistic mode of understanding. The two may not be contradictory as such, but certainly the Divine Life Society leaves it ambiguous as to whether Swami Sivananda was an incarnation of a personal God, like Rama and Krishna, or one who had realised his Brahmanhood. This is a problem that does not seem to arise in the case of Ramakrishna Paramhansa who is clearly seen as the realised soul, although a certain amount of veneration is also offered to him by his followers. At the level of ritual, however, both these traditions, namely, the Divine Life Society and the Ramakrishna Mission, have developed their unique *mantras* to invoke their respective gurus. While members of the Divine Life Society invokes their guru with the *mantra, "om sivanandaya namah"*, the followers of Ramakrishna use the *mantra "om ramakrisnaya namah"*.

Whether they affirm Swami Sivananda's divinity on the basis of a dualistic Vedantic thought or on the basis of a non-dualistic thought, it seems clear that the members of the Divine Life Society perceive their guru as divine. It is possible that the followers of the Divine Life Society may be creating a two level scheme of reality, like the non-dualists. In other words, at the 'lower level' of reality God is personal and at the 'higher level' of reality God is non-personal. But in the case of the non-dualists, the 'lower level' of reality is ultimately unreal and therefore does not exist. However, it is not clear from the writings of the followers of the Divine Life Society whether the idea of God is personal and that their guru, Swami Sivananda, being an incarnation of God is considered ultimately a 'lower' phenomenon and therefore unreal. It seems to me that in the light of their assertion about Sakti as the power of God and the world as her manifestation which is real, one is led to conclude that they do consider the material world as a real manifestation of that Sakti. In that sense, then God as personal and guru as an incarnation of God are statements that are not ultimately unreal as in the case of the non-dualist mode of thinking, but real. Therefore, the worship of the guru is of great significance.

Ethics

One of the most important aspects that the Divine Life Society emphasises in its spiritual path is the ethical dimension of Hinduism. Most of their popular literature deals with the ethical teachings and the ideal Hindu life. It is obvious that their ethical teachings are based on the Hindu epics, namely, the *Ramayana* and the *Mahabharata*. They see the epics as providing a definitive ethical standard for their daily life. For instance, their ethical notion of righteousness is derived from the *Ramayana*. Furthermore, the various characters of the epics represent certain Hindu ideals. Swami Sivananda says:

> Ramayana has a lesson to teach, Sita symbolises the ideal wife, and Lakshmana the ideal brother, and so also Bharata who rises above his mother's worldly sense of values, does not succumb to the lure of throne and power, tries his level best to bring Sri Rama, and failing which, elects to run the caretaker government as an agent of Rama's 'Padukas' (sandals). (Sivananda, 255)

Some of the ethical ideals emphasised by the Divine Life Society are: service, charity, purity and love. Service has to do with both human beings as well as the divine; charity and generosity are important in dealing with not only the poor, but also the family members, one's students and so on. Purity and love are seen as essential in both spiritual as well as mundane activities of life. These ideals are sought through worship and meditation.

The Social Role of Swami Sahajananda

On the basis of the idea that guru/teacher is god or god incarnate, many of the followers of Swami Sahajananda consider him as divine and hence obey his commands and dictates with utmost obedience. He is known to impose strict moral and social discipline among his followers, such as making devotees recite the name of God a thousand times if they arrived late for a *satsangh* and meeting. Swami Sahajananda implemented the ethical values that he derived from his master, Swami Sivananda, most often literally and with great consistency. His social work in South Africa is a direct result of his adherence to those ethical values. Two most important achievements characterise his social work—building schools, clinics and other such projects for the benefit of the poor, mostly the African communities in rural areas; printing and publishing the literature produced in India by the Divine Life Society, mainly the writings of Sivananda and disseminating them among the people in South Africa. Many of his followers saw him as a single-minded social worker who never relied on others. It is not surprising that he did not prepare any of his younger devotees to succeed him. As a result, his eventual passing away on 10 December 2007 did create a vacuum in the organisation for an initial period, until the board of governors of the Divine Life Society of South Africa decided to run the organisation without any spiritual head. It is at the moment driven by community and its lay participation is controlled by a board of governors. It is a rather unique situation for a religious organisation to be without a spiritual head. But at the moment the board of governors do not seem to think of the necessity for such a role. Since the Divine Life Society in South Africa has always remained autonomous in relation to its mother body in India, it is unlikely that the mother body would impose a spiritual head from India. Swami Sahajananda played a significant role in South Africa through much of his social work and completed many social work projects for the poor and needy. The post-Sahajananda Divine Life Society is continuing the work of the founder, but it is too soon to judge whether a spiritual organisation without a spiritual head would continue into the future with the same drive.

Notes

1. It is interesting to note that the Umgeni Road temple (Sri Vaithianatha Isvarar temple) provided space to two major organisations in their initial periods. One is the Divine Life and the other is the Ramakrishna Centre (as it was called at the time).
2. Perhaps, the idea of incarnation is loosely attributed to Swami Sivananda in view of his apparent divine qualities. Also, it must be noted that usually Hindus refer to great men as *avataras* of God. Nevertheless, my major concern here is to understand whether they derive such notion of the *avatara* from a dualistic theism or from a non-dualistic theism. It is my conviction that the followers of the Divine Life Society seem to combine the two.

13 The Hare Krishnas

The International Society for Krishna Consciousness (ISKCON, popularly known as the Hare Krishna movement) traces its roots to the Caitanya school of Vedanta in Bengal. It is, therefore, useful to outline its background briefly and place the contemporary Hare Krishna movement of South Africa in its historical context. Although the devotees of the Hare Krishna group tend to identify themselves as traditional (*sanatana*) Hindus in South Africa, are aware that it was a movement that arose in response to specific historical conditions. In general, three important historical conditions seem to have occasioned the movement in the sixteenth century. First, the presence of the Muslim rule in Bengal which tended to inhibit the free spirit of Hinduism; second, the growing rigidity of the caste system and third, the pervasiveness of popular cults, many of which had Tantric influences (especially the goddess cults in Bengal) (Kennedy, 1–3). It is generally understood that Caitanya's conversion was the result of his visit to Gaya. What really caused such a drastic change in the young scholar, who was only interested in intellectual debates, is not known as the traditional biographies do not say much about it. But once Caitanya began his rather ecstatic and devotional wave, people became attracted to his movement largely because he provided dynamism to the Hindu life in the context of Muslim dominance. People across caste barriers could identify with his devotional religion as opposed to pure ritualism.

Caitanya and His Movement

Caitanya, whose real name was Visvambhar, was born in February 1486. His parents were traditional Vaishnavites who lived in a village called Navadvip in Bengal. Many extraordinary events were associated with his birth and childhood. His father died when he was very young. As he grew up, he emerged as a very bright scholar who revelled in debates. He was married at a very early age, but his wife died while he was away on a tour. He was remarried to a girl named Vishnupriya. He went on a pilgrimage to Gaya to observe certain funeral rites for his father. And when he returned, he was a different man altogether. What really happened in Gaya remained a mystery, but his life thereafter was not the same. He became intoxicated with his devotion for Krishna. That was the beginning of the Caitanya Bhakti movement in Bengal. He gave up his family life and became totally dedicated to the spread of Krishna consciousness throughout India.

The Six Gosvamis

During the life-time of Caitanya, the movement spread mainly within parts of Bengal like Nadia, Puri, Brindaban and Mathura. But it was only after his death that the movement spread to other places, mainly through his six disciples, who later became popular as six Gosvamis. These were: Rupa Gosvami, Sanatana Gosvami, Jiva Gosvami, Gopala Bhatta, Raghunatha Das, and Raghunatha Bhatta. It is pointed out that it was through their work that many Vaishnava centres were reclaimed as sacred sites, including Brindaban (Kennedy, 66). Some of the temples in Brindaban were also built by them. Within Brindaban alone there are one thousand temples and thirty two ghats (sacred banks), all attributed to Caitanya and his disciples. All the six Gosvamis spent most of their time in Brindaban.

Beside the six Gosvamis, the Bengal Vaishnava tradition recognises the work of another three teachers who came later. These are: Srinivasa Acarya, Narottama Datta, and Syamananda Das. The seventeenth century witnessed a great success in terms of the spread of the Vaishnavism in Bengal which was attributed to the work of these three teachers. This time it engulfed not only the whole of Orissa, but spread also to Assam. Sankara Deva, however, was responsible for the success of the Vaishnava faith in Assam, where originally Sakta tradition flourished. The next two centuries, however, saw a major setback to the Vaishnava faith in Bengal because of the resurgence of the Sakta cult. It is said, "[E]ven members of prominent Gosvami families renounced their sectarian faith and wandered off into corrupt cults, which spread their rank growth everywhere" (Kennedy, 77). It is only during the later part of the nineteenth century that a revival of the Vaishnava faith was noticed. This time the reawakening of the Vaishnava faith was through an indirect channel, namely, the Brahmo Samaj, which introduced Caitanya's devotional elements into its practice (Kennedy, 78). By this time, there was a neo-Krishna movement gradually emerging in light of the new literature that was being produced. Most certainly the translation of the *Bhagavad Gita* may have played a role in this regard (Kennedy, 79).

Brindaban as the Sacred Centre

Brindaban (Vrindavan) acquired a special place in the later history of the Bengal Vaishnava tradition due to the work of Caitanya and the six Gosvamis. To the present day it has continued to play a vital role as a confluence of Krishna devotees. It has become one of the most popular pilgrimage centres in India, next only to the city of Benares.[1] The banks of the two rivers, Ganga (Ganges) and Yamuna (Jumna) have traditionally been seen as twin centres of Hindu pilgrimage. Just as river Ganga has a special place in Saiva tradition, the river Yamuna has a special place in the Vaishnava tradition. The river Yamuna has been associated with the birth place of Krishna. The tradition claims that the pilgrimage to the region known today as Braj was started by Krishna's grandson, Vajranab (Brooks, 42). Many Krishna devotees from all over the world, including South Africa look toward Brindaban as their most sacred place. In recent years, especially after the restoration of ties between India and South Africa at the level of people-to-people exchange, many devotees, not only of Indian origin, but also Europeans began visiting Brindaban to experience the Krishna consciousness in the company of Krishna devotees from other parts of the world.

A Brief Account of the Hare Krishnas in South Africa

In 1972, some of the American and British devotees of the Hare Krishna group visited Cape Town and began their activities mainly among the European communities. This was as a result of the initiative of an American devotee who had visited Durban in 1970. Although they were beginning to get a good response from the European community, they realised that their readymade clientele was in Natal where the bulk of the Indian community lived. So, by 1975, they directed their attention to Natal and found wealthy businessmen and other prominent members of the Indian community supporting their activities. In 1975, Swami Srila Prabhupada came to South Africa, and visited Durban and Johannesburg. His visit gave a boost to their activities. About the same time, plans were made to build a temple in the Chatsworth area. Gradually, four major centres emerged in South Africa—Cape Town, Durban, Johannesburg, and Cato Ridge (near Pietermaritzburg). The Cato Ridge provided mainly farm activities. It was subsequently closed down. The Chatsworth temple became a reality by 1985 and catered to the large Indian community. In the absence of clear membership records, it is hard to speculate as to which linguistic group/s most of the members are drawn from. Nevertheless, from an onlooker's point of view anyone who visits the temple on a Sunday gets the impression that most of the devotees come from the Gujarati- and Hindi-speaking families. Other linguistic groups seem to be smaller in number. Previously, the head of the Chatsworth temple was Raghuvir Prabhu, a European, who had been with the temple from the time it came up. He was succeeded by a local South African Indian whose initiated name is Shruti Kirti. He died in mid-1990s. Subsequently, African blacks began to take the leadership of the temple. In October 2010, the temple celebrated its 25th anniversary. According to its website (http://news.isckon.org) currently there are about 700 initiated devotees associated with the temple.

The Hare Krishna temples are open throughout the week. But the main congregational rituals take place on Sundays. The main ritual takes place on Sundays between 10:00 a.m. and 2:00 p.m. At the end of the service, the devotees are offered food which is considered as *prasadam* (grace) of Krishna. On the same day, they also have study groups for those who wish to study the *Bhagavad Gita*, or *Srimad Bhagavatam* regularly. Sanskrit is also taught as part of the study programme. Verses from the *Gita* or *Bhagavatam* are read in Sanskrit and explained in English with the commentary of Srila Prabhupada. In Durban, they also conduct weekly programmes mainly for students at the local university campus.

In Cape Town, their temple is situated ideally in Rondebosch a suburb near the university campus (University of Cape Town) caters mainly to the student community. Every Tuesday and Thursday, the Hare Krishnas organise lunch hour talks on the university campus and distribute vegetarian meals. On Wednesdays, they conduct a service in which the *Bhagavatam* or the *Gita* is studied. On Sundays, there is a service which is attended mostly by the university students. The temple is run by mainly young devotees. One of the very active devotees in the early 1990s was a young woman named Kandarpa Manjari. She was originally an Iranian Muslim, born in the USA. She was sent to South Africa to help organise the Hare Krishna activities but took a liking to Cape Town and chose to live in the temple there. Apart from organising a number of other activities, she also used to lead the singing of the *bhajans* during the service.

Some Features of the Hare Krishnas

In understanding the Hare Krishnas in South Africa, one notices some basic elements that characterise their tradition. Their presence is characterised by, *inter alia*, the sacred chant called "Hare Krishna," the sacred dance, and the sacred chariot. I shall pay special attention to these aspects in describing the Hare Krishna religious phenomenon in South Africa.

Sacred Chant

The Hare Krishnas are easily distinguished not only by their external appearance, but also the constant chanting of the *mantra* Hare Krishna. For the devotees, it is extremely important to chant this *mantra* throughout the day, and believe in its efficacy in purifying their minds and souls. The devotees believe that the *mantra* is chanted in their homes in order to purify the whole place and fill it with the consciousness of Krishna. It is chanted to the accompaniment of a drum. They say that the very vibration of the sound of the chanting accompanied by the drum creates an atmosphere of healing and calms the troubled mind.

The idea of chanting the *mantra* is an old Vedic practice which has survived in later Hinduism to the present day. Each sectarian branch of Hinduism has its own particular *mantra* that they chant in order to invoke their favourite deity. The Vaishnavas, in general, chant *'om namo narayanaya'*, whereas the Saivites chant *'om namah sivaya'*. The Hare Krishnas also developed their specific *mantra* which they say is dear to Krishna himself. In simple terms, it is the invocation of the name of the deity, Krishna. In this sense, Hinduism has later departed radically from the complex *mantra* system which was followed in the context of Vedic rituals. Some Vedic *mantras*, such as *'om bhur bhuvah'* are, however, still in vogue in Hindu rituals. The Hare Krishnas consider that chanting the Hare Krishna *mantra* is sufficient for obtaining the grace of God, because it encompasses all the other *mantras*. For them, it is the life-giving principle which connects them with their life source, Krishna. The significance of the Hare Krishna *mantra* is discussed in a book entitled *Chant and Be Happy: The Power of Mantra Meditation,* based on the teachings of Swami Srila Prabhupada. I shall deal with it later in this chapter.

Sacred Dance

The Hare Krishna devotees express their devotion to Krishna in various dance forms. Their temple ritual, as compared to the traditional temple rituals, is fairly simple. Their ritual is characterised by the dance that they perform in ecstasy. The first part of their worship is mainly singing the *bhajans*, and listening to the teachers' interpretation of the scripture (either *Srimad Bhagavatam* or the *Bhagavad Gita*). The second part of the worship includes singing accompanied by the ritual dance. The Hare Krishna temples are structured in such a way that there is ample space in the hall for the performance of the dance. The devotional element of the Hare Krishnas is best expressed in their ritual dance. It is, perhaps, the most binding force of their tradition. Unlike the dance which one witnesses during the goddess festival and the *Kavadi* festivals the Hare Krishna ritual dance is a communal dance. The performance of the dance is said to be a re-enactment of the original ritual dance that Krishna's (intimate devotees) *gopis* performed. In the case of the goddess and *Kavadi* festivals, only those who are in a trance indulge in the ecstatic dances. But with the Hare Krishnas, it is the whole congregation that performs the dance in unison. As such, the ritual dance in the Hare Krishna temple is highly structured and has specific place and time. It finds its place within the framework of the ecstatic devotion of the devotees. The dance follows the rhythm of the singing and the chanting and in a way it seems to display the spirit of the playful Krishna. It is precisely in the ritual dance that the Hare Krishnas claim to relive, time after time, the presence of Krishna around them.

Sacred Chariot

One of the greatest attractions of the Hare Krishnas in South Africa is their Chariot Festival which used to take place in Durban every year in December. It is an event of celebration and festivities, dramas and shows on Krishna's life as well as on the work of the Hare Krishnas around the world. It is an attraction not only to the devotees, but also to the thousands of uninitiated Hindus and the tourists. December is a summer month in South Africa, a month of vacation and entertainment. In that context, the Chariot Festival presents an occasion for everyone in Durban to come together at a grand religious event filled with entertainment. It is staged at the beachfront for four consecutive days perhaps to attract large numbers. It used to begin in the last week of December, and the Hare Krishna temple at Chatsworth claims that the festival attracts a capacity crowd of 100,000 people. Months before the actual festival, the decoration of the chariot and other preparatory activities begin. Devotees participate in it as part of their devotion to Krishna. However, in 1998, the Chariot Festival was held in May and in 1999, it was held during the Easter holidays (April). Presently, this new timing has become a regularly practice for the staging of the Chariot Festival on the beachfront. However, in 2010 due to the Soccer World Cup arrangements, it was relocated to further north of the previous venue on the beachfront.

The festival is based on the myth which tells of the meeting of Krishna and Radha, his most intimate devotee.[2] The Hare Krishnas take special care in relating that event in the following way:

> Once Lord Krishna, His brother Balarama, and His sister Subadhra journeyed on a chariot to Kurukshetra, India, to observe the ancient Vedic custom of bathing at a holy place during a solar eclipse. On this auspicious occasion, many great devotees of the Lord were reunited with Him. Foremost among them were the devotees from the rural village of Vrindavana, where Krishna had spent His early years before He had left to live as a king in the opulent city of Dvaraka. During Krishna's absence from Vrindavana, the devotees there—especially Srimati Radharani—always thought of Him and longed for His return. So when Srimati Radharani met Krishna at Kurukshetra, She invited Him to come back to Vrindavana and again enjoy loving pastimes with His devotees there.[3]

It is in reliving those mythic moments of the meeting of Krishna and his most beloved devotee, Radha, that the Hare Krishna devotees share the joy and the thrill that surrounds the festival. The Hare Krishnas emphasise the fact that the festival is not merely a remembrance of a past event, but in the actual reliving of the event one really participates in the love of Krishna. The Hare Krishnas point out:

> One shouldn't think that Rathayatra is an empty ritual, a mere imitation of a remote historical event. Although the Jagannatha Deity riding on the chariot may appear to be a wooden statue, He

> is actually Krishna Himself. By Krishna's mercy and omnipotence, He appears as the Deity to give us the opportunity to see Him and serve Him despite our limitations. Though the non-devotees cannot understand how the Deity can be God, the Deity reveals Himself to those who serve Him sincerely.[4]

In other words, in order to understand and accept the inner meaning of the festival one has to be a devotee. The devotees claim that a sympathetic outsider might empathise with their view, but cannot participate in that devotion experienced by the devotees unless s/he is a devotee.

There is a variant of the myth about the festival which traces its origin to the city of Puri in Orissa State (India). It deals with the account as to how the Jagannatha (Lord of the universe) temple in Puri was built. According to the account published in Durban newspapers every year, the story goes as follows:

> King Indradyumna became anxious to establish a temple for Krishna, Balarama and Subadhra. He engaged a sculptor to carve the deities. ... There was a contract between the sculptor and the king that the sculptor should work behind closed doors and that the king would not disturb him. When many days had passed, the king wondered what the worker was doing, and after forcibly opening the door, discovered that the forms were unfinished. The king said that he would nevertheless worship the unfinished deity (sic) and started the temple of Jagannatha.[5]

Within South Africa, the Hare Krishnas relate these stories and myths to illustrate their understanding of the festivals and the rituals they observe. During the festival, the giant chariot is paraded on the second day along the beach as hundreds of devotees pull it manually. Inside the chariot, the images of Krishna, Balarama (his brother) and Subadhra (his sister) are seated, while a Hare Krishna priest performs rituals to the deities. The image of Swami Prabhupada is also placed in the chariot. The devotees throng to get a glimpse of the deity. As the sound of the Hare Krishna *mantra* reverberates, the devotees go into ecstasy.

The festival is praised not only by the devotees that participate in it, but also by the South African Tourism Board. For them the festival is:

> [e]ssentially a presentation of Eastern culture, had proved to be a resounding success, ... an interesting and excellent educational.[6]

Nevertheless, for the Hare Krishnas it seems to be the most effective way of spreading Krishna consciousness. As part of this event, the Hare Krishna devotees distribute food to all the visitors as *prasadam* (grace) of the Lord Krishna. They claim that:

> [A] lot of people have come to Krishna consciousness through prasadam, especially through our Sunday Feast of Krishna at all of our temples around the world. I mean, this process is the only kind of yoga that you can actually practise by eating.[7]

Offering food as the grace of the Lord is their way of inviting people to participate in the Krishna consciousness. For them it is not feeding the poor, but a real participation in the grace of God. It is a form of yoga in itself.

Theological Outlook

Within the Vedantic framework, the Hare Krishnas belong to the dualist school of Madhva, a thirteenth century Vaishnava theologian. One of his disciples, Madhavendra Puri, is said to have had a great influence on Caitanya. Nevertheless, in the hands of Caitanya, the Vaishnava theology underwent a significant modification in light of the influence of the popular singers known as the Radha-Krishna singers. There was also some element of influence from Nimbarka, another thirteenth century Vaishnava theologian (Kennedy, 88ff). The Hare Krishnas believe in a personal God. Krishna is both a historical person and the absolute God at the same time. In that sense, he is identical with the Brahman of the Upanishads. However, for the Hare Krishnas, he is not a formless Brahman, but one who is described with all the auspicious qualities. Kennedy summarises their position well in the following statement:

> Bhagavan, or Hari, is the name given to the Supreme. He is infinite in nature, power and attributes. The creative, destructive and sustaining aspects which appear in Hindu theology as Brahma, Siva, and Vishnu, are manifestations of his nature. All the forms in which the Supreme has been conceived of and worshipped in Hindu thought are included in Bhagavan. He is the source of infinite forms. Of all these forms, that of Krishna is the most perfect. (Kennedy, 92)

The theology of the Hare Krishnas is drawn primarily from the *Srimad Bhagavatam* and the *Bhagavad Gita*. The *Vedas* and the *Brahmasutras*, are further used to support their theological point of view. They also draw heavily from the ritual texts called *Pancaratra*

Agama, especially their teaching of Krishna in the aspects of Vasudeva, Samkarshana, Pradyumna and Aniruddha represented by the symbolism of mace, conch shell, disc, and lotus flower (Prabhupada, 79ff).

The Hare Krishnas believe that the various forms of Krishna are distributed throughout the universe in order to please his devotees. There are 24 forms of Vishnu, which are only a part of Krishna's manifestations. There is, however, no limit to the "expansions and incarnations of Krishna" (Prabhupada, 82). During various ages (*yugas*), Krishna manifested himself in various ways. Accordingly, in the present age, which is known as the Kali age Krishna "incarnates to preach the chanting of the holy name of Krishna" (Prabhupada, 89). Therefore, the chanting of the Hare Krishna *mantra* is of great significance for them. For them, there is nothing greater than the Hare Krishna *mantra*. It is considered a means to liberation. The *mantra* is further identified with God himself. In that sense, it is also the goal of one's life. In accordance with the teachings of Swami Prabhupada, the Hare Krishnas maintain,:

> While the Word, or teachings of God, have enormous power to transform and uplift our lives, just as important are the actual names of God, which are sometimes praised aloud in song or quietly meditated upon. Since God is fully spiritual and absolute, the Vedic scriptures inform us that His holy names are invested with the Lord's full spiritual potencies. God and His name are the same.[8]

Thus, Krishna is considered the name that encompasses everything. Furthermore, meditation on the name of Krishna leads to the awakening of the 'original consciousness'. It is a way of seeing God through the sound. Sound is, moreover, considered as a form or incarnation of God. It is a means to the ultimate good-experiencing ecstasy. And finally, it is a peace formula.[9] It provides not only peace of mind, but also the higher knowledge of the Self and liberates the soul from the cycle of *karma* and rebirth. The most important goal of chanting the *mantra* is to be engrossed in the love of God.

Social Outlook

The Hare Krishnas have a distinct worldview developed by Swami Prabhupada. The discourses in their temples are meant to clarify this worldview to the devotees. It provides an interesting social analysis which is based on traditional Hindu values. Swami Prabhupada divides society into four groups: (i) 'lazy intelligent', (ii) 'busy intelligent', (iii) 'lazy fool', and (iv) 'busy fool'. These are identified with the traditional Hindu caste categories, namely, Brahmin, Kshatriya, Vaishya and Sudra respectively.[10] Prabhupada argues that 'lazy intelligent' person is highly developed in spiritual matters, whereas the next two are not so developed and lack something spiritually. But the 'busy intelligent' person is completely busy in the material world and has no spiritual sense at all. These categories, though identifiable with the traditional Hindu caste categories, are not to be taken to refer to the actual caste system. They are supposed to be the ideal categories which, in the process of the Hindu practice, became reified into fixed sociological groups. In that sense, Prabhupada argues, anyone can become a Brahmin. But it requires training. He further sees no distinction between the European, Indian, etc. In other words, it has nothing to do with race or ethnic background. These are purely spiritual categories that have a hierarchy built into them on the basis of one's spiritual progress. The mission of the Hare Krishnas in the world is to create more Brahmins or 'lazy intelligent' persons. He defines the 'lazy intelligent' person as the one who has control of his/her senses. He points out that the Sanskrit term for the word 'lazy intelligent' is dhira. It is for the intelligent to recognise that the soul is different from the body.[11] Krishna is said to be the lover of the 'lazy intelligent' people (dhiradhira priya).[12] The 'lazy intelligent' person is characterised by the mode of goodness. Prabhupada says:

> The mode of goodness means one must know that we cannot be happy here. That is mode of goodness. And if he thinks, "I am happy", then he is not in (the) mode of goodness. He is in darkness.[13]

Thus, the Hare Krishnas seem to look upon the material world as totally distanced from the higher spiritual development. In that sense, they consider involvement in the material world other than for the sake of Krishna as simply a hindrance to one's spiritual progress.

Activities and Programmes

There seems to be an apparent contradiction in the life of the Hare Krishnas in the sense that while they distance themselves from any active involvement from the material world, they are involved in a major way in the activities of the day-to-day life. Apart from the festivals and ceremonies, they have many activities that make their presence felt in the society. One of the most important activities is the out-reach programme and distribution of literature. They usually gather at a central place in a city during the day, and sing the Hare Krishna *bhajans* and speak to the passers-by about the importance of Krishna consciousness. In the early 1990s they used to engage in this activity in Durban more frequently. However, now they seem to have quietened and seem to focus more on their temple-based spiritual activities and social work.

Their evangelistic outreach is quite analogous to the method used by charismatic Christian groups to evangelise. Nevertheless, the way the Hare Krishnas see it is different. For them, it is sharing the Krishna consciousness to those who are caught up in the worldly bondages of *karma*. At the same time distribution of literature brings them their financial support. Although they distribute their literature free, they do seek contributions from the public who pay some attention to their conversations about Krishna. Perhaps, to the outsider it may seem like a contradiction. On the one hand, they seem to dissuade people from becoming caught up in the mundane activities of life so that they are free from their karmic bondage. But on the other hand, they seem to be engaged in an active campaign for funds to support their organisational network. Often their critics look at the imposing temple structure in Chatsworth and ask if that is not an indulgence in material prosperity. The Hare Krishnas, nonetheless, counter such criticisms with the answer that everything is done for the sake of spreading Krishna consciousness. Their supporters point out that often in an effort to spiritualise the world, one needs the material things, such as wealth. During one of my conversations, a Hare Krishna devotee pointed out to me that they are essentially spiritual people. But in order to spiritualise South Africa, they need a university that is based on the principles of Krishna consciousness. And it requires money to build a university for the dissemination of Krishna consciousness.

There are a number of other programmes that the Hare Krishnas pursue as part of their service to Krishna. 'Food for Life' is a programme under which they feed the poor. Nearly 10,000 meals per month are offered to the people in poorer townships around Durban alone. All Hare Krishna centres are involved in this feeding project. The food is cooked at the temple and offered to Krishna before it is distributed. Again, it is seen as an offering of Krishna's grace to people in need rather than as a mere social welfare programme. In other words, although the Krishna devotees seem to be involved in the mundane activities of life, those activities are transformed into religious acts and given deeper spiritual meaning.

Notes

1. The significance of the region of Mathura on the bank of Yamuna is attested by the Chinese pilgrims, Fa Hien (400 C.E.), and Hiuen Tsang (634 C.E.). In 1830, a French scholar attested, Next to Benares, Brindaban is the largest purely Hindu city I have seen." See Brooks, 39–43.
2. In the mythology of Krishna, Radha is portrayed as one of his cousins and is said to be deeply in love with Krishna. She was never married to Krishna, but he is said to have had a special love for her. Nevertheless, the later interpreters of the myths allegorise the relationship between Krishna and Radha in terms of love that exists between the Lord and the devotee. The Hare Krishna followers also perceive Radha-Krishna relationship in that light. Radha is considered Krishna's "most beloved devotee".
3. *Back to Godhead* (magazine of the Hare Krishna Movement). Vol. 16, No. 8, 1981, p. 7.
4. Ibid.
5. *Natal Mercury*, Tuesday, December 24, 1991, p. 9 (parenthesis is mine).
6. Ibid.
7. *Chant and Be Happy: The Power of Mantra Meditation.* (Los Angeles: The Bhakti Vedanta Book Trust, 1983, p. 20.
8. Ibid., p. 69.
9. Ibid., p. 92 ff.
10. *Conversations with Srila Prabhupada.* Vol. 16 (September 1975 October, 1975), (Los Angeles: The Bhaktivedanta Book Trust, 1989), p. 307ff.
11. Ibid., p. 313.
12. Ibid., p. 314.
13. Ibid., p. 317.

14 The Satya Sai Baba Followers

In the present chapter, I shall explore the role of the Satya Sai movement in shaping the Hindu presence in South Africa. I shall also discuss its teachings in the light of the general Hindu thought. I shall base my account of Sai Baba's teachings on the accounts of the devotees themselves. The Satya Sai Baba movement in South Africa is a relatively recent phenomenon compared with the other Hindu organisations. *The Hindu Heritage in South Africa,* published in 1960, does not make any mention of the Sai movement in South Africa, although under the category of New Currents, it mentions other organisations, such as the Divine Life Society and the Ramakrishna Centre (Nowbath, Chotai and Lalla, 1960). Unlike most of the organisations which were either founded by local individuals or foreign visitors, the Satya Sai movement seems to have sprung up as a natural outcome of people's interaction with Sai Baba. As such, there is no single founder of the movement in South Africa. The people who became devotees of Sai Baba formed groups at various centres in South Africa in an effort to share their experiences of Sai Baba and strengthen their faith in him. The devotees built shrines and temples for the activities related to Sai Baba all over South Africa. Today, there are more than 50 branches of Sai organisation all over South Africa. All their activities are coordinated by the umbrella body, 'Satya Sai Baba Central Council of South Africa', located in Chatsworth (Durban).

The Sai movement in South Africa, like it's counterparts elsewhere, is founded on the four cardinal principles, namely, Truth, Education, Love and Peace. These four principles appear quite prominently in all their books, pamphlets, and other literature. They do not seem to have a great deal of literary activity and social welfare programmes like those organised by the other major Hindu organisations in South Africa. They focus more on spiritual meetings, and *bhajans*. Nevertheless, their growth within the Hindu community during the last two decades might be considered phenomenal. This raises the inevitable question as to why so many Hindus are becoming attracted to the Sai movement, and how this phenomenal growth has taken place.

The main reason for the Hindus becoming attracted to the Sai group is that it seems to provide the healing touch and a sense of belonging directly to an incarnation of God. For all the devotees of Sai Baba, he is God in human form. Most of the accounts and testimonies that the devotees give about Sai Baba relate to healing in one form or another and relief from suffering. Some claim to have been saved from some dangerous situation, such as accidents and others claim to have been cured by Sai Baba of cancer and other diseases. When people experience such miraculous healing they tend to share those experiences with their friends and relatives, who in turn, become either curious or may even be convinced and become followers of Sai Baba. Thus, the sharing of their experiences of Sai Baba is, perhaps, the most effective way in which the popularity of the movement is growing, bringing more devotees into the fold. During most of my interviews, I found that the devotees tended to ask the newcomers to share their experiences of Sai Baba. This sharing of the experiences of Sai Baba not only provided a common bond among the devotees, but also became an effective vehicle through which they could attempt to convert the rest of the society.

As a result of this growing tendency among the devotees to spread the message of Sai Baba, there are countless stories and anecdotes about his miracles all over South Africa. Extraordinary claims are often made by the devotees about the "miracles" of Sai Baba. Some of the accounts given by the devotees include falling of ash from the ceiling of the house, and honey dropping in front of the sacred lamp that most Hindus keep in their homes and so on. Often any small event in the family is seen as a miraculous intervention of Sai Baba in the lives of the devotees. For instance, one of the devotees related to me a small event that had taken place within his family. He (devotee) said that his daughter was due to be married in June, but when they visited Sai Baba in India, he told them that the marriage will take place in February of that year. And it so happened when they returned to South Africa, the boy's father came to him and suggested that the marriage should take place in February. Such accounts are innumerable in South Africa and form the basis for individuals becoming either interested in this movement or becoming converted to the movement.

The Sai devotees identify themselves with the *mantra* "om sai ram". It is used in greeting other devotees. As a testimony to their devotion to Sai Baba, the devotees wear the picture of Sai Baba either in a ring or in a locket hung around the neck. It seems to serve as a talisman which, they claim, has some spiritual power to protect the bearer.[1]

Every year hundreds of devotees from South Africa visit Sai Baba in India and receive his personal *darshan*. And every year they come back with new experiences and spread his message. The devotees gather for worship every Sunday in their respective branches and spend time singing the *bhajans* of Sai Baba and worshipping him.

Background of the Sai Movement in India

The Sai devotees claim that Sai Baba's birth was heralded by the Hindu scriptures thousands of years ago. He was born on November 23, 1926, in Puttaparti, a small village in Andhra Pradesh. At the age of eight he is said to have begun showing signs of unusual behaviour. He began performing "miracles" like finding missing items, being able to tell who stole an item and so on. His early leanings towards spiritual matters and his ability to perform "miracles" disturbed his parents so much that they even took him to local exorcists and doctors for treatment.

Finally, on May 23, 1940, Sai Baba declared himself as the incarnation of the Sai Baba of Shirdi in India and demanded that he be worshipped. The final declaration came on October 20, 1940, when he is said to have appeared simultaneously inside and outside a temple during the performance of a ritual. Such appearances of Sai Baba simultaneously in two places have been recorded by his devotees in most instances many years after he was worshipped as Sai Baba (Kanu, 25–36). After this incident, he told his family members again that they should give up trying to change him and accept that he was the incarnation of God.

The devotees of Sai Baba establish his claim to divinity on the basis of the Hindu scriptural authority, mainly from the *Bhagavad*

Gita (4: 7–8). They rephrase the verses from *The Gita* in the following statement:

> For the protection of the virtuous, for the destruction of evil and for establishing righteousness on a firm footing, I incarnate from age to age. Whenever asanti (discord, restlessness) overwhelms the world, the Lord will incarnate in human form to establish the modes of earning prasanti (supra-peace) and to re-educate the human community in the ways of peace. (Kanu, 38)

Thus, the mission of Sai Baba is to restore the lost divinity in human beings and make them aware of their inner divinity. He is quoted as saying, "Realising the Lord within you as the motivator is the task for which He comes in human form" (Kanu, 38). Thousands of Hindus in India as well as Europeans have became his devotees over these few decades and helped to spread his message throughout the world. Sai Baba claims that he would live until the year 2021 C.E., and would reincarnate "a year later to complete his work" (Kanu, 44). It is not clear from the statements that his devotees make whether he claims to be the only incarnation of God at the present time or whether he considers the possibility of other Godmen/women elsewhere.

Further, it is also not clear whether his return means the continuation of the cycle of divine incarnations as understood within the Hindu worldview or whether in a limited sense he returns just one more time to finish what he had started. Nevertheless, as far as his devotees are concerned he is a Godman in their midst and that when he leaves his physical body he would return to it again. They claim that Sai Baba would return not just in spirit but in physical form. In this sense, Sai Baba's claim to return is different from that of Jesus' promise to his disciples that he would send his spirit. His second coming is not understood in a physical sense, but in eschatological sense. That is, Jesus would come the second time when the whole world comes to an end and all human beings are judged for their deeds. On the contrary, Sai Baba's claim to return in the physical form is perhaps well within the Hindu worldview, because there is no such final end to the world within the cosmology of the Hindus. Although the idea of *pralaya* signals the end of the world, it also means beginning of another cycle of the world.

Place of Miracles in Sai Baba's Work

As noted above, the Sai devotees in South Africa, place great emphasis on the miracles of Sai Baba like their counterparts elsewhere. There are innumerable miracles that the devotees claim on behalf of Sai Baba. Wherever his devotees are, the main thrust of their experience of Sai Baba seems to be recounting the number of times they experienced his miraculous intervention in saving their lives or helping them under difficult circumstances. Many western devotees, like Howard Murphet (*Sai Baba: Man of Miracles*) and Phyllis Krystal (*Sai Baba: The Ultimate Experience*) write about the "miracles" that they experienced in their lives.

However, within Sai Baba's teachings, those "miracles" seem to function as a means of attracting the devotees' attention toward him. He says that what people call "miracles" are in fact seen by him as his "visiting cards". That is his way of introducing himself. In other words, he seems to presuppose that people do not approach him as Godman unless he performs "miracles." His devotees record him as saying, "You will understand Me only through my work. That is why sometimes, in order to reveal who I am, I show you My 'visiting cards'—something you call miracle" (Kanu, 58). His devotees even draw parallels between him and Jesus in the way both seemed to have used miracles as signs of their divinity. Kanu explains the theory of miracles as understood within the circles of Sai Baba in the following statement:

> Miracles have the magnetic power to draw people toward the centre of the divine magnetic field, the Avatara Himself. To man, miracles are an important proof of an avatara's divinity; so, it is as if he demands them. That is why the lives of Jesus Christ and Sai Baba are filled with signs and wonders. (Kanu, 10)

Thus, the miracles have a double role to play. On the one hand, they prove to the devotees that Sai Baba is divine, and on the other, they establish a bond between him and his devotees. It is seen both as establishing a metaphysical claim and an expression of divine grace. They demonstrate to the devotees his transcendental nature as the divine, and at the same time his immanence in their midst so that they can experience him and receive from him various material benefits. It is this two-fold function, one a transcendental role and the other an immanent role, that makes the "miracles" of Sai Baba integral to his teachings and ministry. It seems coherent with what he tries to teach and achieve as his mission.

Sai Baba's Teachings

According to his followers, the teachings of Sai Baba include not only religious but also secular matters. His purpose is to move people in the direction of God and make them more humane in their conduct, behaviour and lifestyle. To begin with, he seems to instil a feeling of devotion in the followers towards himself. He asks them, "Bring what you have: your sorrows and grief's, (your) worries and anxieties. And take from Me joy and peace, courage and confidence" (Kanu, 10). Invariably all devotees go to him because of some need or the other. And that gives them the occasion for directing their devotion towards him. In other words, an expectation of receiving something from him seems to be the cause of their devotion towards Sai Baba. So, he takes needs of the people as occasions for his teachings. He seems to make a distinction between the divinity in human beings and God Himself. His devotees claim that God can come in human form in order to reawaken the innate divinity in humans. In that sense, he is God incarnate who has come down to alleviate the suffering and pain of the devotees.

After having convinced his followers through his miracles, he sets out to convey his teachings to them. He teaches that "Godhead (Supreme Consciousness) is invisible, and formless. You visualise It as you wish and pray to It and derive consolation and strength" (Kanu, 10). He further says:

> I have not come for publicity, or to gain devotees or disciples. I am yours and you are Mine. Where then is the need for publicity? I do not just lecture, I teach a mixture of useful things for your mental health and moral regeneration. Take my words as medicine which is necessary for your spiritual health. (Kanu, 10)

All his teachings are directed towards making people aware of their spiritual needs and developing spiritually. His teachings, therefore, emphasise the need for character building and discipline. He asks his devotees to remove from their minds all forms of "anxiety, fear and ignorance" and engage in "good deeds, good company and good thoughts" (Kanu, 59).

Courage and confidence are two important aspects that he asks his devotees to develop. He says:

> What is needed today is right effort, courage and faith. For courage you must have self-respect. Never call yourself a sinner, born in sin or bred in sin. That kind of self-condemnation ill becomes a child of God [*sic*]. In every one of you, God is the moving-spirit, the very soul; how then can you be evil? You are

> here fulfilling God's purpose according to His will, His plan, His law. He has endowed you with many faculties so that you may seek Him and reach Him. You are, therefore, not a helpless (and) neglected individual under sentence of death; you are an ever-blissful soul, born in a rich heritage which is yours for the asking. Only ... so many of you do not ask. Have faith in your destiny and work gladly to attain it. (Kanu, 62)

The way Sai Baba interprets human destiny has to do with his overall emphasis on the divinity of human beings. Divinity is the natural condition of human beings and they should live up to that condition. According to his teachings, it is precisely because humans are inherently divine, that he does not think in terms of their being born in sin. He further states that such categories as sin are alien to the very nature of human beings. It is when truth is defied that human nature tends to become allied with the qualities that are categorised as sin. Sai Baba emphatically affirms, "Man is divine, take it from me. He is really here on a sacred mission for a divine purpose" (Kanu, 64). He also says that one has the potential to "become the instrument of Divine Power if he has acquired the two essential qualities: Truth and Divine Love" (Kanu, 64).

According to his philosophy, people can reach God through love and faith which are the two most essential guides in their spiritual pursuit. He says that one has to approach God with an attitude of love and surrender. He recognises a distinction between the love that people have for the divine and pure divine love. He describes pure divine love as a "stage (reached) when only service to the Lord matters and is its own reward" (Kanu, 72). As such, devotion to God is not devoid of any actions, but rather all actions are performed with an attitude of total surrender to God.

To pursue such a path of devotion, one does not need great knowledge and worldly riches. The divine love itself provides the "energy and (the) powers of concentration" to enable one to go towards total "liberation of consciousness" (Kanu, 72). Nevertheless, Sai Baba does prescribe a certain spiritual discipline and the study of the sacred scriptures. These are to enable individuals to gain control of their mind and gradually cleanse it of all impurities and evil thoughts. This cleansing is seen as both internal and external. Study of the scriptures provides one with divine thoughts, and discipline enables one to practise those thoughts. There are two goals of life, he says. Those are—to work for the good of the world and to attain liberation. This is the highest goal. It is also seen as the ultimate realisation of the self.

Phyllis Krystal, an English devotee of Sai Baba, who lived in the USA, has written a book on him giving her own account of how she experienced him. She closes her book with the following verse which seem to summarise Sai Baba's teachings in a nutshell:

> I love you all every single one
> For deep within I see
> Beneath the ego layers
> Your own Divinity. (Krystal, 254)

Thus, Sai Baba's teachings seem to combine a two-fold doctrine—humans are inherently divine and that God comes in human form to lead them to their destiny which is divinity.

Sai Baba's Teaching and its place in the Hindu Thought

Sai Baba's teachings are a recasting of the traditional Hindu Upanishadic ideas which speak of the latent divinity in all human beings. While he declares himself as incarnation of God, he seems to recognise the divinity in other human beings and seeks to rekindle it by his message. In other words, by making the assertion that he is the incarnation of God, he affirms a personal God. But on the other hand, by affirming the divinity in all human beings he seems to affirm the 'Brahmin-hood' in all. While he invites his devotees to come to him for divine grace and receive blessings, he also addresses them as "*pavitratmasvarupas*" (forms of the pure self) and "*premasvarupas*" (forms of love). In other words, in his view the divine form radiates not only through Sai Baba, but also through his devotees and in fact through the entire universe.

In his teachings, Sai Baba introduces ideas related to Hinduism through anecdotes and stories from the *Puranas* and the *Upanishads*. Thus, in his teachings, Sai Baba combines both a personalistic as well as a non-personalistic view of the divinity. Brahman is both personal and non-personal. He basis his teachings on the *Bhagavad Gita* and the *Srimad Bhagavatam* and conveys the idea that God comes in human form to help human beings. In this sense, Krishna, an incarnation of Vishnu (Narayana), becomes quite central to his teaching. He says:

> Thinking of the name of Krishna, one can lose one's consciousness. Thinking of Brahma (Brahman) one can become

> identical with Brahma (Brahman). So also, by constantly thinking of Krishna, one can become identical with the Lord. (*Bhagavatam* n.d.: 13. Parenthesis mine)

Thus, the divinity is perceived as personal Lord as long as people are caught up in the empirical world. Emphasising the need for the personal Lord, he says:

> All actions of a Jiva must be directed toward Vasudeva. It is impossible for us to seek directly the unmanifested form of God. Since you have a body, with a form and a name, it is very difficult for you to recognise the unmanifested form of God. So long as you have attachments in the world, it becomes possible for you to comprehend the Lord only through a name and a form. (*Bhagavatam* n.d.: 13)

He further says that God takes the form that the devotees seek. The form of God is dependent on the actions and prayers of his devotees. Thus, the best way to approach God is to sing the name of God concentrating on his form. The name and the form of God are the best way to attain him (*Bhagavatam* n.d.: 31).

The transcendental principles, namely, Purusha and Prakrti are identified in his teaching with Lord Krishna and Radha. The two are not only inseparable, but also identical to each other. He says:

> Because Prakrti and Paramatma are identical with each other, it is one single entity. Without Prakrti or creation, there is no Krishna, without Krishna we will not be able to see creation. We cannot have a cloth without the thread and the thread without the cloth. The oneness of the cloth and the thread exemplifies the aspect of Radha and Krishna. (*Bhagavatam* n.d.: 54)

In this sense, the teaching of Sai Baba is deeply rooted in the tradition of *Srimad Bhagavatam*. He brings in Hindu philosophical ideas from the *Upanishads* and the *Vedanta* to support his teaching. In many ways, it fits into the traditional model of Hindu thought, especially Vaishnava teaching. In a loose sense, he combines both the theistic Vedanta and the non-theistic Vedanta. In his discourses, he freely uses the ideas from both the *Srimad Bhagavatam* and the *Bhagavad Gita*. He moves freely from the idea of 'devotion to the Lord' to the Upanishadic idea of 'identity with God'. For instance, he identifies the devotion of the *gopikas* (Krishna's devotees) with the Upanishadic idea of oneness with Brahman. He says:

> The gopikas understood that all this was indeed mithya or unreal. Gopikas are not like ordinary women. They had practised several types of sadhana and they had this aspect of Brahman showing in them with effulgence. They were born as if they had come only to understand this aspect. The gopikas were ideal individuals who had been rishis in their previous births. They knew that if they fully understood Brahman, they would become identical with Brahman. They were establishing their unity with divinity. (*Bhagavatam*, 72)

Sai Baba identifies Krishna with Brahman, and says that Brahman alone is the real or truth. In the Upanishadic fashion, he speaks of Brahman as infinite, indescribable, permanent, having no beginning or end, unequalled, unique and so on. He further attributes all the auspicious qualities to Brahman. And at the same time he speaks of Brahman as having no blemishes or evil qualities. (*Bhagavatam*, 98f). Again it is quite in line with the Vedanta developed by many Vaishnava teachers of the medieval period.

Continuing this line of thinking, Sai Baba speaks of God as Purushottama (most superior being). He says that God in human form is called purusha and as the formless one he is *Purushottama*. As *Purushottama*, God is known as *prajnanam brahma* (Brahman, the Knowledge). Sai Baba describes Brahman as supreme bliss (*ananda*) (*Bhagavatam*, 212f).

In line with traditional Hindu teaching, Sai Baba affirms that at the time of death, the soul transmigrates according to its karmic influence while the body is discarded. Thus, the purpose of education is to overcome the cycle of birth and death. By education he means acquiring the knowledge of God. Taking his examples from *Srimad Bhagavatam*, he points out that "The Gopikas had that kind of good education which relieved them of this cycle of death and birth" (*Bhagavatam*, 108). In order to acquire divine knowledge, the devotees must develop concentration through meditation. He says that the human mind has the tendency to run fast and uncontrollably. It is necessary, he says, that the mind rests sometimes. And this rest is possible only through concentration (*dhyana*) (*Bhagavatam*, 114–115).

While this concentration enables one to realise the divinity, Sai Baba suggests that for the ordinary people service of the Lord or his incarnation is an effective way of realising God. For, in serving other human beings as forms of God one is really serving God. He further suggests that everyone should cultivate a form of God as a first step towards God-realisation (*Bhagavatam,* 164). Again, he cautions that whatever path one chooses, the essential thing is to develop devotion to God. For, "Devotion to God is the only path for salvation" (*Bhagavatam,* 194).

As mentioned earlier, the teaching of Sai Baba is essentially in line with the traditional Hindu thought, mainly the Vaishnava branch. In recasting those ideas in his metaphysical scheme, he puts special emphasis on the need for a form of God or an *avatara*. It is that need that he claims to fulfil for the devotees whom he has drawn from all over the world. There seems to be no doubt in the minds of his devotees that he is the *avatara* of God, the very God who dwells in the hearts of the devotees.

The South African phenomenon of the Sai Baba movement has certainly overtaken the growth that was witnessed in the 1990s with regard to the Hare Krishnas. However, because their movement is not based on membership as such, the lay devotees of the Sai movement are visible even in other neo-Hindu organisations. In other words, the phenomenon of the Sai movement in South Africa seems to blur the boundaries of organisations. In South Africa, its organisational structures are not as strong as those for instance of either the Ramakrishna Centre or the Divine Life Society. It looks more like a people's movement with no centralised organisation or management. It does not even have its own website fully constructed and functional. There seems to be, however, a Facebook-based youth movement around the Satya Sai movement.

Note

1. Most traditional Hindus wear some talisman to ward off evil. Mahatma Gandhi, for instance, mentions in his autobiography, the talisman that his mother placed around his neck when he was young.

15 Afterword

There exists among many Hindus a perception that philosophical Hinduism is "higher" than the ritualistic Hinduism, and many consider the latter as if it is the "lower form" in their religious growth. Unfortunately, this kind of tendency also exists among scholars. For instance, in the early studies of the anthropology of religion, we are familiar with the distinction between "higher religions" and the "lower religions" or "folk religions". The early Orientalist interpretations have contributed to the idea that Sanskrit-based rituals belong to the "higher" form of Hinduism and the non-Sanskrit rituals belong to the "lower" form of Hinduism. This unfortunate categorisation of ritual has skewed our understanding of ritual. This hierarchical understanding of ritual is complicated further by juxtaposing it with philosophical Hinduism. Thus, we have become accustomed to thinking that there is "lower" ritual and "higher" ritual in Hinduism, and there is "lower" Hinduism which is ritualistic and "higher" Hinduism which is philosophical and based on Sanskrit texts. The neo-Hindu tendency to look down upon image-centred rituals is only a recent phenomenon which developed during the mid-nineteenth century mainly in response to the Christian missions and western educational influence. In spite of these new tendencies, hundreds and thousands of South African Hindus continue to see the temple and domestic rituals as basic to their religious life.

The tendency of placing the ritualistic Hinduism and philosophical Hinduism hierarchically is largely due to our skewed reliance on Hindu texts to document the practice of Hinduism. Such text-based constructions of Hinduism still tend to dominate our scholarly research. But in recent years, historians of religions are beginning to see the significance of the popular traditions based on the vernacular and are beginning to look at the context and text together. A case in point is Alf Hiltebeitel's masterly work on the cult of Draupadi, (Hiltebeitel, 1988) a tradition which has survived among South African Hindus to this day. Firewalking (as it is known in KwaZulu-Natal) is, perhaps, the most dominant tradition among Hindus in South Africa and has become a pan-Hindu tradition. An originally Tamil-Telugu tradition, it has spread beyond its borders and has become assimilated into the North Indian tradition. In South Africa, the Gujarati, Hindi, Tamil- and Telugu-speaking people participate in it, and it is beginning to draw some European participants also.

In the foregoing chapters, I have presented Hinduism in South Africa based on observed rituals and not on texts, orally transmitted life-stories, and myths. I have juxtaposed this temple-based ritual Hinduism with that of the neo-Hindu organisations of the nineteenth and twentieth centuries. The tension between ritual and philosophy exists within Hinduism as it does in most religions. The tendency to move away from ritual towards philosophical orientation can be seen as an internal dynamic within the older Hinduism. But the postcolonial Hinduism in its tendency to move away from ritual is clearly due to the western influence. The long Muslim rule in India had already prepared the ground for a gradual disinterest in ritual. The Islamic emphasis on 'One God' contributed to a rethink about the Hindu notion of 'God.' As the western Christian missionaries began their activities in India with their initial judgmental attitude toward Hinduism, many educated Hindus such as Gandhi, Tilak, Vivekananda, Aurobindo Ghosh and others have contributed toward a reconceptualisation of Hindu doctrines on 'God.'

While the neo-Hindu groups, under the influence of the Orientalists, began their work by moving away from ritual Hinduism and by affirming philosophical Hinduism, eventually they also integrated in many ways various aspects of ritual Hinduism. This return of ritual in almost all the neo-Hindu organisations is what makes the early Orientalist constructions problematic. This means, it is not easy to separate temple-oriented ritual Hinduism and philosophical Hinduism. After all, almost all the Vedantic philosophers, such as Sankara, Ramanuja, Madhva, Vallabha, Caitanya and others whose philosophical schools were introduced through neo-Hindu movements in the west were intensely involved in their daily ritual activities in the temples despite the fact that they gave special significance to philosophical orientation. They worshipped their beloved deities (*ista devatas*), namely, Siva and Parvati, Vishnu and Lakshmi, Krishna and Radha and Rama and Sita. They did not isolate philosophical ideas from their ritual context, but rather integrated the two.

Evidently the majority of the Hindus tend to practise what we have called the traditional (*sanatana*) forms of Hinduism and a minority of Hindus follow the philosophical trends established in institutions like the Ramakrishna Centre. In the following pages, I shall reflect on how the two ostensibly divergent approaches in Hinduism seem to interact, thus providing coherence to the total understanding of Hinduism in South Africa.

In chapters 1 and 2 we have noted the general background of the South African Hindus and the emergence of Hinduism in South Africa. In chapters 3 to 14, we have noticed two main features of South African Hinduism—first, there are those who consider themselves Sanatanist Hindus who follow the traditional ritualistic Hinduism. Their lifestyle is characterised by ritual performance either in the temple or at home. Second, there are those who play down ritual in their life and tend to identify themselves with what is known as reformed Hinduism, or the neo-Hindu organisations. Nevertheless, even while playing down the ritual activity, the second group tends to identify itself with the more philosophical Hinduism which includes devotional singing, meditation, listening to discourses, reflection and so on, which I would tend to call a sublimated form of ritual activity. All their devotional singing and meditation ends with the offering of *arati* which is the most important part of the Hindu ritual observed by the traditionalists. In order to describe the two types of orientation adequately, I shall use the categories, namely, 'ritualistic' approach for the former group and 'cognitive' approach to refer to the latter group.

In other words, there are two ostensibly polarised types of Hindu phenomena that we notice in South Africa. One is a phenomenon based on traditional ritual activity, and the other is based on thought, reflection, meditation, etc., cognitive activities. The former emphasises doing or action, whereas the latter emphasises thought and reflection.

The two types of phenomena, though appearing polarised, are not radically separable. In other words, it does not mean that the performer of ritual does not reflect on what s/he is doing, nor does it mean that the philosophically-oriented group rejects any form of ritual radically. The two groups of Hindus need to be seen as emphasising two different aspects of the Hindu tradition, while at the same time interacting closely. The ritual-oriented Hindus appear to perform their rituals without any thought or reflection, whereas the more philosophically-bent Hindus seem to be playing down the ritual performance in their life.

Whether one is engaged in ritual activity or intellectually-oriented activity, both must be viewed as important ways of attempting to "know the divine". In that sense, both the ritual activity and the intellectually-oriented activity have a cognitive element in them. I am not concerned with the evaluation of the effectiveness of either one of the approaches, but rather concerned with how the two approaches; either independently or in a combination function at the level of interpretation and how the two approaches are integrated at different levels, namely, at the level of the devotee's experience, and at the level of interpretation which is rendered by the scholar.

In terms of their religious experience, the two groups are not mutually exclusive, although typologically they can be differentiated as such. Those who are oriented toward rituals have no difficulty in associating with the philosophically-oriented neo-Hindu organisations and participating in their activities, while the intellectually-oriented neo-Hindus do not seem to have any difficulty in associating with the ritualists and affirming the effectiveness of ritual activity even in their own organisations. A case in point is that, while thousands of ritual-oriented Hindus often participate in the activities of the neo-Hindu organisations (e.g., discourse, meditation camps, and so on), many neo-Hindu organisations make use of ritual activity (e.g., offering *arati*, and celebrating festivals with grand ritual paraphernalia).

This study confirmed that in understanding religious phenomena, we need to take into account both the ritual dimension and the philosophical dimension as part of a whole. The question is—how do we interpret the relationship between action and thought? Can there be a theory or theories of religion that would satisfactorily address both these aspects of religion?[1] One way of resolving it is to note that both the ritual actors of a tradition and the intellectually-oriented religious people as well as the outside theoreticians who study the religious traditions seem to admit that ritual is an expression of the system of beliefs and myths of a religious tradition. That is, ritual is what gives concrete expression to the abstract concepts of belief and myth. Nevertheless, several questions arise for our consideration. First, those who consider themselves intellectually-oriented tend to look down upon the ritualists as though ritual activity is the 'lower' form of religion. So, the question is whether ritual activity is the 'lower' form of religion that people give up as they move upward in their spiritual pursuit. Certainly, some philosophically-oriented organisations tend to think that way in the South African context. The neo-Hindu organisations, which are primarily dominated by the Vedantic philosophy, presented to the west by people like Swami Vivekananda, seem to emphasise this way of thinking. Even the Arya Samaj, though affirming the Vedic ritual, tends to emphasise the idea of "monotheism" and seeks to impress upon its adherents to break away from the image-centred worship which is characterised by them as the 'lower' form of religion. But for the average Hindu in South Africa, participation in ritual both daily and during festivals seem to give coherence to what he or she does in life. There seems to be an intrinsic connection between their material needs and ritual activities.

Second, is ritual activity devoid of meaning? What does it mean to say that ritual is devoid of meaning? Does it mean that ritual acts have no meaning attached to them? Or does it mean that the performer often does not know the meaning? It seems to me that the question is not so much whether the performers of ritual knew the meaning of their ritual acts or not, but rather to recognise the fact that at the time of performing the ritual actions they seem to be totally unconcerned about the meaning and significance attached to them. *They concentrate on doing it right.* Often they are not even aware of the fact that they are mispronouncing many words of the chants or *mantras* or hymns. It seems the utterance of those words at the right time is more important than thinking of the meaning or whether or not they are pronouncing them correctly. For instance, I have often heard people saying "ayogara" when they are supposed to be saying "Haro Hara". It took me a few days to connect the two. Perhaps, they knew that they were referring to Siva (Hara) but as far as they are concerned it seems to make no difference whether they say "ayogara" or "Haro Hara". I later realised that it was one of those problems of pronouncing Sanskrit words faced by a Tamil. Words and their meaning seem to be conjured up by the intention that is behind them. The participants use those words despite the fact they are unaware of the meaning. The listener may hear it differently but the devotee seems to be aware of the fact that s/he is referring to Siva. And we are able to see it only in the context of ritual.

Furthermore, does "meaninglessness of ritual" and "purposelessness of ritual" mean the same? Can ritual activity be meaningless and yet purposeful? I have not come across any Hindu in South Africa who takes part in a ritual without any purpose. There is always a motive or purpose for which the ritual is performed. It might be that people often do not know the meaning of every aspect of the ritual, or the symbols and myths which are involved in it. Moreover, a person might not even be thinking about the ritual while s/he is performing it. But there seems to be no indication of a ritual without a purpose. It is always associated with some material benefit (e.g., wealth, success in business), if not for the sake of attaining salvation (*mukti*). The care and fear with which the ritual actions are performed reveals the concern for effectiveness in securing the desired result.

Third, even if we were to attribute some meaning to the ritual actions of the devotee, it is seen only as an afterthought and not prior to or at the time of the performance. Nevertheless, such philosophical meanings given to the ritual do not seem to displace the action. Thus, ritual is the most dominant form of Hindu religious orientation in South Africa and seems to be the most integrating force within the Hindu community. This is clear from the history of the Hindus in South Africa. At a time when there were no philosophical discourses available to the Hindus, the temple and domestic rituals were the only way in which they could identify themselves as Hindus. It is the ritual activity in the temples and at home that brought the community together. In the early days, people of all linguistic backgrounds could come together at the rituals performed either on the occasion of a festival or at some domestic ceremony. Ritual, as a means of integration within the Hindu community, is still an important factor. The goddess festivals and other rituals which are performed at the temples during festivals continue to draw people of all backgrounds within the Hindu community. Ritual activity continues to bind them, and provide them with a sense of identity as Hindus. As such, rituals are motivated by various factors, such as economic factors, cultural identity and religious orientation. Furthermore, ritual activity motivates the devotees to perpetuate their life-world. It provides inspiration in their lives and coherence to their worldview by externalising their feelings, aspirations, goals, inner experience and hidden meanings. In this sense, rituals provide integration both at the level of social life and also at the level of their inner experience. They provide coherence between what they do in their daily life and what they do in their religious life.

Just as the temple and domestic rituals of the Hindus provide us with some insight into their worldview, the neo-Hindu religious organisations and institutions also provide us with some insight into the various denominational dynamics of the South African Hindus. Furthermore, with their special emphasis on the philosophically and intellectually-oriented Hindu tradition, they also provide coherence to the ritually constructed worldview. In spite of their overt emphasis on philosophy it must be noted that they spend a lot of time singing and chanting during their corporate meetings. In fact, this activity seemed to me more prominent than philosophical discourses. Whether it is the Ramakrishna Centre or Divine Life Society or Arya Samaj or the Hare Krishnas, during their corporate meetings (*satsanghs*) all of them spend a great deal of time singing and chanting. The discourse on a philosophical topic of their choice is often given no more than ten or twenty minutes. Their average meeting (*satsangh*) lasts at least two hours which means nearly three fourth of the time is spent singing and offering *arati* at the end. These ritual activities are of great importance even in the neo-Hindu organisations which claim to play them down.

While ritual seems to appeal to a greater number of devotees, we also notice that the denominational Hinduism based on the neo-Hindu philosophical traditions has been successful among some people. The success of the neo-Hindu denominations is, however, due largely to their ability to integrate ritual (such as, *bhajans*, the offering of *arati*, festivals and so on) into their field. This is not to belittle the significance of philosophical traditions, but to note that the average Hindus who are usually drawn by the temple rituals, visit the neo-Hindu organisations mainly when festival ceremonies are conducted by the neo-Hindu organisations. For instance, the attendance for the philosophical discourses at the religious organisations is often very minimal. But when they have a festival like the "festival of chariots" or Sivaratri, the Hindu community attends in large numbers. In other words, ritual, as a social dynamic, seems to have a more integrating force even in the philosophically-oriented religious institutions. That is to say, even when the average Hindus become attracted to the neo-Hindu organisations, often it is not necessarily to the philosophical thought but rather to the ritual activities such as singing and so on which provides a sense of social and group identity. Thus, the intellectual activity that is encouraged in the neo-Hindu organisations has to be somehow expressed in concrete acts so that the average Hindus can participate in it more effectively. Without such intellectual activity being translated into ritual activity, the devotees cannot seem to have an effective religious experience. In order to evoke such feeling in a devotee, an intellectual conception has to take the form of a physically experienced act.

Whether Hindus in South Africa visit a temple or a neo-Hindu organisation their deep commitment to their Hindu tradition and culture is evident. It is with the desire to perpetuate their Hindu world in a foreign land that they established vernacular schools which often functioned both as centres of education as well as those of religion. The nature of their vernacular teaching is intensely religious. As the old apartheid laws gave way to new ways of living in South Africa a new era of Hinduism is emerging. Hindus in South Africa are no longer expected to live in separate locations and as they move on into a more open society they would have to devise new strategies of perpetuating their Hindu religious traditions. By building temples and religious institutions in places where they lived, Hindus have created a unique geography for themselves. But as they move away from their traditional geographical locations, the temple and religious institutions become gradually distanced from them in a physical sense. They might move away from the former temples, but they will build new ones in the new locations to which they move. A case in point is the current attempts of the Hindu community that is fast growing in the Umhlanga suburb, a former 'whites only' section of Durban. They are currently raising funds to build a new temple in this suburb. Building a temple might be a religious act, but to the extent that it carries the signature of the community that lives there, it is at the same time an identity marker. If this is an indication of the future evolution of Hinduism, the sociology of Hinduism in South Africa needs to take these new developments that are unfolding in the country. Nevertheless, the future of Hindus in South Africa is wide open to new expressions. How they would relate themselves to the temples and religious centres, how they would perpetuate their worldview, the new ways they would devise, and the forms of religious orientation they would follow, will form at least some of the most important content of the books written in future. This book anticipates all that and attempts to contribute to it.

Note

1. In her recent work, Catherine Bell explores the relationship between ritual action and cognitive dimensions. See Catherine Bell. *Ritual Theory, Ritual Practice*. (New York: Oxford University Press, 1992). Her work critically analyses previous theoreticians, such as Emile Durkheim, and complements the works of scholars, such as Clifford Geertz.

Appendix

Perceptions and Attitudes of South African Hindus[1]

A sample survey has been conducted to gain an insight into the perceptions and attitudes of the South African Hindus. About 1,000 questionnaires were distributed and we received 331 responses. The survey thus includes a total of 331 individuals primarily from the Natal region, but also from Johannesburg and Cape Town. About 10 per cent are drawn from Cape Town, 15 per cent from Johannesburg and the remaining from the Kwazulu-Natal province. This distribution of the questionnaire in the above fashion is in the light of the fact that the bulk of the Indian community lives in the Natal region. Within the Natal area special attention was given to Chatsworth, Verulam, Tongaat, Phoenix, Reservoir Hills, Overport (in Durban), Pietermaritzburg, and Ladysmith.

Among the total number of respondents, 45 per cent were male and 55 per cent were female. Four age groups, as shown in Table 1 below, were identified among the total number of respondents:

Table 1
Age Groups

(in %)

Age	*Total*	*Male*	*Female*
18–24	28	32	33
25–34	21	20	22
35–44	27	33	23
45+	23	25	21

Similarly, following four language groups were identified among the total number of respondents:

Table 2
Language

(in %)

Language	*Total*	*Male*	*Female*
Telegu	11	7	13
Tamil	37	40	34
Hindi	38	34	41
Gujarati	15	19	11

These groups were identified according to the level of education as shown below in Table 3:

Table 3
Education

(in %)

Level of Education	*Total*	*Male*	*Female*
Below Matric	31	24	36
Above Matric	30	34	26
Matric	40	42	38

Seven major groups according to denominational affiliations were also identified with an additional group claiming anonymity (see Table 4):

Table 4
Hindu Denomination

(in %)

Denomination	*Total*	*Male*	*Female*
Sanatanist	32	32	32
Arya Samaj	4	4	4
Hare Krishna	7	9	5
Divine Life	10	9	10
Satya Sai Baba	11	11	10
Saiva Siddhanta	9	11	7
Ramakrishna	10	7	18
Anonymous	18	18	18

Self-Understanding

A set of questions were asked to ascertain how the different constituent groups among the South African Hindus understand themselves in terms of their religion. Of the total male respondents, 94 per cent consider themselves Hindu, and 91 per cent consider religion as an important aspect of their life. Among the female respondents 95 per cent consider themselves Hindu and 88 per cent consider religion as important. We have cross-checked these responses according to the various age groups and found the following responses:

The Age Group of 18–24

Ninety per cent said that they consider themselves Hindu, and 85 per cent of them think that religion is important in their life. Only 39 per cent of them said that one has to be always involved in religious activities at the temple and at home in order to be a Hindu.

The Age Group of 25–34

Ninety-six per cent think of themselves as Hindu and 82 per cent of them think that religion is important in their life. A total of 52 per cent of them said that in order to be a Hindu one has to be always involved in rituals at the temples and at home.

The Age Group of 35–44

Ninety-eight per cent think of themselves as Hindu and 96 per cent think that religion is important in their life. In all, 54 per cent of them think that one has to be involved in temple and domestic rituals in order to be a Hindu.

The Age Group of 45+

Ninety-five per cent think of themselves as Hindu and exactly the same percentage of them think that religion is important in their life. About 58 per cent of them think that one has to be involved in temple and domestic rituals in order to be a Hindu.

If we consider the above responses carefully, we notice that there is no significant change in the responses for the questions about whether or not they consider themselves as Hindu and whether or not religion is important in their life. In all the categories, a significant majority of them responded affirmatively. But, how that Hindu identity and being religious translates into one's life practice seems to give us some interesting pattern. In general, 52 per cent of the male respondents think that one has to be involved in ritual activities at the temple and at home in order to be a Hindu. And 49 per cent of the female respondents think the same. If we disregard the difference between the male and female responses to the above question being negligible, one might assume that about half of both male and female respondents give importance to rituals and about half of them do not.

However, when we look at the responses according to the various age groups, it appears that there is a gradual rise in the percentage of responses of the older age groups. In the age group 18–24: 39 per cent, in the age group 25–34: 53 per cent, in the age group 35–44: 54 per cent, and the age group 45+: 58 per cent.

In other words, the older the age group is the higher the percentage of people who said that rituals at temple and at home are important. The difference between the youngest group and the oldest group is especially obvious. In other words, the older one becomes, the greater is the tendency to be involved in ritual activities.

We shall see how the educational background affected the responses to the same questions.

Below Matric

Ninety-four per cent consider themselves Hindu, and exactly the same percentage think that religion is important in their life. A total of 60 per cent of them said that one has to be involved in rituals in the temple and at home in order to be a Hindu.

Matric

Ninety per cent consider themselves Hindu, and 90 per cent think that religion is important in their life. Around 52 per cent of them said that one has to be involved in rituals in the temple and at home in order to be a Hindu.

Above Matric

Ninety-two per cent consider themselves Hindu, and 86 per cent think that religion is important in their life. About 42 per cent of them said that one has to be involved in rituals in the temple and at home in order to be a Hindu.

The percentages vary for the three groups on the first two questions, namely, whether or not they consider themselves Hindu, and whether or not they think religion is important in their lives. However, on the question of rituals, a similar pattern that we noticed in the category of age groups emerges here as well. That is, there is a consistent decline in the percentage of responses as the educational level goes up. Thus, Below Matric-60 per cent; Matric-52 per cent, and Above Matric-42 per cent indicate that there is a correlation between the level of education and intellectual understanding of the kind of religious activities people should involve themselves in. In other words, the percentage of those who prefer to be involved in rituals in temples and at homes happens to be on the higher side for the Below Matric group. However, it would be unfair to draw the conclusion that those who are less educated are more involved in the rituals, because we have noted earlier that the older people get the more they tend to be involved in rituals. In other words, even the more educated ones are also, perhaps, more involved in rituals as they grow older.

The only conclusion that we can safely draw from the above analysis is that a significant majority of the respondents belonging to all the age groups and all the educational levels consider themselves Hindu and that religion is important in their life. But how they tend to practise their religious life seems to vary according to the age groups and the level of education. Of course, the finding that older persons are more involved in religious activities, especially rituals, fits with the traditional mode of Hindu life. In other words, the traditional Hindu lifestyle fosters the idea of becoming more religious as one becomes older. Thus, our finding affirms the traditional Hindu idea of four stages of life in which the last two stages are more geared toward spiritual aspects of life. Whether spiritual life is oriented towards ritual activities or more intellectual and cognitive activities is an option that depends on the intellectual and cognitive orientation of the individuals.

The traditional Hindu way of life provides the options of both ritual and intellectual pursuit. It also provides a third alternative in which the two can be combined, namely, the path of devotion. In our analysis above, we have noted that the group belonging to the higher educational level tends to be less involved in rituals. But our analysis has also shown that the older one gets the more one is involved in rituals. Thus, it may be safer to assume that while higher educational level makes one lean towards the intellectual and cognitive approach to one's religious life, the age factor seems to temper it and lead one towards a certain amount of rituals as well. Thus, a combination of the two may be seen as the best possible means to gain an insight into the religious life of the Hindus in South Africa.

This way of understanding the Hindus also fits with the fact that a great many of them have a dual sense of self-identity. That is, many of them have identified themselves with both the traditional ritualistic mode of Hinduism (Sanatanist) and the neo-Hindu way of life, such as the kind of life fostered by the neo-Hindu organisations in South Africa (e.g., Ramakrishna Centre, Divine Life Society, and so on).

Religious Belief and Practice

In an effort to understand the depth of their theological outlook and how that relates to their actual religious practice, I asked another set of questions.

Table 5

Religious Belief and Practice

(in %)

Category of Belief	*Male*	*Female*
Life after death	85	75
One God	91	83
Plurality of Gods and Goddesses	36	39
All deities ultimately one	91	84
Religious myths	58	61
Legends about saints	64	63
Historical character of epics (*Ramayana* and *Mahabharata*)	76	75
Incarnation of God in human form	61	56
Godmen as incarnation of God	30	23
Karma and rebirth	87	82
Accidental death and disease as punishment for past deeds	54	48
Trance	50	52
Miracles, visions and dreams	62	61
Material prosperity depends on religious practice	58	55
Astrology	61	52
Consult priest to ward off evil	45	40

Male Respondents

As the Table 5 shows 85 per cent of the male respondents admitted a belief in life after death; 91 per cent believed in one God; 36 per cent believed in plurality of gods and goddesses;[2] 91 per cent believed that all the deities ultimately represent one reality; 58 per cent believed in the religious myths; 64 per cent believed in the legends about the saints; 76 per cent believed in the historical character of the epics (the *Ramayana* and the *Mahabharata*); 61 per cent believed in the idea of incarnation of God in human form; only 30 per cent believed in the modern-day godmen as incarnations of God; 87 per cent believed in *karma* and rebirth; 54 per cent believed that accidental death, disease, etc., are punishments for one's past deeds; 50 per cent believed in trance; 62 per cent believed in miracles, visions, and dreams; 58 per cent believed that their material prosperity depends on their religious practice; 61 per cent believed in astrology; and 45 per cent consulted a priest or some such person to ward off evil.

Female Respondents

The Table 5 also reveals that 75 per cent believed in life after death; 83 per cent believed in one God; 39 per cent believed in the plurality of gods and goddesses; 84 per cent believed that all the deities ultimately represent one reality; 61 per cent believed in religious myths; 63 per cent believed in the legends about saints; 75 per cent believed in the historical character of the epics (the *Ramayana* and the *Mahabharata*); 56 per cent believed in the incarnation of God in human form; 23 per cent believe in modern-day godmen as incarnations of God; 82 per cent believed in *karma* and rebirth; 48 per cent believed that accidental death, disease, etc., are punishments for past deeds; 52 per cent believed in trance; 61 per cent believed in miracles, visions, and dreams; 55 per cent believed that their material prosperity depends on their religious practice; 52 per cent believed in astrology, and 40 per cent believed in consulting a priest or some such person to ward off evil.

These responses indicate a relatively higher level of cognitive belief. Many of these beliefs are culturally imparted and therefore part of their Hindu worldview. With the exception of the question on the belief in the plurality of gods and goddesses, and on the question of "godmen," all other questions register an average of above 50 per cent positive responses. There is not much of difference between the male and the female responses. In other words, the male respondents are no more or no less traditional than their female counterparts. Both male and female respondents registered a low percentage of positive response on the "plurality" question as well as on the "godmen" question. Both male and female respondents affirmed a neo-Hindu trend of perceiving all deities as representing one reality in the ultimate sense. This suggests that the Hindus, in general, tend to have a universalistic idea of reality.

It may be suggested that the Hindus in South Africa, though distanced from their original home (India), continue to uphold their traditional worldview. It seems fundamental to their existence to continue to live in the traditional worldview, and share in the traditional beliefs for it gives them not only meaning for their existence, but also a distinct identity of their own in the middle of other cultural groups. Nevertheless, there are occasions when they seem to step out of their traditional mode of thinking and share the agnosticism of the modern scientific worldview.

The combination of their traditional mode of thinking with the modern way of perceiving things is obvious in many different areas of their life. In order to understand the interaction between tradition and modernity,[3] we asked a number of questions on family, women, language, race, politics, modern society in general and other religions.

Family

These sets of questions dealt mainly with marriage. A mixture of traditional worldview and modern worldview is affirmed by the questions on marriage.

Table 6

Family and Marriage

(in %)

Views on Marriage	*Male*	*Female*
Marriage is sacred	92	90
Sanctity of marriage	90	83
Hindu wedding ceremony leads to happy marriage	58	42
Both partners are equal	95	90
Arranged marriage	23	27
Divorce an option	30	38
Children must be raised according to Hindu ideals	79	74
Preference of sons over daughters	22	21
Daughters must be raised with greater discipline	55	49
Sons must be raised with greater discipline	37	48

Male Respondents

As the Table 6 shows 92 per cent affirmed that marriage is sacred; 90 per cent believed in the sanctity of Hindu marriage; and 58 per cent believed that the Hindu wedding ceremony leads to a happy marriage. However, 95 per cent affirmed equal status of both partners in marriage; and only 23 per cent believed in arranged marriages. Again, with regard to the question of divorce 30 per cent considered divorce as an option, and 79 per cent believed that children must be raised according to Hindu ideals. However, they indicated a low level of discrimination between sons and daughters as only 22 per cent preferred sons to daughters, and only 18 per cent preferred daughters to sons. But there seems to be some indication of difference between the way girls are treated and the way boys are treated as 55 per cent thought that their daughters must be raised with greater discipline, and 37 per cent thought that sons must be raised with greater discipline.

Female Respondents

The trend among the female respondents is also much the same as shown in Table 6. While 90 per cent affirmed that marriage is sacred; 83 per cent believed in the sanctity of Hindu marriage, and 42 per cent (considerably less than the male respondents) believed that the Hindu wedding ceremony leads to happy marriages. However, 90 per cent affirmed equal status of both partners in marriage, and only 27 per cent believed in arranged marriages. Again, with regard to the question of divorce, 38 per cent (higher than the male respondents) considered divorce as an option, and 74 per cent believed that children must be raised according to Hindus ideals. Nevertheless, like their male counterparts, they indicated a low level of discrimination between sons and daughters—only 21 per cent preferred sons to daughters, and only 20 per cent preferred daughters to sons; but there seems to be not much of difference between the way the girls are treated and the way the boys are treated—49 per cent thought that their daughters must be raised with greater discipline, and 48 per cent thought sons must be raised with greater discipline. The question of marriage and raising of children are clearly seen as part of their religious domain, and not simply matters of the secular world. In both areas the traditional Hindu worldview is affirmed. Nevertheless, considering their general tendency towards orthopractice regarding matters of marriage, 30 per cent male and 38 per cent female option for divorce may seem somewhat unusual, and is indicative of how their social values are gradually changing and coming to grips with the changing social reality in South Africa.

Women

These questions were intended to ascertain the views on women and their role in society.

Male Respondents

As the Table 7 reveals, 79 per cent of male respondents considered women to be equal to men, and 85 per cent thought that women could compete with men in the modern world of science. However, 73 per cent thought that women should follow the religious

Table 7
Gender Equality

(in %)

	Male	*Female*
Women equal to men	79	85
Women could compete with men	85	95
Women to follow husband's religious practice	73	61
Men should follow wife's religious practice	10	18
Women should be traditional in their lifestyle	66	58
Women are more religious than men	47	53

practices of their husbands' family; only 10 per cent of them thought that men should follow the religious practices of their wives' family; 66 per cent thought that women must be traditional in their lifestyle, and 47 per cent considered women to be more religious than men.

Female Respondents

Similarly, 85 per cent of female respondents considered women to be equal to men, and 95 per cent thought that women could compete with men in the modern world of science. However, 61 per cent thought that women should follow the religious practices of their husbands' family; only 18 per cent of them thought that men should follow the religious practices of their wives' family; 58 per cent thought that women must be traditional in their lifestyle, and 53 per cent considered women to be more religious than men.

The responses of both men and women are very close. Both have registered a significantly higher percentage of positive responses for the question of equality and competition in the modern world of science. Nevertheless, when it comes to religious matters both men and women seem to affirm a traditional Hindu point of view. In the traditional Hindu view, women seem to be more religious than men, and that they also are expected to follow the religious practice of their husbands' family. For instance, if a woman is married to a man whose family is more inclined toward ritualistic way of life, she is expected to follow the same way of life. In other words, the traditional Hindu worldview expects the wife to conform to her husband's religious way. This traditional worldview is affirmed by both male and female respondents. As noted earlier, marriage and family are areas of life inseparable from their religious worldview. Thus, religious practice is tied up with the question of marriage, and seems to be a key factor in the choice of marital alliances, and furthermore in shaping the family life.

It seems likely that in the face of the fast changing modern world, men as well as women have come to terms with the fact that both of them are equally competing, and that the traditional bias against women cannot stand in the context of the modern worldview. Nonetheless, both men and women tend to remain in the traditional worldview in matters of religious behaviour. This clear separation of secular and religious worlds is also visible in other areas of their life.

Language

Like religious identity, linguistic identity is also vital to the Hindus in South Africa. A set of questions were asked to ascertain their linguistic identity. About 64 per cent male respondents and 64 per cent female respondents thought that marriages within the same linguistic group were better. By the same token, the marriages outside the linguistic boundaries do not necessarily lead to unhappy life—48 per cent male respondents and 54 per cent female respondents did not think that marriages outside the linguistic group lead to an unhappy life. Nonetheless, the linguistic identity is more pronounced in the area of ritual—68 per cent male respondents and 73 per cent female respondents preferred worshipping in their own vernacular. In other words, language and religion seem to be inseparable from each other. The significance of the vernacular in their life is seen in the following—91 per cent male respondents and 92 per cent female respondents thought that the younger generation should learn their (Indian) vernaculars; and 93 per cent male and 89 per cent female respondents thought that Indian vernaculars should be taught in schools and colleges. This does not necessarily mean that the younger generation saw their vernaculars as important as the older generation did. What is reflected in the responses above seems to represent the ideal but not the actual reality. The basic medium of instruction and communication being English seems to be a major factor that the younger generation had to take into account as they prepared for their careers.

Race

A set of questions were asked to ascertain how Hindus in South Africa perceived and related themselves to other racial groups. About 86 per cent of the male respondents and 80 per cent female respondents thought that members of other races could be Hindus;

78 per cent male and 73 per cent female respondents said they were comfortable with living with other races in the same neighbourhood; 64 per cent male and 65 per cent female respondents did not consider racial integration as a threat to the preservation of the Hindu culture, and 72 per cent male and 73 per cent female respondents thought that it was good for their children to be exposed to other cultural values. However, only 30 per cent male and 32 per cent female respondents considered inter-racial marriages happy; 17 per cent male and 20 per cent female respondents liked it if their children married whites, and 17 per cent male and 19 per cent female respondents liked it if their children married Blacks.

These questions were asked on a hypothetical basis, and, therefore, no real conclusions can be drawn from them as to what the real situation is going to be in South Africa with regard to the issues of race. Nevertheless, the above responses do indicate the present mindset of the Hindus in South Africa. As long as there is no real inter-racial mixing in terms of marriages, and so on, the Hindus do not seem to mind the integration of the different races on a loosely related level. Here, marriage is seen to be the limit where the integration stops. Thus, the issue of marriage seems to be tied up with the basic identity as to who they are, not only in terms of their religion and language, but also in terms of their ethnicity and colour.

Politics

These questions were intended to understand how the Hindus in South Africa view politics. The question of politics is another area that reveals the interaction between religious and secular matters in the lives of the Hindus in South Africa. Only 14 per cent male and 14 per cent female respondents said they were involved in politics; 45 per cent male and 32 per cent female respondents thought that religion and politics are inter-related; 40 per cent male and 32 per cent female respondents thought that heads of religious organisations should be involved in politics; 49 per cent male and 45 per cent female respondents thought that heads of religious organisations should provide guidance to their followers in making political options, and 34 per cent male and 28 per cent female respondents thought that religious leaders should make political statements.

Although a majority of them are not involved in politics and see religion and politics as separate entities, a fair amount of them (about 45% male and 32% female) seem to see the inter-relatedness of religion and politics. Those who consider the inter-relatedness of religion and politics may not constitute the majority, but nonetheless it is a significant number of people. In other words, a significant number of people seem to be departing from the traditional mode of thinking, that is, the idea that religious and secular matters are separate. This trend, perhaps, has to do with the intense political climate of South Africa. In fact, if one looks at the history of the South African Hindus (for that matter the South African Indian community in general), from the beginning their life in this country has been enmeshed in political controversies. For instance, the "Indian question," namely, whether or not to repatriate (or expatriate!) all Indians to India was shelved only in the 1950s. In that sense, it is no wonder that a significant number of Hindus see politics as an integral part of their life in South Africa. Since most Hindus are overtly religious, there is scope to see religion and politics as becoming more and more interconnected.

Seen from this perspective, it makes sense for a significant number of people (49% male and 45% female) to seek political guidance from their religious leaders. However, the percentage of people expecting their religious leaders to make political statements is far less (34% male and 28% female). In other words, while they seek guidance from their religious leaders on political matters, they, nonetheless, do not seem to think it wise for the leaders to make political statements that would commit them one way or the other. They see politics affecting their entire life which includes their religious life but on the other hand they seem to be treading a safe path keeping a safe distance from politics. Thus, they are not only not involved in politics, they do not expect their religious leaders to make political statements that would implicate them. Seen from the standpoint of their minority status, this approach of safe distance from politics is a characteristic strategy that the Hindus in South Africa generally adopted from the very beginning.

Modern Society

One of the things that is increasingly becoming a concern of the Hindus in South Africa is the modern lifestyle that the younger generation is adopting in the present climate of South Africa. Their concern is expressed mainly in relation to their children and their upbringing. A set of questions were asked to ascertain the views of Hindus as to how they saw modern society mainly in relation to the younger generations. A careful look at the responses in the age groups above thirty-five years reveals the fears and the uncertainties of the older generation.

35–44 Age Group

Seventy-seven per cent said that they were concerned that their children might be exposed to bad habits at the university; only 15 per cent allowed their children to late night parties, and 86 per cent thought that their children must be taught their Hindu faith in schools.

45+ Age Group

Sixty-one per cent said that they were concerned that their children might be exposed to bad habits at the university; only 26 per cent allowed their children to late night parties, and 79 per cent thought that their children must be taught their Hindu faith in schools.

It is interesting to note a lower percentage rate is registered in the age group above forty-five years. Nevertheless, the common concern for the children is clear in the majority of the respondents. The concern to impart the Hindu faith to their children is especially obvious among both age groups. This concern makes sense when it is seen in light of the growing trend toward more liberal and non-committal religious attitude that is manifest in the Hindu community. As mentioned earlier in this chapter, the traditional worldview (in the sense of their general Hindu identity and belief in God, etc.) is affirmed more on the social level. That is to say that the traditional categories, such as caste, affiliation to a denominational organisation, affiliation to a temple, and so on, are becoming less meaningful. This does not mean that these categories have ceased to exist among the Hindus in South Africa completely. But a new way of understanding their Hindu identity is becoming manifest.

A total of 80 per cent male and 79 per cent female respondents did not think that caste is important to be a Hindu; 76 per cent male and 71 per cent female respondents thought that one does not need to be of Indian origin to be a Hindu; 89 per cent male and 89 per cent female respondents thought that one does not need to go to any Hindu organisation to be a Hindu; 77 per cent male and 81 per cent female respondents thought that one can be a Hindu without performing rituals at a temple, and 60 per cent male and 60 per cent female respondents thought that one can be a Hindu without performing any rituals at home. Nevertheless, 83 per cent male and 82 per cent female respondents thought that Indian language and culture is important to be a Hindu.

In other words, this modernist way of understanding who a Hindu is, more open and liberal. Except the affinity for one's language and culture, all other traditional categories seem to be becoming, if not meaningless, at least less relevant. The advantage of this kind of perception of being a Hindu without the traditional appendages is that it gives scope for them to become more integrated into the other worldviews around them and also enables them to develop a more tolerant view of the people of other faiths and ideologies. However, the negative side of it is that they can be deprived of their traditional religious sources which are, perhaps, essential in order to be informed of their faith and practice.

Other Religions

Perhaps, it is this loose way of understanding themselves as Hindu without the traditional paraphernalia that seems to have influenced their positive and assimilative attitude to other religions. These questions were intended to understand the Hindu perception of other faiths.

Eighty-two per cent male and 84 per cent female respondents thought that other religions are equally good; 89 per cent male and 89 per cent female respondents believed in the unity of all religions; only 15 per cent male and 13 per cent female respondents thought that people of other faiths must become Hindus, and 42 per cent male and 32 per cent female respondents thought that Hindus have better values than others. Nevertheless, 76 per cent male and 71 per cent female respondents thought that it is not good for Hindus to become converted to other religions.

While they display a great deal of openness to other religions, they certainly see conversion to other faiths as being detrimental to their own Hindu identity. In other words, one's Hindu identity seems to be synonymous with the linguistic and cultural identity. What seems to matter is the preservation of the Hindu culture and through it their identity as Hindus. It is in this light one may have to understand the majority of respondents' desire to have their language and culture as well as Hindu faith taught in the schools.

Some General Observations

In the light of the above analysis, some general observations can be made, more in terms of theoretical issues, rather than conclusions. I have identified seven larger theoretical issues some of which I have discussed at some length in the last chapter.

First, as noted in the above discussion, the South African Hindus combine both the ritual approach and the cognitive approach or what I might call action-reflection in terms of their religious life. This does not mean that every Hindu in South Africa is both doing and reflecting at the same time. What it means is that there are those who give more weight to doing (ritual action) and others who give more weight to reflection or thought. In statistical terms, it is difficult to say exactly what percentage of them are ritually, oriented, although majority of them seem to be involved in ritual action. Nonetheless, in the wake of the neo-Hindu organisations, there is a general interest among many Hindus to seek more reflection-oriented religion. That is, they are beginning to be more interested in the study of their philosophies and so on. Although statistically it is possible to show that there are some visible groups who are involved mainly in rituals, and there are those involved in more thought-oriented activities, such statistical findings need to be tempered with some caution. In some sense, the Hindus cannot be separated so easily because they seem to be moving freely between ritual orientation and philosophical orientation. Only when someone asks a question as to whether they are more inclined this way or that, they tend to make those choices. Therefore, such a separation of the two groups is the creation of the way we ask questions in the data collection, rather than their real existence as clearly definable groups.

Second, they combine both traditional mode of thinking and modernist rational way of thinking in terms of their theological outlook. What this means is that the South African Hindus are struggling to combine their traditional worldview with the modern scientific one. And they seem to do this quite consciously. Their choices of what falls into the traditional worldview and what falls into the modern scientific worldview seems to be quite selective.

Third, in terms of their religious belief and practice, they tend to affirm the traditional worldview. But in terms of their social world in the context of science and technology they tend to affirm the modernist worldview. This is reflected, among others, in the areas of status of women in society. Thus, though to a large extent religious and secular worldviews of the South African Hindus overlap, they do distinguish between the two on select issues.

Fourth, the intrinsic relation between the religious identity and linguistic identity is clear among the South African Hindus. This is further coupled with the ethnic identity. Thus, religion, language and ethnicity form the core of the South African Hindu identity.

Fifth, again in matters of politics there is a mixture of both traditional mode of thinking and the modernist mode of thinking. Although majority of the Hindus are not involved in politics, they see politics affecting their life as a whole. While they expect guidance from the religious leaders, they do not expect them to make political statements.

Sixth, on the social level the Hindu worldview is modernist and not traditionalist. Thus issues, such as, caste, religious denomination, and rituals are not the defining factors for their identity. In other words, they can be Hindu without having to participate in any of those categories. The major defining factors in terms of their social identity are language and culture.

Seventh, thus there is a broadening of the scope of the Hindu identity based on broader terms of language and culture. Although from the standpoint of a larger South African society it may not be broad enough, when one looks at it from within the Hindu society it is a much broader identity. In other words, even though each family or individual may have different ways of living their religious life, what matters is the language identity and the overall Indian cultural identity. Language identity and cultural identity are intrinsic to each other. These two are the main factors for the South African Hindu identity. Often religious and cultural aspects overshadow the language identity. In that sense, it is perhaps this broader meaning of being Hindu which is the reason why it is not difficult for most Hindus to attend any Hindu festival or rituals organised by any Hindu denomination, be it Hare Krishna or Ramakrishna, or the traditional Hindu temple.

Notes

1. In this survey, all figures are rounded off to their nearest numbers. This survey is not intended as a purely technical one from a social scientist's point of view. It is meant to give some rough trends among the Hindus in South Africa.
2. I asked this question to cross-check as to how many might answer positively. The 35.57 per cent who indicated that they believed in the plurality of gods and goddesses also indicated their belief in one God. This means, that this percentage of respondents are believers in both one God and in the plurality of gods and goddesses. They seem to have no difficulty in affirming two seemingly opposed views on the ultimate reality (or realities).
3. Although the two categories, namely "tradition" and "modernity" are far more complex than they are taken to be, for the purposes of this analysis I have used the terms simply to refer to the dichotomy between the old inherited worldview and the new acquired worldview in the light of modern scientific and technological changes in human society.

Bibliography

Books

Aiyar, P. Subramania. *The Indian Problem in South Africa*. Durban: The African Chronicle Printing Works, 1925.

Alexander, H. *Gandhi Through Western Eyes*. London: Asia Publishing House, 1969.

Arkin, A.J., K.P. Magyar and G.J. Pillay, eds. *The Indian South Africans*. Pinetown (South Africa): Owen Burgess Publishers, 1989.

Basham, A.L. *The Origins and Development of Classical Hinduism*. Boston: Beacon Press, 1989.

Beal, J.D. *Class, Race & Gender: The Political Economy of Women in Colonial Natal*. (Unpublished M.A. Thesis) Durban: University of Durban-Westville, 1982.

Bell, Catherine. *Ritual Theory, Ritual Practice*. New York: Oxford University Press, 1992.

Bell, Kenneth N. and W.P. Morrell, eds. *Select Documents on British Colonial Policy 1830–1860*. Oxford: The Clarendon Press, 1928.

Bhagavantam, S. ed. *Summer Showers in Brindavan 1978*. Prasanti Nilayam, Puttaparti: Sri Satya Sai Education & Publication Foundation, n.d.

Bhana, S. ed. *Essays on Indentured Indians in Natal*. Leeds: Peepal Tree Press, 1991.

Bhana, S. and B. Pachai, eds. *A Documentary History of Indian South Africans*. Cape Town: David Philips, 1984.

Bhana, S. ed. *History III Projects*. (Unpublished Reports by History Students). Durban: University of Durban-Westville, 1984 and 1985.

Bhana, S. *Indentured Indian Emigrants to Natal 1860–1902: A Study Based on Ships Lists*. New Delhi: Promila & Co., Publishers, 1991.

Bharati, Sudhananda. *Mystic Treasure* (English rendering of Tamil hymns). Durban: Saiva Sithantha Sangam, 1976.

——. *The Revelation of Saint Meikander*. Durban: Saiva Sithantha Sangam, 1972.

——. *Yoga for All.* Durban: Saiva Sithantha Sangam, n.d.

Brain, Joy B. "Natal's Indians: From Co-operation through Competition to Conflict, in *Natal and Zululand: From Earliest Times to 1910: A New History,* edited by Andrew Dummy and Bill Guest. Pietermaritzburg: University of Natal Press, and Shuter & Shuter 1989, pp. 249–273.

——. *Movement of Indians in South Africa: 1860–1911.* (An Unpublished manuscript) Durban: University of Durban-Westville, n.d.

——. "Religion, Missionaries and Indentured Indians." in *Essays on Indentured Indians in Natal,* edited by Surendra Bhana. Leeds, UK: Peepal Tree Press, 1991, pp. 209–225.

Brooks, Charles R. *The Hare Krishnas in India.* New Jersey: Princeton University Press, 1989.

Chant and Be Happy (The Power of Mantra Meditation). Los Angeles: The Bhaktivedanta Book Trust, 1983.

Chettiar, S.M.L. Lakshmanan. *Folklore of Tamil Nadu.* New Delhi: National Book Trust of India, 1980.

Chidananda, Swami. *The Philosophy of Sakti Worship* (originally published as *God as Mother*). Durban: Divine Life Society of South Africa, 1960.

Chirkut, Sheila. *Hindi Instruction in the Indian Primary Schools in South Africa.* M.A. Thesis. Durban: University of Durban-Westville, 1993.

Conversations with Srila Prabhupada. Vol. 16. Los Angeles: The Bhaktivedanta Book Trust, n.d.

Currin, T.E.V. *The Indians in Durban: An Exploratory Study of the Roman Catholic Indian Minority, with Special Emphasis on the Sociological Aspects of Conversion.* (Unpublished M.A. Thesis). Durban: University of Natal, 1962.

Davis, R.H. *Ritual in an Oscillating Universe: worshipping Siva in medieval India.* New Jersey: Princeton University Press, 1991.

de Bruyn, A.C.S. *The Role of the Indian Woman.* (M.A. Thesis) Durban: University of Natal, 1985.

Desai, M. *Gandhi: An Autobiography.* London: Phoenix Press, 1949.

Diesel, A. "Hindu Firewalking in Natal." in *Journal for the Study of Religion,* vol. 3. No. 1. March 1990, pp. 31–39.

Dummy, Andrew and Bill Guest. *Natal and Zululand: From Earliest Times to 1910: a new history,* edited by. Pietermaritzburg: University of Natal Press and Shuter & Shuter, 1989.

Dunuwila, Rohan A. *Saiva Siddhanta Theology: a Context for Hindu-Christian dialogue.* Delhi: Motilal Banarsidass, 1985.

Durkheim, Emile. *The Elementary Forms of the Religious Life.* (Translated by Joseph Ward Swain). London: George Allen & Unwin, 1982.

Ferguson-Davie, C.J. *The Early History of Indians in Natal.* Johannesburg: South African Institute of Race Relations, n.d.

Fransen, H. *Three Centuries of South African Art*. Johannesburg: A.D. Donker/Publisher, 1982.

Gandhi, M.K. *My Experiments with Truth: An Autobiography*. Ahmedabad: Navajivan Publishing House, 1972 (first published in 1927).

Geertz, Clifford. *Local Knowledge: Further essays in Interpretive Anthropology*. New York: Basic Books, Inc., Publishers, 1983.

——. *Works and Lives: The Anthropologist as Author*. Cambridge, UK: Polity Press, 1988.

Grossert, J.W. *Hindu Temples of Natal*. (Unpublished M.A. Thesis). Durban: University of Natal, 1942.

Gupta, Giri Raja, ed. *Main Currents in Indian Sociology*. New Delhi: Vikas Publishing House (Pvt) Ltd., 1983.

Hardy, F. *Viraha Bhakti: The Early Krishna Devotion in South India*. Delhi: Oxford University Press, 1983.

Hattersley, A.F. *The British Settlement of Natal*. Cambridge: The University Press, 1950.

Henning, C.G. *The Indentured Indian in Natal 1860–1917*. New Delhi: Promilla & Co., Publishers, 1993.

Hiltebeitel, Alf. *The Cult of Draupadi. (Mythologies: from Gin gee to Kurukshetra)*. Chicago: The University of Chicago Press, 1988.

Hiralal, Kalpana. *The Natal Indian Trader: A Struggle for Survival 1875–1910*. (Unpublished M.A. Thesis), Durban: University of Durban-Westville, 1991.

Hofmeyr, J.H. and G.C. Oosthuizen. *Religion in a South African Indian Community*. (Report, number 12, October 1981). Durban: Institute for Social and Economic Research, University of Durban-Westville, 1981.

Holiday, I.G. "Natal and Indentured Indian Immigration," *The Economic Society of South Africa*. (March 1940) 52–59. Johannesburg: Hayne and Gibson, 1940.

Jain, Prakash, C. "Five Patterns of Indian Emigration" pp. 7ff. in *Global Migration of Indians: Saga of Adventure, Enterprise, Identity & Integration*. New York: National Federation of Indian-American Associations, 1989.

Kanu, Victor. *Sai Baba, God Incarnate*. London: Sawbridge Enterprises, 1981.

Karashima, Noboru. *South Indian History and Society*. Delhi: Oxford University Press, 1984.

Kennedy, Melville T. *The Chaitanya Movement: a study of the Vaishnavism in Bengal*. London: Oxford University Press, 1925.

Klostermaier, K.K. *A Survey of Hinduism*. New York: State University of New York Press, 1989.

Kondapi, C. *Indians Overseas 1839–1949*. London: Oxford University Press, 1951.

Krystal, Phyllis. *Sai Baba: The Ultimate Experience.* Shaftesbury, UK: Element Books Limited, 1990.

Kuper, Adam. *Anthropologists and Anthropology: The British School 1922–72.* Middlesex, UK: Penguin Books, 1975.

Kuppusami, C. *Religions, Customs and Practices of South African Indians.* Durban: Sunray Publishers (Pvt) Ltd., 1983.

Life of Sri Ramakrishna. Calcutta: Advaita Ashrama, 1977.

Meer, Fatima. "Indian People: Current Trends & Policies," in *South Africa's Minorities.* (Edited by Peter Randall). Johannesburg: The Study Project on Christianity in Apartheid Society, 1971, pp. 13–32.

Meer, Fatima. *Portrait of Indian South Africans.* Durban: Avon House, 1969.

Meer, Y.S. *Documents of Indentured Labor: Natal 1851–1917.* Durban: Institute of Black Research, 1980.

Mesthrie, Uma Shashikant. *From Sastri to Deshmukh: A Study of the Role of the Government of India's Representatives in South Africa (1927–1946).* (Unpublished doctoral thesis) Durban: University of Durban-Westville, 1987.

Mikula, Paul, Brian Kearney and Rodney Herber. *Traditional Hindu Temples in South Africa.* Durban: Hindu Temple Publications, 1982.

Monier-Williams, M. *Sanskrit-English Dictionary.* Oxford University Press, 1920.

Motwani, Jagat K. and Jyoti Barot-Motwani eds. *Global Migration of Indians: Saga of Adventure, Enterprise, Identity & Integration.* New York: National Federation of Indian-American Associations, 1989.

Naidoo, S.R and D. Bramdaw. *Sastri Speaks.* Pietermaritzburg: The Natal Press, 1930.

Naidoo, T. *The Arya Samaj Movement in South Africa.* Delhi: Motilal Banarasidass Publishers, 1992.

——. *The Temple at Melrose.* (No details of publisher available).

Nanda, B.R. *Gandhi and his Critics.* Delhi: Oxford University Press, 1985.

Narayana, Ananta, N. *From Man to God-Man.* Durban: Divine Life Society of South Africa, 1979.

Nischalananda, Swami. *Footprints in the Sand.* Durban: Swami Nischalananda Memorial Publications (Pvt) Ltd., n.d.

North-Combes, M.D. "Indentured labour in the Sugar Industries of Natal and Mauritius," in *Essays on Indentured Indians in Natal.* edited by S. Bhana. Leeds: Peepal Tree Press, 1991, pp. 12–87.

Nowbath, R.S., Sookraj Chotai, and B.D. Lalla. *The Hindu Heritage in South Africa.* Durban: The South African Hindu Maha Sabha, 1960.

Oosthuizen, G.C. *Pentecostal Penetration into the Indian Community in South Africa.* Durban: Human Sciences Research Council, Pretoria South Africa, 1975.

Pachai, B. ed. *South African Indians: The Evolution of a Minority*. Washington, DC.: University Press of America, Inc., 1979.

——. *The History of the Indian Opinion, its Origin, Development and Contribution to South African History, 1903–1914.* (Doctoral Thesis, University of South Africa, Pretoria) Found in the Archinve Year Book of SA, Oct., 11, 1962.

——. *The International Aspects of the South African Indian Question 1860–1971.* Cape Town: C. Struik (Pvt) Ltd., 1971.

Pandian, J. "The Sacred Symbol of the Mother Goddess in a Tamil Village: A Parochial Model of Hinduism." in *Main Currents in Indian Sociology*. edited by Gin Raja Gupta. New Delhi: Vikas Publishing House (Pvt) Ltd., 1983, pp. 198–214.

Pather, S.R. ed. *1860–1960: A Century of Indians in South Africa.* Durban: Cavalier Publishers, n.d.

Paton, Alan. *The Story of the Group Areas Act.* Durban: Clarendon Press, n.d.

——. *Towards the Mountain: An Autobiography.* Cape Town: David Philip Publishers, 1980.

Peterson, Indira Viswanathan. *Poems to Siva: The Hymns of the Tamil Saints.* Princeton: Princeton University Press, 1989.

Pillay, Govindamma. *An Investigation into the Caste Attitudes that Prevail Amongst Hindus in the Durban Metropolitan Area.* (Unpublished M.A. Thesis). Durban: University of Durban, Westville, 1991.

Prabhakaran, V. "Tamil Lexical Borrowings in South African Telugu." in *South African Journal of Linguistics*, 1994:12:1, pp. 26–31.

Prabhupada, Swami, A.C. Bhaktivedanta. *Chant and Be Happy.* Los Angeles: The Bhaktivedanta Book Trust, 1991.

——. *The Science of Self-Realization.* New York: The Bhakti Vedanta Book Trust, 1988.

——. *The Teachings of Lord Caitanya.* Los Angeles: The Bhaktivedanta Book Trust, 1988.

Prayer Book of the Saiva Sithantha Sungam of South Africa. Durban: Saiva Sithantha Sungam of South Africa, n.d.

Randall, Peter. ed. *South Africa's Minorities.* Johannesburg: The Study Project on Christianity in Apartheid Society, 1971.

Ranganathananda, Swami. *Sarada Devi: The Crowning glory of Indian Womanhood.* Durban: The Ramakrishna Centre of South of Africa, 1985.

Reader, Ian. *Religion in contemporary Japan.* Honolulu: University of Hawaii Press, 1991.

Rhoodie, N. ed. *South African Dialogue.* Johannesburg: McGraw Hill Book Company, 1972.

Robinson, Sir John. *A Life Time in South Africa.* London: Smith, Elder & Co., 1900.

Rocher, H.J.W. *A Study of the Theory and Practice of the Hindu Religious Tradition Among a Selected Group of Tamil-Speaking Hindus in South Africa: A Sociological Approach.* (Unpublished M.A. Thesis). Pretoria: University of Pretoria, 1965.

Saradananda, Swami. ed. *Tirukkural of Tiruvalluvar.* Durban: Ramakrishna Press, 1991.

Sastri, Natesa S.M. *Hindu Feasts: Fasts and Ceremonies.* New Delhi: Asian Educational Services, 1988.

Satprakashananda, Swami. *Sri Ramakrishna's Life and Message in the Present Age.* St. Louis, Missouri: Vedanta Society of St. Louis, 1976.

Sharma, Satyapal. *Know Your Religion, (Part I).* Pietermaritzburg: Veda Dharma Sabha, 1986.

Sharpe, E.J. *The Universal Gita: Western Images of the Gita.* London: Duckworth, 1985.

Shastri, Shukla Shri Tileswar Nath. *Shri Satyanarana Vrat Katha.* Durban: D. Roopanand Bros., n.d.

Shukla, U.D. *Perceptions of the Ramacharitmanas of Goswami Tulsidas Amongst Hindi-Speaking South Africans.* (Unpublished M.A. Thesis). Durban: University of Durban-Westville, 1989.

Shulman, David Dean. *Tamil Temple Myths: Sacrifice and Divine Marriage in the South Indian Saiva Tradition.* Princeton: Princeton University Press, 1980.

Singh, N. *A Study of the Divine Life Society with Special Reference to its Socio-Religious Implications in South Africa.* (Unpublished M.A. Thesis). Durban: University of Durban-Westville, 1986.

Sivananda, Swami. *Essence of Ramayana.* Durban: Divine Life Society of South Africa, 1960.

——. *Lord Krishna, His Lilas and Teachings.* Durban: Divine Life Society of South Africa, 1961.

Smart, Ninian. *Worldviews: Crosscultural Explorations of Human Beliefs.* New York: Charles Scribner's Sons, 1983.

Smith, W.C. *The Meaning and End of Religion.* New York: Harper & Row, 1978.

Sookial, A. *A Socio-Religious Study of the Hare Krishna Movement in South Africa.* Durban: Nermic, 1986.

Studies on Sri Ramakrishna. Calcutta: The Ramakrishna Mission, 1988.

Sugirtharajah, Sharada. *Imagining Hinduism: A Postcolonial Perspective.* London: Routledge, 2003.

Swamigal, Thiru Ramalinga. *Garland of Grace.* Durban: Saiva Sithantha Sangam, 1971.

Swan, Maureen. *Gandhi: The South African Experience.* Johannesburg: Ravan Press, 1985.

The Complete Works of Swami Vivekananda. Vol. 1. Calcutta: Advaita Ashrama, 1986.

Thevaram Mini Sermons. Durban: Verulam Kalay Kazhagam, n.d.

This is a Story of the Indian People, Their Origin, Growth and Development, a monograph with no author's name. Durban: University of Durban-Westville Documentation Centre, n.d.

Thomas, Timothy N. *Indians Overseas: A Guide to Source Materials in the India Office Records for the Study of Indian Emigration 1830–1950.* London: The British library, 1985.

Thurston, Edgar. *Castes and Tribes of South India.* Madras: Government Press, 1909.

Vedalankar, Pt. Naradev. *Arya Samaj: Its Ideals and Achievements.* Durban: Arya Pratinidhi Sabha, n,d.

——. *Hindu Polity and Administration*. Durban: Arya Pratinidhi Sabha, n.d.

——. *Religious Awakening in South Africa.* Durban: Arya Pratinidhi Sabha, 1950.

——. *Shastra Navanitam: A Concise Study of Hindu Scriptures.* Durban: Veda Niketan, 1981.

——. *Arya Samaj: Its Ideals and Achievements*. Durban: Veda Niketan, 1971.

Venkatesananda, Swami. *Gurudev Sivananda.* Durban: Divine Life Society of South Africa, 1961.

——. *Caste, Culture and Socialism,* Calcutta: Advaita Ashrama, 1988.

——. *Chicago Addresses,* Durban: The Ramakrishna Centre of South of Africa, 1989.

——. *Lectures from Colombo to Almora.* Calcutta: Advaita Ashrama, 1990.

——. *Practical Vedanta.* Calcutta: Advaita Ashrama, 1987.

——. *The Complete Works of Swami Vivekananda.* Vol. 1. Calcutta: Advaita Ashrama, 1986.

——. *The Complete Works of Swami Vivekananda.* Vol. 2. Calcutta: Advaita Ashrama, 1987.

——. *The East and the West.* Calcutta: Advaita Ashrama, 1990.

Vivekananda, Swami. *Complete Works of Vivekananda.* Vol. 2. Calcutta : Advaita Ashrama, 1987.

Waiz, S.A. ed. *Indians Abroad.* Bombay: The Imperial Indian Citizenship Association, 1927.

Wilson, H.H. *Religions of the Hindus*. Delhi: Cosmo Publications, 1978.

Souvenirs, Pamphlets, Magazines, Reports, etc.

Arya Pratinidhi Sabha, South Africa, Golden Jubilee 1925–1975.

Arya Pratinidhi Sabha, South Africa: 67th Annual Secretarial Report, 1991.

Arya Pratinidhi Sabha, South Africa: Souvenir 1985.

Back to Godhead (The magazine of the Hare Krishna Movement), Vol.16, No. 8.

Higher Taste (Official publication of the Bhakti Yoga and Vegetarian Society-University of Cape Town), March 1991, and March 1992.

Hindu Dharma (Official Journal of the Hindu Alliance of South Africa), August 1986.

Hinduism Today-Africa Edition, Vol. 12, Nos. 4,6,7, 1990.

Hinduism Today-Africa Edition, Vol. 13, Nos. 1,3,4,5,6,7, 1991.

Indian Opinion. No. 1, Vol. LIX., 1961.

"Karthigai Theebum Prayer" (A pamphlet distributed by the Saiva Sithantha Sungam of South Africa, n.d.)

Mother Sarasvati (A Pamphlet). Distributed by Saiva Sithantha Sangam of South Africa.

Navalar, Swami Sivananda. *Maha Shivaratri* (Pamphlet). Durban: Saiva Sithantha Sangam of South Africa, n.d.

Nischalananda, Swami. *Dedication.* (A Pamphlet). Durban: The Ramakrishna Centre of South Africa, n.d.

Official Year Book of South Africa, 1993.

Ramakrishna Centre of South Africa: 1942–1992 Golden Jubilee.

Report of Activities of the Ramakrishna Centre of South Africa, 1991.

"Saivite Light," (A quarterly publication of the Saiva Sithantha Sungam of South Africa). Vol. 1, No. 3, 1968; Vol. 2, No. 4, 1969; Vol. 3, No. 1, 1969.

Shree Radha-Krishna Mandir Souvenir Brochure 1988.

Shri Vishnu Temple: Diamond Jubilee Celebrations 1907–1982.

Souvenir Brochure of Arya Pratinidhi Sabha, 1988 in Honor of Pt. Naradev Vedalankar.

Statistics South Africa 1996 and 2001. (http://www.statssa.gov.za/census01/html/RSAPrimary.pdf). (visited on 22.03.2012).

Stree Vaithianatha Easvarar Alayam, Souvenir Brochure 1989.

Stri Siva Subramaniar and Mariammen Temples: Centenary Brochure 1885–1985.

Swamigal, Panrimalai. *Mahasivaratri: The Day of Deliverance,* (a typed monograph). Released by Siva Nyana Sabha of South Africa.

The Daily News, Tuesday, December 24, 1991.

"The Gracious Light," (A quarterly publication of the Saiva Sithantha Sunagam of South Africa). Summer 1974, Summer 1976, Autumn 1977.

The Jyoti (A quarterly published by the Ramakrishna Centre of South Africa). Vol. 15, January–March 1990.

The State: A South African National Magazine, 1909, Vol. 1.

Veda Dharma Sabha, Pietermaritzburg, Souvenir Brochure 1909–1984.

Index

Abhishekam, 69, 70, 71, 74
Advaita, 143, 151, 173, 238, 240, 241
African National Congress, 144
Agama, 39, 44, 48, 50, 83, 151, 193
Alvar, 50, 64
Ananda, 120, 206
Andhra Maha Sabha, 106, 107, 118, 119, 120, 122
Angalamman, 27, 28
Anglo-Boer War, 11
Ankalesvari, 90, 91, 93
Ant hill, 93
Antyeshti, 139
Apartheid, 14, 45, 144, 149, 163, 215, 238, 239
Appar, 82, 152
Artha, 52, 64
Arya Samaj/Samajists
  contribution of, to South African politics, 144–45
  in South Africa, 137–40, role in spreading religious awareness, 140–44
  teachings of, 142–44
Arya Yuvak Sabha, 29
Aryan Benevolent Home, 140, 145
Asiatic Trading Bill, 11
Aurobindo Ghosh, 126, 209
Avatara, 183, 201, 207
Ayodhya, 78, 83
Ayurveda, 162

Bad Luck Prayers, 39, 62
Banyan Tree, 39
Bell, Kenneth N. and W.P. Morrell, 23
Bhai Paramanand, 12, 137, 148
Bhajan, 62, 63, 105, 107, 120, 121
Bhakta, 164
Bhana, S. and B. Pachai, 13
Bhana, S., 9, 19, 52
Bhavani Dayal Sanyasi, 138, 139, 146
Bhudevi, 37, 77
Bilva Tree, 75, 84
Brahmo Samaj, 124, 186
Brain, Joy B., 10, 11, 24, 25, 29
Braj, 186
British East India Company, 20
British Government, 11
British Imperialism, 8
Brooks, Charles R., 186

Cato Manor, 25, 27, 28, 40, 43, 47, 87, 150
Cella, 26, 35, 36
Chaitanya, 237
Chant, 83, 188, 189, 196, 236, 239
Chettiar, S.M.L. Lakshmanan, 94, 95
Chidambaram, 44
Chidananda, Swami, 178
Chinmaya Mission, 126, 127, 129, 130
Chirkut, Sheila, 110
Christian Missionaries, 20, 30, 31, 124, 125, 136, 209

Christmas, 162, 172
Circumambulation, 35, 40, 57, 73
Class Areas Act, 12
Colonial Born Indian Association, 12, 148
Coolie Commission, 25
Coolies, 25
Currin, T.E.V., 53

Dada Abdhulla, 30
Darsana, 71
Davis, R.H., 153, 154
denominationalism
  in South Africa, emergence of, 128
Deepavali Cheer Society, 109
Department of Indian Affairs, 14
Dhyana, 206
Diesel, A., 51, 87, 92
Divine Life Society
  in South Africa, 174; activities/ programmes of, 175–76
Dravidian, 36, 47, 76, 84, 101, 135
Dunuwila, Rohan A., 152, 153
Durga, 92, 106, 120, 136, 178

Easter, 95, 162, 190
Eisteddfod, 119
Electoral Commission, 14
Emperumal Temple, 37
European Colonists, 10
European Merchants, 10
European Settlers, 10

Ferguson-Davie, C.J., 17
Festival of Chariots, 215
Flag post, 35, 68, 69, 93
Fransen, H., 24, 26, 27, 28
Free Passenger, 10
Funeral Ceremonies, 43, 57, 58, 59

Gandhi, M.K., 30, 31, 32, 43, 209
Gangai amman, 61, 90, 93, 97, 177
Garbhagriha, 92
Gaya, 19, 184, 185
Gentoo, 16, 20, 21
Gingee, 92
Girana Soni Hitvardhak Mandal, 107
Girana Sonis, 107
Goddess Festival, 62, 87, 97, 189
goddess worship
  in South Africa, 89–100
Gokhale, 12
Gokula Temple, 37
Gopalal Temple, 28
Great March, 12
Grossert, J.W., 26
Group Areas Act, 13, 14, 144, 239
Gujarati community
  in South Africa, 107–10
Gujarati Mahila Mandal, 108
Gujarati Vedic Society, 108, 109
Gurukal, 42
Gurupuja, 114, 150, 157, 177

Hanuman Jayanti, 67, 177
Hare Krishna Movement (ISKCON), 184
  activities/programmes of, 194–96
  features of, 188–94
  in South Africa, 186–88
Henning, C.G., 9, 10
Hiltebeitel, Alf., 91, 92, 209
Hindi Pracharini Sabhas, 139
Hindi Siksha Sangh, 112
Hindi community
  in South Africa, 110–12
Hindu Alliance, 130, 136, 241
Hindu festival(s)
  basic structure of a, 68–70
  in South Africa, celebration of, 70–82
Hindu Maha Sabha, 29, 31, 32, 131, 138, 148, 238

Hindu Reform Society, 137
Hindu religious/temple activities
in South Africa, 24–25, 105–7, worship pattern, 38–40, 86; celebration of, 70–82
Hindu Tamil Institute, 112, 113
Hindu Temples
in South Africa, construction of, 35–38; priesthood in, 42–43
Hindu Trinity, 59, 120, 121, 158
Hindu Young Men's Association, 29, 112
Hofmeyr, J.H. and G.C. Oosthuizen, 49, 50
Homa, 60, 93
House of Delegates, 14, 41

indentured Indians
in South Africa, 9
Indenture system, 8, 9, 10
Indian Advisory Council, 14
Indian Education, 12
Indian emigration, 8, 19, 237, 241
Indian immigrants, 9, 16, 21, 38, 43
to South Africa, 16; cultural background of, 16–19
Indian Labourers, 8, 17, 23, 41
Indian Merchants, 10
Indian National Congress, 12
Indian Opinion, 12, 239, 242
Indians
in the global context, 7–9
Isipingo Temple, 90, 95, 97, 99
Indian traders
in South Africa, 10
Islam, 125, 138, 139

Jagannatha Temple, 37
Jew, 172
Jhanda, 56, 60, 61, 64, 177
Jiva Gosvami, 185

Kalasam, 69, 88, 94, 101
Kali age, 193
Kali, 27, 78, 92, 101, 166, 178, 193
Kama, 52, 64
Kanu, Victor, 199, 200, 201, 203
Karakams, 88, 94
Karma Yoga, 174, 176
Kartavarayan, 97
Karttikaidipam, 38, 67, 81, 82, 156
Kashmir Saivism, 151
Katha, 59, 60, 61, 65, 112, 177, 240
Kathiawad Hindu Seva Samaj, 107
Kathiawad Pattani Soni, 107
Kattiri, 64, 67
Kennedy, Melville T., 184, 185, 192
Klostermaier, K.K., 124
Kodi, 35, 36, 68
Krishnajanmastami, 77, 142
Kriya, 154, 156
Krystal, Phyllis, 204
Kshatriya, 194
Kumbha Mela, 162, 173
Kumbha, 68, 162, 173
Kumbhabhishekam, 39
Kumkum, 60, 62, 69, 73, 94
Kuppusami, C., 58
Kurma Venkata Reddy, 188
Kurukshetra, 190, 237
Kusa grass, 60

Lohar caste, 16
Lord Russell, 23

Madhavendra Puri, 192
Madhva, 192, 209
Madras Presidency, 26, 27, [illegible]
Magazine Barracks, 27
Mahabhishekam, 93
Mahalaya Amavasya, 78, 79
Maharshi Sudhananda Bharati, 155
Mahasakti, 156

Mahasamadhi, 164
Mahesvara, 120, 180
Mandela, 14, 145
Mangalasutram, 40
Manikkavacakar, 151, 152, 157
Marriage ceremonies, 40, 43, 57
Mathura, 77, 85, 196
Mathuraiviran, 61, 97
Matsya Purana, 77
Mauritius, 8, 27, 64, 75, 139, 238
Maya, 171, 178, 179
Meer, Y.S., 9, 19
Merchant Class, 10, 11
Meykandar, 117, 151, 152
Mikula, Paul, Brian Kearney and Rodney Herber, 17, 27, 28, 35, 36
Mithya, 206
Mochi, 107
Mohrrum, 138
Moksha, 51, 64, 75
Motwani, Jagat K. and Jyoti Barot-Motwani, 9, 10, 11, 12, 13
Mt. Edgecombe, 24, 26, 27
Mudras, 63
Muhurtam, 41
Mukti, 213
Murti, 59, 69, 71, 74, 83

Nagara style, 35, 36
Naidoo, S.R and D. Bramdaw, 13
Naidoo, T., 51, 145, 146
Nanda, B.R., 31
Narakasura, 78
Narayana, 65, 204, 238
Narottama Datta, 185
Natal Government, 20, 23, 24, 25, 33
Natal Gujarati Parishad, 108
Natal Indian Congress, 11, 29, 144, 163
Natal Province, 90, 118, 169, 217
Natal Tamil Conference, 113
Nataraja, 117
Nationalist Party, 13
Navadvip, 184
Navagrahas, 39
Navaratri, 59, 67, 172, 177
Neem, 93, 95, 96, 97
Nelson Mandela, 14, 145
neo–Hindu organisations/ movements in South Africa, 123–28; features of, 131–33
New Castle Tamil Association, 12
Nimbarka, 192
Nischalananda, Swami, 127, 161, 162, 163, 164, 165, 166, 167, 168, 169, 170, 171, 172
Non-dualism, 155
North-Combes, M.D., 8
Nowbath, R.S., Sookraj Chotai, and B.D. Lalla, 18, 24, 29, 61 ,78, 113, 118, 119, 140, 141, 142, 163, 197

Oosthuizen, G.C., 53
Orality, 103
Orissa, 19, 47, 185, 191

Pachai, B., 12, 13, 14
Padma Purana, 77
Pakistan, 13
Pancaratra Agama, 50
Pandavas, 66, 77
Pandit Karamchand, 139
Pandit Pravinsingh, 139
Pandit Ramgovind Trivedi, 139
Pandu, 91
Para Brahman, 178
Paramahamsa Sacchidananda Yogesvarar, 118
Paramatma, 205
Parattassi, 21, 41, 67, 78, 79, 80, 85
Pariahs, 22
Parsees, 17
Parvati, 38, 156, 210
Pasa, 153
Passenger Indians, 10, 16, 22, 28

Passive Resistance, 13, 138, 144
Pasu, 83, 153
Pasupata, 151
Patel, 107
Pati, 83, 153
Pattani Social Club, 107
Pattani Sonis, 107
Perumal, 26
Peterson, Indira Viswanathan, 82
Phalguna, 75
Pilgrimage, 75, 120, 185, 186
Pitrpak, 80, 81
Poll Tax, 11, 32
Poturaju, 97
Prabhupada, Swami, 193, 194
Pradyumna, 193
Prakrti, 205
Prasadam, 187, 192
Prasanti, 200, 235
Pretoria Hindu Seva Samaj, 12
Proselytization, 139
Puja, 56, 69, 74, 75, 96, 177, 178
Purohit Mandal, 140, 141
Purusha, 205, 206
Purushottama, 206

Quaker, 30, 31

Radha Krishna Temple, 109
Radhakrishnan, S., 118
Radharani, 190
Raga, 72
Raghunatha Bhatta, 185
Raghunatha Das, 185
Raghuvir Prabhu, 136, 187
Railway Barracks, 27
Raja Yoga, 164
Rajputs, 16
Ram Mohun Roy, 124
Rama Rao, 119
Ramakrishna Order, 161
Ramakrishnaites
  in South Africa, 159–61
Ramanavami, 67, 75, 76, 142
Ramanuja, 50, 151, 209
Ravana, 76, 78, 83
Reader, Ian, 86, 87
Rebirth, 80, 193, 223
Representative Government, 11
Responsible Government, 11
Rishikesh, 174
Rudra, 151
Rupa Gosvami, 185

Sadasiva, 120
Sadhaka, 176
Sadhana, 206
Saiva Agamas, 151, 152
Saiva Siddhanta
  in South Africa, 155–56
  of South India, in historical perspective, 151–52; teachings of, 152–55
Saiva Vazhipattu Kazhagam, 112
Saivism, 64, 106, 150, 151
Sakta Cult, 185
Sakti Puja, 178
Sambandar, 82, 113, 115, 152, 157
Sambrani, 73
Samkarshana, 193
Samskaras, 29, 32, 141
Sanatana Dharma, 126
Sanatana Gosvami, 185
Sandhya, 56, 141, 148
Sankara Deva, 185
Sankara, 185, 209
Sannyasin, 63
Saradananda, Swami, 115, 116, 161
Sarasvati, 56, 119, 136, 177, 242
Sarojini Naidu, 12

Sarvadeshik Arya Pratinidhi Sabha, 139, 140, 147
Sastri College, 12
Sastri, Natesa S.M., 79
Satsangh, 62, 63, 169, 182, 214
Satyagraha, 20, 29, 138
Satya Sai movement, 197
- in India, 199–200
- in South Africa, 197–99
- teachings of, 201–4; in Hindu thought, 204–7

Saurashtra Hindu Association, 107
Second River Temple, 27, 87, 90, 94, 97, 101, 102
Sharpe, E.J., 123, 124, 125, 126
Shukla, U.D., 51, 110, 111
Shulman, David Dean, 81
Siddhanta Ratna, 141
Sikhara, 27, 35
Sindhur, 60
Singh, N., 174, 175, 176, 177
Siringa, 97
Sita, 37, 61, 78, 182, 210
Siva Nyana Sabha, 112, 242
Siva Purana, 81, 84
Siva Subrahmanya Alayam, 150
Sivananda, Swami, 133, 155, 156, 174, 175, 176, 179, 180, 181, 182
Six Gosvamis, 185, 186
Six-foot Dance, 61, 92, 93, 97, 101
Skanda Purana, 81
Slavery, 7, 8
Small-pox, 95
South Africa
- celebration of Hindu festivals in, 70–82
- Gandhi in, 30–32
- Hindu communities/organisations in, 107–21, 123–33
- Hindu priesthood in, 42–44
- Hindus customs and practices in, changes in, 40–42
- Hindus temples in, 35–38
- indentured Indians in. 9
- Indian immigrants to, 16–19
- Indian traders in, 10
- religious organisations in, 105–7
- ritual observation in, 54–63; changes in, 40

South African Indian Congress, 139
South African Indian Council, 14
South African Tamil Institute, 112
South African Vanik Association, 107
Springfield Training College, 13
Sri Maha Vishnu, 37
Sri Siva Subrahmanya and Mariamman Temple, 90
Sri Vaithianatha Isvarar Alayam, 161
Sri Vishnu Temple, 112
Srimad Bhagavatam, 77, 87, 189, 192, 204, 205, 206
Srinivasa Acarya, 185
Srinivasa Sastri, 12, 113
Srirangam, 50
Stambha, 68, 69
Sthanikal, 42
Suddhi, 139
Sudra, 194
Sundaramurti, 114, 152, 157
Supreme Brahman, 178, 179, 180
Supreme Consciousness, 202
Surat Hindu Association, 12
Suratis, 107
Surya, 56
Swami Arjunananda, 155, 156, 157
Swami Chidananda, 178
Swami Mangalanand Puri, 29
Swami Purushottamananda, 161, 166, 168, 173
Swami Saradananda, 122, 161, 163, 164, 168, 169, 171

Swami Shivapadananda, 163, 164, 168, 169
Swami Sivananda Navalar, 155, 156
Swami Srila Prabhupada, 187, 189
Swami Venkatesananda, 180
Swami Virajananda, 160
Swan, Maureen, 10
Syamananda Das, 185

Talisman, 199, 207
Tamil community
  in South Africa, 112–17
Tamil Protective Association, 106, 112
Tamil Saivism, 151
Tamil Vedic Society, 112
Tamizh Manram, 112
Tantric, 42, 48, 184
Telugu community
  in South Africa, 117–21
Terukkuttam, 92, 101, 112
Thai Pongal, 66, 67, 72
Thai Pusam, 67, 72
Theosophical Society, 125, 138
Thomas, Timothy N., 8, 9
Tiru Navukkarasar, 114, 157
Tirumantiram, 152
Tirumular, 152
Tiruvacakam, 151, 152, 155, 161
Tongaat South Vishnu Temple, 89
Transitional Executive Council, 14
Transvaal Gujarati Parishad, 108
Tricameral Parliament, 14, 20
Trident, 62, 94
Tulsidas, 110, 111, 240
Turmeric, 60, 62, 69, 93, 94

Umbilo Temple, 25, 27, 97
United Nations, 13
Universal Brotherhood, 143
Upanayana, 139
Upanishads, 43, 135, 161, 178, 179, 192, 204, 205
Utsava, 69, 70, 71, 74, 83

Vaishnavism, 50, 51, 64, 185, 237
Vallabha, 209
Valli, 38, 73
Valmiki, 111
Vaniks, 107
Vanniya, 16
Varuna, 77
Vasishta, 161
Vasudeva, 77, 193, 205
Veda Dharma Sabha, 28, 29, 32, 33, 110, 138, 144, 240, 242
Vedalankar, Pt. Naradev, 137, 138, 139, 140, 142, 143, 147
Vedas, 104, 125, 142, 146, 147, 148, 151, 192
Venkatesananda, Swami, 180, 181
Verulam Kalai Kazhagam, 112, 113
Verulam Siva Sabai, 112
Victorian, 35
Vidya, 142
Villiparatam, 91, 92
Villiputturar, 92
Vinayaka Caturthi, 67
Virasaiva, 153
Vishnupriya, 185
Visistadvaita, 155

World Parliament of Religions, 160

Yajna, 93
Yama, 79, 80, 84, 114
Young Men's Hindu Association, 12
Young Men's Vedic Society, 112